POPE PIUS XII LIBRARY, ST. JOSEPH COL.

3 2528 08057 7812

D1563233

Redefining Fatherhood

Redefining Fatherhood

NANCY E. DOWD

NEW YORK UNIVERSITY PRESS
NEW YORK AND LONDON

NEW YORK UNIVERSITY PRESS
New York and London

2000 by New York University
ALL RIGHTS RESERVED

Library of Congress Cataloging-in-Publication Data
Dowd, Nancy E., 1949–
Redefining fatherhood / Nancy E. Dowd.
p.   cm.
Includes biblographical references and index.
ISBN 0-8147-1925-2 (cloth : alk. paper)
1. Fatherhood. 2. Fathers.   I. Title.
HQ756 .D588 2000
306.874'2—dc21   00-008628

New York University Press books are printed on acid-free paper,
and their binding materials are chosen for strength and durability.

Manufactured in the United States of America

10 9 8 7 6 5 4 3 2 1

To Zoe & Zachary

Contents

Acknowledgments

I have been blessed with extraordinary help during the course of this project, particularly from fine research assistants. Ellen Ham, Darian Wagner, and Linnea Schram provided wonderful research. The heaviest load, however, was carried by brett zeeb, to whom I owe a deep debt of gratitude. Rosemary Howard, who was instrumental in completing my first book, again provided invaluable assistance in completing this manuscript. My secretary, Carol Velasques, strongly supported this project throughout. The entire staff of the Legal Information Center of the Levin College of Law provided outstanding research assistance, particularly with respect to gathering multidisciplinary sources from a range of collections.

The University of Florida Levin College of Law has generously supported my research and writing, providing several research leaves which allowed me to complete this project in relatively short time from conception to completion. I also benefited from additional research funds provided to me as a Trustee Research Scholar.

I benefited from comments made during several conferences on various portions of the book, including the Governor's Conference on Responsible Fatherhood during the summer of 1998; a conference held in honor of the late Professor Mary Joe Frug at Villanova Law School in the fall of 1998; and the 1999 annual meeting of the Law and Society Association.

During the course of my research, I also benefited from comments from, and conversations with, Bill Marsiglio, David Leverentz, Barbara Bennett Woodhouse, Patricia Bradford, Martha Fineman, Joan Williams, Nancy Levit, Sharon Rush, Walter Weyrauch, and Michelle Jacobs.

My editor, Niko Pfund, has been unswerving in his support, believing in this project from the start, even as his own time as a father began.

It is the friends that always get you through. My thanks to Jane Pendergast, Dorota Haman, Marty Peters, Paul Dodds, Kevin Conlin, and Bob Luehman. My sister, Patty McDermott, is always there for me. My dad continues to tell me stories. Countless friends, and some strangers, have shared stories of men who nurture, and I have watched many fathers feeding, carrying, comforting, and caring for their children in public spaces.

But my greatest inspiration is my children. I thank them for their unlimited, unquestioned, unqualified love and support and for teaching me, every day, what really matters.

Redefining Fatherhood

Introduction

Fathers parent less than mothers. Both within and outside of marriage, they nurture their children (and stepchildren and children in general) far less than mothers do. Not only do fathers parent less, but they abandon their children to a remarkable extent, again far exceeding such conduct by women.

That this conduct occurs is troubling. That we seem to accept it is disturbing. That we care about it so little speaks volumes. Imagine the same patterns characterizing mothers. I suspect that such conduct in mothers would be viewed with widespread alarm. Our complacency may be tied to our limited view of what it means to be a father. Perhaps such behavior does not significantly violate our idea of fathering. Our complacency may also assume that fatherhood has limited significance for men, and that men who exhibit this pattern experience little or no emotional or psychological pain as a result of their disconnection from their children.

At least two things suggest that this latter assumption is false. First, alongside the pattern of limited, disconnected fatherhood is evidence of a small but increasing number of fathers who are significantly involved as caretakers of their children. Second, a strong fathers' rights movement has arisen that unites around the common proposition that the legal system disregards the desire of fathers to nurture their children.

We know far less about fathers than we know about mothers. We tend to count fathers less, notice them less, and understand less about the correlations between fatherhood and child care, and between fatherhood and wage work. We do know, however, that most fathers function differently from mothers. Traditionally, we expected that to be the case: we presumed that fathers worked for wages and that mothers cared for children and the household. This traditional ideal is now a minority family form. Less than 10 percent of families with children under age eighteen conform to the pattern of a single male breadwinner and female stay-at-home spouse. Nevertheless, we retain the traditional model, cloaked in egalitarian, gender-neutral ideology.

The gendered differential of fathers' and mothers' parenting persists, although in somewhat modified form. The presence of children rarely changes men's wage work patterns. Men continue to do wage work with little or no break, temporary or otherwise, because of children. Most fathers take little time off when children are born or adopted and most do not change the type of work they do or the hours they work in order to meet the new demands of parenthood. In contrast, most women take some leave at the birth or adoption of their children. Women are far more likely to accommodate work to family, and therefore to make changes in their wage work patterns by their choice of job, by their choice of hours, or by working part time. In a majority of two-parent families with young children, although both parents often continue to work in the wage workforce, one parent stays home full time to care for children under two, and less frequently to care for children under six. The parent that stays at home and does the caretaking is nearly always the mother.

Caretaking patterns of mothers and fathers are similarly distinctive. On the whole fathers do not perform an equal share of caretaking or housework, regardless of the wage work status of the mother. Fathers take on some domestic tasks. Mothers, however, commonly do a "second shift" of household work in addition to their wage work. To the extent that men provide greater domestic help, therefore, it does not double the nurturing available to children. Men's actions generally conform to an unequal rather than a coequal caretaking role. In this model, the secondary caretakers have the power and the money in the relationships, and their caretaking is overwhelmingly economic.

The contemporary reconstruction of traditional gender roles is even more evident, and the pattern even more strongly gendered, in divorced families and families where the couple never marries. Most single-parent fathers are divorced. Eight percent are widowers, 25 percent are never married, and the rest are divorced (Dowd 1997a:49). While most single fathers are unmarried, some remarry, and they do so to a greater degree than do single mothers (41 percent versus 23 percent) (Dowd 1997:a49). Most single fathers do not have primary or sole custody of their children, although the number of single fathers with custody is increasing. The percentage of children living with their mothers is 87 percent and with their fathers 13 percent (Rawlings 1994:5–7).

The income of single-parent fathers with custody is roughly double that of mothers with custody (Bureau of National Affairs 1989:16). Nevertheless 18 percent of single-father families live in poverty. Few fathers receive child support. Courts order less child support for fathers than for similarly situated mothers (Downey 1994:142).

Most single-parent fathers are noncustodial, occasional fathers. The income of single-parent fathers without sole or primary custody is significantly greater than that of men who are primary caregivers (Dowd 1997a:21, 48–49). Many fathers do not pay child support at all, or pay erratically or incompletely. Economic irresponsibility has given us the "deadbeat dad" as a paradigm and scapegoat. So widespread has been the pattern of fathers' failing to pay full or even partial support—even when support is ordered (and in many cases it is not), that the deadbeat dad often seems to be the norm.

Single fathers' noneconomic links with their children range from regular visitation to a severing of all but the legal relationship. According to one national survey, fathers averaged only two visits per month several years after divorce, and almost half the children in the study had not seen their fathers even once the previous year. The strongest predictor of ongoing contact is the father's relationship with his former wife rather than the strength of his paternal involvement with his children prior to divorce. Lack of visitation occurs in about 50 percent of all cases, and upward of one-third of children in divorced families do not see their fathers at all after the first year of separation (Czapanskiy 1991:1449). Ten years after divorce, only 10 percent of children have regular contact with their fathers; and sadly, 66 percent had no contact in the prior year (Furstenberg and Cherlin 1991).

Never-married fathers are even less likely to nurture their children than divorced fathers. Paternity is established for only 30 percent of nonmarital children. Thus 70 percent of nonmarital children have biological fathers but not legal fathers. The degree to which such fathers nurture or economically support their children is largely unknown.

Three patterns of fatherhood are suggested by this data about fathers. One pattern, typified by the small cadre of single-parent fathers with sole or primary custody and an even smaller proportion of married fathers, is men who father like mothers in both substance and style. A second pattern, evident in the data on two-parent heterosexual families, is men fathering as a secondary parent, supporting mothers in their full-time parenting role. In such families, fathers and mothers do not parent differently simply in style, but also in form and function. The third pattern is that of men fathering as limited or disengaged nurturers. Such fathering occurs both in intact and divorced families, among married and never-married fathers, and in single and dual wage-earner families. These fathers sometimes support their children economically, but in many instances they do not do even that. These fathers may have only a biological or legal link to their children. A nurturing relationship with their children may never have existed or may have deteriorated over time.

To a remarkable degree, legal notions of fatherhood reflect fathering divorced from nurturing. The model of fatherhood embedded in the law is predominantly biological and economic within the marital framework. It accords with historic concepts of fathers as property holders in relation to their children. Support for the nurturing aspect of fatherhood is very limited, hidden, and indirect. The view expressed in U.S. Supreme Court decisions that biology alone should not permit unmarried fathers to assert parental rights would seem to suggest that the Court also expects them to play a nurturing role. On the other hand, it appears that the Court would simply like them to legitimate their relationship with the mother through marriage rather than expand their relationship with their child from a merely biological to a nurturing role (Dolgin 1997).

A stronger case for a nurturing role might be found in the move toward gender neutrality in the law, and the elimination of sex stereotypes. The goal of eliminating gender bias in the law by encouraging gender neutrality suggests that men can (although not necessarily that they should) nurture their children as mothers do. In this manner law might support either of the two nurturing patterns of fatherhood. Historically, however, law has viewed fatherhood as ownership and children as property, controlled by and responsible to the patriarch. The perpetuation of a merely biological and economic definition of fatherhood is apparent in much modern law, which silently accepts lack of nurturing as unremarkable.

Examples of this marital-biological-economic model are evident in adoption, paternity/legitimation, and divorce law. Under most adoption statutes, the establishment of a biological connection to a child is sufficient to entitle a father to determine whether his child may be placed for adoption, even if he is unwilling to care for the child himself. The father's consent may be unnecessary only if he has abandoned the child, but abandonment is commonly understood in economic terms as failure to contribute to the support of the child during the pregnancy or after birth. In a notable departure from this view, in 1995 the Supreme Court of Florida expanded the notion of support to include psychological and emotional support by finding abandonment even when the biological father had provided some economic assistance but was abusive toward the mother (*In re Adoption of Baby E.A.W.* 1995).

The historic property orientation of fatherhood, defined in biological terms, remains at the core of the concept of legitimation and the establishment of paternity. Fatherhood is defined by the status it can confer upon children, rather than in terms of responsibilities, obligations, relationship, or nurturing. The concept of legitimacy embodies a blatant example of stigma intertwined with gender hierarchy. Legitimacy is father-controlled and father-related. Status is conferred through the father, epitomized by the father's gift of his name to his children. Theoretically, we no longer treat legitimate and illegitimate children differently, or at least significantly differently, although in reality they are treated quite differently. Illegitimate children are less likely to be the beneficiaries of child support, and lower support is ordered on average than for marital children, whose legitimacy is automatic. In addition, the status of illegitimacy continues to have strong significance. This is reflected in another Florida case where the Supreme Court of Florida was confronted with the status of a child born when the marital couple had separated but had not yet divorced, and the child was conceived by the wife with a man other than her husband (*Department of Health and Rehabilitative Services v. Privette* 1993). The court refused to acknowledge the biological facts, on the grounds that to do so would delegitimate the child, who ordinarily would benefit from the legal presumption that every child born during a valid marriage is legitimate.

The related area of paternity law is a glaring example of the law's discouraging fathering. The rate of paternity establishment has remained steady at approximately 30 percent of all non-marital births (Wattenberg 1993:214–15). The rates by state range from a high of 67 percent in Michigan to a low of 14 percent in Louisiana and 20 percent in New York. The process of establishing paternity is not inherently difficult, given genetic testing. Nevertheless, the rate of establishment remains stubbornly low. One study identified the reasons for this as connected to the quasi-criminal or criminal nature of some proceedings, triggering heightened procedural and evidentiary standards that slow the process (Wattenberg 1993:214–15). Even with respect to voluntary acknowledgment, many existing procedures are cumbersome and invasive.

The disincentives to establishing paternity lie both with these structural barriers and limited commitment of public funds. If the purpose of the paternity process is to protect men from becoming fathers, then the process works quite well, although overinclusively. If public policy is better served by establishing the paternity of all children, then the statutory structure and its implementation are clearly lacking. If encouraging the nurture of children is our goal, then paternity might be recast as an opportunity to support fathers' nurture instead of as a defense of men's property and name. According to one survey, most children involved in paternity cases were not conceived in casual encounters (Wattenberg 1993). Approximately two-thirds of the fathers were present at the births of their children. Nearly 85 percent of fathers who do not marry the mothers of their children nevertheless continue their relationship with the mother during the pregnancy, and for some period thereafter, commonly two to three years (Williams and Williams 1989:5). Little in our legal structure, however, actively supports those father-child connections or encourages their continuation.

In addition to reflecting a biological definition of fatherhood, these legal structures also reflect the view that fatherhood is a chosen, voluntary status, rather than one automatically or involuntarily conferred. To use Karen Czapanskiy's terms, fathers are treated as volunteers, while mothers are draftees (Czapanskiy 1991:1415–16, 1449). But as Czapanskiy and others have also pointed out, the choice of whether, and to what extent, to father exists even when paternity and legitimation are not at issue. Nothing in the law supports fathers' nurturing nor sanctions the lack thereof during or after marriage. Particularly after divorce, when the law is far more intrusive in the lives of fathers and mothers, fathers are not legally sanctioned for failing to spend the time with their children to which they had committed themselves under custody and visitation schemes. At the same time, most custody and visitation schemes envision only a limited fathering role. For example, a typical court order usually sets up a schedule of visitation or shared parenting that is far more unequal than a fifty-fifty division of parenting time or tasks. Joint physical custody is the norm in only a minority of divorce cases. The vast majority of divorce cases presumes very limited nurturing by fathers.

The dominant expectation and focus of the divorce model is economic fathering or the payment of child support. Financial responsibility is equated with adequate fathering in a way that would never be acceptable for mothers. The extension of this vision to nonmarital families, triggered by the establishment of paternity in order to obtain child support, promotes the model of the economic father. The inclination to accord fewer rights of visitation and custody to nonmarital fathers actually enhances the economic model of fatherhood for nonmarital fathers.

The strongest countercurrent to the biological and economic definition of fatherhood is the implicit model of nurturing suggested by the elimination of gender bias and the adoption of gender neutrality in family law. Fathers' rights activists claim that the courts largely ignore this approach and fail to see fathers as nurturers. The issue of whether the courts act in a gender-neutral manner is disputed. What cannot be disputed, however, is that the vision of neutrality and its presumed link to gender equality remains unclear and undeveloped. There is remarkably little discussion regarding our understanding of the current context of fatherhood, what the goal of fatherhood is, and what the means are of achieving that goal. The vacuum tends to be filled with an economic model. The pattern of postdivorce fathering and nonmarital fathering as limited or nonexistent nurturing is accepted as *natural*.

Part of the agenda for a reconstructed fatherhood must be a careful examination of these and other legal structures and concepts that reflect our legal vision of fatherhood. We must understand this context in order to rethink our legal vision of fatherhood. I am not claiming that a reconstituted definition of fatherhood would be a magical solution to the patterns we see. Rather, I would argue that changes in the law are necessary to a redefined fatherhood. For married fathers, the law neither imposes nor supports a particular fatherhood role. Respect for family privacy is highly valued, and therefore the allocation of responsibilities and the definition of roles are left largely to individual choice. But the law controls fatherhood for unmarried or divorced fathers to a significant degree, imposing obligations and limitations on fatherhood through child support and custody/visitation, as well as regulations governing paternity and adoption. The model defined outside of marriage inevitably defines the implicit view of what the model should be within marriage. Although law may not cause the patterns, it does little to encourage or support a different vision. But first we have to identify what that vision should be.

A new model of fatherhood is not hard to envision because we have pieces of it already. We look to the roles fathers play when they become the primary caretaker or a coequal, separate caretaker and we look to the model of motherhood. These nurturing roles are essentially the same. Fathers who nurture can provide us with gender-specific information critical to understanding both why so few fathers do nurture in this fashion and in what ways this model of fatherhood can be supported. The motherhood role gives us a fuller, richer context to draw from in constructing a nurturing model, because more mothers have lived the practice of nurturing and because mothers have been more closely studied than fathers. A comparison of the motherhood model with that of fathers who nurture can also expose the issues and problems that must be addressed by a reconstructed vision of fatherhood. Most obviously those issues include the devaluation of motherhood, the norm of a single primary caregiver as part of the existing nurturing model, and the unresolved conflicts between work and family roles.

Fathers do not possess a unique style of parenting. Fathers who parent alone do so like mothers—they nurture. Good parenting is neither sex-specific nor sex-related. The attributes of good parenting are more strongly associated with mothering, but the connection is cultural, not biological. When men are primary parents, by choice or by circumstance, they parent as well as, and like, women. Men are not essential to healthy child development because they are unique; rather, they contribute to healthy child development by providing the benefit of direct nurture, as well as indirect nurture by their support of the primary caretaker. A father's presence correlates with more income, and sufficient economic resources correlate with greater childhood success.

The claim that fathers are essential (and unique) nevertheless remains powerful. For example, David Blankenhorn not only argues that men have something unique to offer as fathers, but also that fatherhood is essential to men as a civilizing influence to men's aggression (Blankenhorn 1995). Men's belief in their own uniqueness is essential, in his view, to giving men a reason to connect with their children; and that connection is essential to becoming a good man. Fatherhood, according to Blankenhorn, "is society's most important role for men. First, fatherhood, more than any other male activity, helps men to become good men. . . . [S]econd, fatherhood privileges children" (Blankenhorn 1995:25). Blankenhorn further states, "As a social role, the deepest purpose of fatherhood is to socialize men by obligating them to their children. . . . More than any other cultural invention, fatherhood guides men away from violence by fastening their behavior to a fundamental social purpose" (Blankenhorn 1995:65).

Central to Blankenhorn's position is an acceptance of the view that men are violent, self-centered, individualistic, and materialistic. One must see fatherhood as necessarily gendered to convince men that they possess unique abilities as fathers that children need for successful development, and to combat men's negative predispositions. Blankenhorn rejects an androgenous model of parenting, arguing that gender-specific roles are essential to meet children's needs. In his view, coresidency with children and a parental alliance with the mother are necessary preconditions for fatherhood. In short, fatherhood works only within a heterosexual marital norm through defined, gender-specific roles regarded as complementary.

However, we know that fatherhood is a cultural role, not a biological role. If our goal is to promote nurturing fathers, our model is an androgenous one based on the experience of fathers who have parented as sole or primary parents. It is also apparent that the cultural role of motherhood is a well-developed nurturing model that can be emulated by fathers. If we label nurturing as mothering, will we deter men from fathering? I suspect that some would argue that we would. The argument would go something like this: to use motherhood as a model puts men off and makes them feel excluded and presumptively inadequate. Therefore, if we are serious about reorienting our definition of fatherhood, let us not begin with terminology that will defeat our goal. On the other hand, an argument can certainly be made that motherhood is precisely the model that we should use. It honors and validates the parenting that women have been taught and have performed. At the same time, it rejects the gender essentialism that has limited parenting to mothers and women to motherhood, to the exclusion of other choices and roles.

At least several other questions must be addressed. Do we envision variations in this nurturing model of fatherhood? We have inherited a pattern of significant uninvolvement or limited involvement by fathers in nurturing. Do we envision fatherhood as a role that requires a high level of nurturing, so that any other kind of fathering relegates a father to some other status, or without status at all? Mothers tend to be held to a single implicit standard. Is that a good thing? If that standard is not good for fathers, we should, of course, also question it for mothers.

Another question generated by a motherhood model is the relationship between nurturing and wage work. Fatherhood has always been strongly linked to the breadwinner/economic model. Motherhood (and even potential motherhood), on the other hand, has been an automatic disadvantage in wage work. Although adoption of the motherhood model does not require us to adopt this negative consequence, the relationship between fatherhood and work must be revisited. We have never fully envisioned what this change would look like or what it would require in terms of structural change. Because men stand in a different relationship to work and family, resolving those conflicts requires a new perspective.

Finally, both the nurturing by the small band of fathers who are primary or sole caretakers and the nurturing by most mothers function on a single-parent model. Whether it is a two-parent relationship, or one where the parents are living in separate households, in general one parent does all, or substantially all, of the nurturing. If we accept that as a given, then a reenvisioned fatherhood is one which aims to give fathers an equal opportunity to be the primary or sole parent. On the other hand, if we want to move toward a two-parent model of parenting, rather than simply redistribute responsibility or restructure opportunity, then we must think through exactly what that means. Furthermore, we have to consider how a dual- or multiple-parent model works when the parents do not share the same household. Finally, if we decide to embrace a dual-parent model, we must do so without stigmatizing those who do function as single parents.

The challenges to redefining fatherhood lie not, I think, in envisioning what fatherhood might be. Notwithstanding the difficulty of thinking about the subject innovatively and the deep structural changes required, those hurdles can be overcome. More difficult are the changes required in concepts of masculinity, especially male violence and homophobia, and men's relationships with women and other men. Men's socialization continues to emphasize qualities in conflict with good parenting. Parenting challenges men to adopt characteristics traditionally viewed as unmanly. Reconstructing fatherhood requires thinking about the models that are passed on to boys as well as supporting men in different ways. The combination of socialization and structural constraints makes it seem "natural" that mothering and fathering are substantively different, gender specialized, and differentiated, even while the ideology of equal parenting hides the inequality of parenting responsibility and care.

Our tasks are manifold. First, we must address the question, how do we as a society see male gender roles and how do we respond to the evident lack of value attached to nurturing in concepts of masculinity?

Second, the problem of male violence toward partners and children, and its relationship to the promotion and acceptance of violence and force as male characteristics, confounds any effort to further empower men as fathers. One of the real dangers of a reconstituted definition of fatherhood, coupled with a greater entitlement of fathers to preserve their relationships with their children, is that the redefining will be done at the expense of women and children. Any strategy giving men more rights or power increases the risk of giving power where significant and widespread abuse already exists. The problem of gender violence, commonly male on female, must be confronted.

Third, it is essential that we break the hold of homophobia as a constraint against reconstructing fatherhood. Homophobia not only pushes men away from nurturing work by labeling it "women's work," but also pushes men away from nurturing children as being somehow unmanly. It also affects the kind of nurturing men do. It deters us from learning analytical or practical concepts of a different masculinity or a different fatherhood from gay fathers or gay culture.

Fourth, gender challenges also include reconceptualizing partnership. This includes both male-female and male-male partnerships involved in raising children. Fathers often serially or multiply parent children to whom they may or may not have biological, adoptive, or marital ties, but to whom they may have strong social connections. The challenge is to envision nurture as children need and experience it, not as adults often see it.

Finally, if we are to envision and define fatherhood differently, we are faced with the clear challenge of making this inclusive of all fathers—Black, Latino, Asian, Native American, European, poor, blue collar, middle class, rich, married, unmarried, stepfathers, foster fathers, gay, straight. We currently make it difficult or impossible for many men to achieve the breadwinner ideal. If we are to make nurturing fathers a reality for all children, we must learn from our diversity and include all men in our vision. Many of these issues have to do with problems of dominance and hierarchy, the price that men pay for racialized patriarchy, whether or not desired.

How these challenges translate into legal policies and structures that might support a reconstructed vision of fatherhood suggests a complex agenda. Policies that expressly condemn or promote a particular gender role may raise a number of concerns. I certainly see a role for the state in promoting and supporting strong families, even to the detriment of what we have identified as weak or lesser family forms. That justification could be used to support what we identify as "good" fatherhood. Whether we would be willing to condemn and root out destructive influences (especially violence and negative gender roles that undermine men's ability to be egalitarian toward women and nurturing toward children) might depend on whether we characterize such an effort as legitimate state support for egalitarian gender roles or as censorship and a denial of free expression. Since the state has rarely acted with that goal in mind, many might find this not only suspect but also dangerous. Efforts to combat male violence might benefit from ongoing reforms to combat domestic violence. On the other hand, the orientation of many domestic violence strategies is to address violence in a crisis situation, rather than to prevent battering in the first place. Finally, movement on some gay and lesbian rights and the emergence of a vibrant jurisprudence concerning issues of sexual orientation are other legal developments that could help in the reconstruction of fatherhood. The problem, however, is how do you get a patriarchal system to give up privilege, even when it is self-destructive? Perhaps the only way is that it be sacrificed from within, by men themselves.

In this book I hope to contribute to the process of thinking through these challenges by describing the context of fatherhood, by examining the status of fathers under the current law, and by proposing a re-definition of fatherhood centered on nurturing. In Part 1, I explore the present context of fatherhood. Chapter 1 presents a snapshot of fathers based on demographic and statistical information. Chapter 2 summarizes interdisciplinary research on the character of fathering and provides a clearer picture of fatherhood in action and over the life course. Chapter 3 focuses specifically on how fathers combine work and family. Chapter 4 examines the available research on particular subgroups of fathers, including Black, gay, and divorced fathers. In chapter 5, I summarize the data and the patterns of contemporary fatherhood.

In Part 2, I provide an overview of the primary legal frameworks that affect fathers. Traditionally, fathers were defined within the framework of marriage. That common law view remains a significant part of constitutional cases on fatherhood which I discuss in chapter 6. The legal treatment of biological fathers, both unmarried and married, is discussed in chapter 7, by examining paternity, adoption, and repro-ductive rights. Although traditionally biology alone was insufficient to define legal fatherhood, the trend is toward increasing legal rights and obligations based solely on biology. The other major trend, rein-forcement of fatherhood as an economic role, is discussed in chapter 8, which focuses on custody and child support.

In Part 3, I offer a redefinition of fatherhood centered around nur-ture. I articulate my redefinition in chapter 9 rejecting marital, bio-logical, and economic definitions in favor of social fatherhood defined by the quantitative and qualitative nurture of children. The challenges to that redefinition are discussed in chapter 10. In the final chapter, I explore the policy implications of my redefinition in terms of eco-nomic support, work-family restructuring, and cultural education.

I am the mother of a son and a daughter, and have always considered the job of raising my son, at least with respect to issues of gender and sexism, to be far more difficult and challenging than those relating to my daughter. For my daughter, I want to prevent doors from closing simply because she is a girl; for my son, I want to close the door of privilege that is open simply because he is a boy. For my daughter, I see my task as supporting her sense that she can do anything, that no one can deny her an opportunity or an experience because she is a girl. General notions of equality support my efforts; nevertheless, the more subtle, hidden structural and cultural messages that contradict widespread notions of gender equality are frustrating. For my son, on the other hand, while I want to support his consciousness that everything is open to him, I also wnat to help him resist the notion of privilege which comes to him simply because he is male, as well as to refuse to accept the limitations which are the quid pro quo for privilege. Dominant notions of equality do not seem to support me in that regard; rather, they seem to have grafted a commitment to gender equality onto a male role model without much challenge to the underlying concept of maleness, or without generating an alternative model. Nowhere is this more apparent than in the concept of fatherhood.

My dilemma is twofold. First, children are remarkably perceptive and honest. If I were to ask my son what fathers do, and how they are different from mothers, I suspect his answer would reflect his perceptions of the fathers that he knows, as well as how he sees fathers functioning in the world around him, and in the pictures, movies, and commercials that he sees. Undoubtedly, his perceptions would reflect the realities of fathering: most fathers do not significantly nurture their children.

Second, there are few role models for me to point him to. Neither real nor imagined fathers engage in nurturing in a visible, common, ordinary way in the world in which he lives. He knows plenty of great fathers. But he knows that they are not the norm. Fathers who are actively engaged in nurturing tend to be treated as unusual, different, and extraordinary, and he no doubt notices that.

When I began this book, my son (then four years old) crawled up on the sofa beside me and announced,

"When I grow up, I want to be a Superhero."
"Does that mean you're going to be a daddy?" I asked.
"No," he responded with great certainty.

"Why not?" I asked.
"Because Superheroes have to fly around and save people," he said.

I hoped then that when he grew up, being a dad would be as important to him, and to our society, as being a Superhero. As I finished this book, he was having a conversation with his older sister about what he was going to be when he grew up. With the total confidence and assuredness that six-year-olds can muster, he said he was going to be a writer, an artist, and an astronaut, and that he was going to adopt several children. I hope he will achieve all his dreams. This book is an effort to support him, and all boys and men, in the dream and reality of nurturing children.

PART I · CONTEMPORARY FATHERS

CHAPTER 1

The Context of Fatherhood

It's Father's Day. This year, we will honor fathers by making them more visible. We will not give them a *day off* but rather a *day on*, a day at the center of things. Mothers will be asked to step back, to absent themselves from the lives of their children, so that the roles of fathers can be more clearly seen. What will we see? If mothers are absent, unavailable and invisible, how will children experience fathers? For some children, life will be no different because their fathers are their primary or sole parent. They will continue to be taken to school, to the doctor or dentist, will continue to be cared for at home for the flu or a sore throat, will continue to be shuttled to after-school activities, to be watched in a play, soccer, or t-ball game, to be dropped off at the mall, or helped with homework. They will continue, largely unaware, to be the object of their fathers' planning, worry, and discussion. These children will call, page, beep, or otherwise communicate; when they fall or are hurt, their fathers will be there or come to their aid.

For another, much larger group of children, life will change to some degree, and perhaps even to a significant degree. Their fathers will have to do the things that their mothers usually do. It will feel like part, or half, or even most of their world has significantly changed. Not only will their own father be taking on work and planning which he usually does not do, but many other fathers will do so as well. Indeed, these children might be surprised to learn that some men they know outside their own household are fathers. The switch to father care might cause confusion, frustration, and nervous surprise. Fathers about to leave on business trips might have to cancel their plans or take their children with them. Fathers may be embarrassed when they don't know the names of their children's friends or teachers.

Yet another group of children may simply find themselves alone. Whether unknown, physically distant, or emotionally cut off, these children would have no father available to parent them. Some of them have never known, and will never know, the identity of their fathers, because no legal or social paternity exists for them. Some of them have fathers who are no longer part of their household, and cannot or will not be found. Some of them live in households where the men, although biological fathers or stepfathers, do not know how to parent or feel no desire or obligation to do so. These children are also alone.

Some children might have more than one man caring for them, such as both a biological father and a stepfather. Others might have a stepfather, cohabitant, or boyfriend of their mother caring for them. A few might have male relatives such as grandfathers as their caretakers. Other men, without a biological, legal, or social relationship with children, will be unlikely to do much caretaking as a matter of communal or social practice. If the children need paid caretakers to replace their fathers, it will be difficult to find men with experience or an interest in doing such work. Indeed, fathers who need babysitters will have a difficult time finding teenage or college males with the experience or inclination to care for children. If Father's Day is celebrated during a school day, after-school programs might be canceled or severely limited for the day, and many elementary and middle schools would be forced to close or alter their lesson plans.

How will men experience this Father's Day? For some, it will be validating, a time when their positions would be valued and understood, their expertise obvious, their accomplishments recognized. Some might brush off overblown praise by seeing this as simply doing what it means to be a parent. For some, it will be a welcome challenge and expansion of their time with their children. Fathers without legal status who are engaged in nurturing children will be made visible and feel valued for their nurture and care.

For many fathers, however, taking on sole care of their children might well be confusing, frustrating, and difficult. The day will expose their lack of competence, without direction or understanding of what to do; it might even be terrifying, fearsome. For yet another large group, absent from their children, this Father's Day would be no different from all the other days when they did not connect, care for, or care about their children.

For some fathers, making visible their care will create a double bind. Visible fathering might be perilous or threatening to their job security. An open acknowledgment of their caring and nurturing, and of the demands that their children make, or conflicts with meetings, erratic schedules, and long-distance travel could threaten their employment or hinder their advancement.

And then the next day things would return to normal.

To begin thinking about fatherhood, we must expose the context within which we operate. In order to measure where we are against what we think fatherhood ought to be, we need to know how fathers function and what fatherhood looks like. What we know tells us a number of significant things about fatherhood. First, fathers' patterns of nurture are starkly asymmetrical as compared to those of mothers. A small proportion of fathers are sole or primary caregivers, or co-equal caregivers. A larger proportion are secondary parents. Sadly, a substantial number of fathers are largely absent as nurturers and fail to provide economic support as well. Second, the life patterns of fathers are significantly different from those of mothers. Men are more likely to be "serial fathers" parenting a succession of children as they enter and leave households. Mothers are more often "linear mothers." Men are more likely to nurture the children with whom they share a home. Third, there is a strong correlation between male nurturing and the strength and health of men's relationships with the women with whom they share children. Men rarely parent alone. Finally, the nature of men's nurture is neither unique nor essential. Fathering has significance for children because nurture and care has significance for child and adult development.

Our state of knowledge about fatherhood is provisional and tentative. Most of the work on fatherhood has been done only since the

1970s, when various disciplines began to examine the role of fathers. Even today, researchers disproportionately study mothers. Demographic information also reflects interest in the patterns and life course of women and children, but not of men and children. Designing policy without adequate information about current conditions or the effects of reforms may lead to perverse consequences if premised solely on theoretical assumptions or models. While we need to know more, existing patterns are the premise for social and cultural redefinition of fatherhood.

BASIC PATTERNS

Fatherhood is a common life experience for nearly all men. Almost 90 percent of men marry, and nearly 90 percent of these become fathers (Snarey 1993:32). Most become fathers by normal reproductive means, although with an infertility rate of 15 percent, some use reproductive technologies while others adopt (Snarey 1993:224). Many men become fathers outside marriage. Nonmarital births account for 30 percent of children born each year, although some of these parents marry or cohabit. Men may also connect with children as stepparents, in legally formal or informal relationships. Most become first-time parents in their twenties or early thirties (Dobrin et al. 1996; Lerman 1993:32). Fathering a child, defined as creating a child, is a common experience for men.

Fathering in the sense of nurturing children, however, is not a common experience for men (Mackey 1985). Researchers agree that currently two patterns of fatherhood predominate. First, there is a growing, but small, proportion of men who are significantly involved in the nurture of their children. Second, there is a dominant mode of fatherhood which involves minimal or no caretaking, with no other connection or contribution to the children (Dowd 1997a; Furstenberg 1992; Gerson 1993; Radin 1994). These two patterns of abandonment and involvement coexist. The pattern of involved fathers, however, is not one of coequal or equal coparenting. The best estimates are that truly coequal fathers either within marriage or in postdivorce families account for a mere third of highly involved fathers (Gerson 1993:181).

Certainly an increasing number of fathers are engaged in the care of young children. These arrangements are often viewed as necessary to replace a mother when she does wage work. The arrangement is rarely viewed as an independent obligation or desire on the part of the father. Also included among involved, nurturing fathers are single fathers, men who are the sole or primary parent of their children. Although numerically small, they are nonetheless a dramatically increasing proportion of single-parent families. While most single-parent families are mother-headed, recent figures show that 17 percent of all single-parent families are father-headed (Bureau of Census 1998b:1). Four percent of working fathers are single parents, compared to 23 percent of working mothers (Levine and Pittinsky 1998:21).

The dominant pattern of fatherhood, however, is one of abandonment or lack of connection. This pattern has persisted and grown with the increase in nonmarital births and with the high rate of divorce, but it cannot be explained simply by those two phenomena. Currently, the number of children whose fathers are not present in the home is 23 million, compared to 8 million in 1960 (Horn 1997). Forty percent of all children do not live with their fathers and, more distressing, it is estimated that the rate will rise to 60 percent for children born in the 1990s (Horn 1997). Forty percent of children in father-absent homes have not seen their fathers at all during the previous year. Only one in six sees his or her father at least once a week (Horn 1997). Only one-quarter of nonmarital fathers visit their children consistently beyond age four (Lerman 1993:45). On the other hand, many men who do not live in the same household as their children still parent them; disconnection and abandonment are not automatic by virtue of not sharing the same household.

The presence of a father in the household of children does not guarantee active and significant nurturing. Physically present fathers may have very little contact with their children. Contemporary parents in general spend roughly 40 percent less time with children than did parents in the previous generation (Horn 1997). In two-parent households, mothers still dominate in the care of children and the fathers' nurturing contribution is often insignificant or meaningless (Dowd 1989a and 1997a). In single-parent households, women are far more likely to be the custodial parent. Approximately 1.6 million men were custodial parents in 1992, compared to 9.9 million women (Bureau of Census 1995a:1).

The basic caretaking patterns of American fathers are remarkably similar to fathers in other cultures. One review of a hundred and eighty-six societies describes fatherhood as consistently characterized by economic providing, serving as a role model, protecting family members, and functioning as an authority figure. While capable of nurture and caregiving, fathers consistently did less direct child care work than mothers (Bruce, Lloyd, and Leonard 1997). Across cultures, fathers tended to engage more with older children, and more with sons than with daughters. Fathers rarely provided more than a few hours of care per day, and on average always less direct care than did mothers. The level of a father's involvement was strongly correlated with his relationship with the child's mother and increased when both parents shared the same household.

A significant proportion of American men do not even support their children economically. Thus, even if economic support is viewed as caretaking, it does not radically change the picture of disengaged fathering. Here again, American fathers mirror the patterns of other cultures (Bruce, Lloyd, and Leonard 1997). Men are more likely to support children when they are married. They are also more likely to support their children when their income is higher, although fathers with a college education are less likely to support their children than high school dropouts. Other characteristics associated with higher support levels are race (because of its high correlation with income) and the financial needs of the provider.

In 1988, the average child support payment received by custodial parents constituted 7 percent of family income, or roughly $2,700 annually (Bureau of Census 1992a:10). Men paid a higher percentage of their income as child support than women. Higher child support is associated with *greater* labor force participation by the recipient. The addition of support, if reliable and steady, provides the financial resources to fund child care, which in turn permits custodial parents to work (Veum 1993).

Fathers benefit less frequently from child support, but the economic consequences of nonsupport or nonpayment are generally less dramatic for them. The most common reason for a father not being awarded child support is his failure to pursue an award or his refusal to accept one (Bureau of Census 1995a:2). For fathers who do have awards, child support represents a less significant proportion of their income than for mothers who have awards—7 percent for men versus 17 percent for women. Men are also less likely to have support actually paid to them. Mothers' overall incomes remain lower than fathers', generally half that of custodial fathers. Not surprisingly, then, the poverty rate for mothers is two-and-a-half times that for fathers, and more than four times that for married couples with children (Bureau of the Census 1995a:2–3).

The inadequacies of child support and the declining availability of welfare contribute to children's high poverty rate. Nationally, one in four preschoolers lived in poverty in the mid-1990s. The rate varies from one in ten in New Hampshire and Utah, to four in ten in Louisiana (Li and Bennett 1996:84). The rate for children of all ages is approximately one in five (Bureau of Census 1996b:3). Poverty rates are higher for female-headed families and families of color. An exit from poverty is unlikely for both groups of families (Bureau of Census 1996b:5). Welfare programs have not made a serious dent in this regard, although one in seven Americans participates in a means-tested assistance program, including 33 percent of Blacks, 10 percent of whites, and nearly 30 percent of Hispanics. Nearly 25 percent of all children receive some benefits, and most frequently they live in female-headed households (Bureau of Census 1996c:1). The median length of time for which they receive benefits, however, is less than three-quarters of a year (Bureau of Census 1996c:1; Li and Bennett 1996:84).

Some men do not support their children economically not because they are unwilling to pay, but because they are unable to do so. Real wages have fallen, fewer jobs pay a living wage, and a large proportion of the youngest men in the population, aged eighteen to twenty-four, earn poverty-level wages (Kimbrell 1995:109). The most destitute are homeless men, whose average age is thirty-five, and only a quarter of whom are employed full- or part-time (Kimbrell 1995:281). A single income is usually insufficient to support a family. From 1960 to 1988, for example, average household net income declined by 6 percent while mortgage payments increased from 14 percent to 44 percent of an average homeowner's gross income (Snarey 1993:13). The inability of men to support or adequately support their children is strongly race-related.

Researchers frequently note that voluntary payments of child support correlate positively with visitation (Veum 1992). However, the rate of visitation is less frequent than the rate of child support payment (Veum 1992). Men who have never been married are more likely than divorced fathers to visit but not pay support. More than a third of fathers who neither visit nor pay support have remarried. More Black fathers than white fathers, and more high school dropouts than high school graduates, visit but pay no child support. Fathers who both pay child support and visit are most likely to be employed. Those who paid child support usually worked more than two thousand hours per year and had three times as much annual income as those who did not pay support. Those who do not pay child support have a tendency to work less and have low earnings. Finally, among those who visit, non-payers of support are more likely to visit daily while payers are more likely to visit once a week. Nevertheless, child support payments and visitation are closely related, whatever the degree of visitation (Veum 1992).

SERIAL PARENTING

The lifetime patterns of men's fathering suggest a pattern of serial parenting rather than linear, lifelong parenting (Furstenberg 1992; Jacobsen and Edmondson 1993; Marsiglio 1997; Seltzer and Brandreth 1994). Men parent the children who reside with them and thus may parent more than one set of children over their life course. Rarely does a man parent several groups of children differently and simultaneously. The data suggest a "social fathering" pattern which may change or modify the perception of fathers' disengagement. At the same time, the quality of this fathering may be less engaged and less socially supported.

Men's serial parenting is indicated by a number of studies on family transitions that point to diversity and fluidity in fathering patterns. This includes transitions in and out of fatherhood, as well as the fathering of children both within and outside the father's household. A 1991 study examining the economic status of children found that nearly 10 percent of the families studied had experienced a transition in family form during the previous three-year period (Bianchi 1995). About 6 percent of the children who began the period with two parents had an absent father by the end of the study; nearly 3 percent of the children who began the period with an absent father had a mother who had either remarried or reconciled with their father by the end of the study. Only about 3 percent of the children had an absent mother and lived with their father only during this period (Bianchi 1991:2). The breakdown differed by race: just over a third of Black children lived continuously with both parents during the period as compared to over two-thirds of white children. Among Hispanic children, two-thirds lived continuously with both parents during the study period.

When fathers moved out of the household, family income dropped dramatically. Although children in two-parent families and single-parent families had stable or increasing incomes, because single mothers earned so much less, half of the children nevertheless were in poverty (Bianchi 1995). When a father departs the household, the decline in income is attributed to the loss of his income to the household. Children who lost their fathers often came from households that were less well off to begin with (Bianchi 1995). Coincidentally, fathers' labor force attachment declined when they left a two-parent household. In two-parent households 81 percent of the fathers worked, whereas only 67 percent of the absent fathers worked. The amount of earnings provided to children was nearly a third greater for those fathers living in two-parent households. Earnings were not easily replaced by mothers. Working mothers often increased their hours of work but for meager returns. Mothers not in the workforce were frequently unsuccessful in entering the workforce or in working full-time (Bianchi 1995).

The high rate of family transitions coupled with the custody patterns for single-parent households translates into complex fathering patterns. Looking at the composition of children's households it is apparent that fathers frequently nurture their children (if they do so) from a separate household, or legally (or otherwise) stepparent children with whom they share a household. Fifteen percent of all children live in a blended family. Living with a half-sibling is the most common blended family form, followed by living with a stepparent, and finally with a stepsibling. Blended families are equally common among two-parent and single-parent families, reflecting the more common blending of children but not necessarily of parents (Bureau of Census 1994a).

A 1994 report found that approximately 75 percent of American children lived with two parents and 24 percent with one parent, and a very small percentage lived with neither parent (Bureau of Census 1994a). Half of all American children lived in a family composed of two biologically related parents and biological siblings. The other half lived in a household which might include a single parent, stepparent, grandparent, another relative, or nonrelatives. Of children who lived in mother-only families, 20 percent lived with an adult male as well. In father-only families, children were twice as likely to live with an adult female. In both single-mother and single-father households, about 20 percent of adults lived with an adult of the same sex, most commonly a relative, usually a grandparent. Thus, children in two-parent families commonly lived in a blended family, while those in single-parent households frequently had a father or mother figure in their household.

Family patterns are sharply racially differentiated: white children were nearly twice as likely as Black children, and considerably more likely than Hispanic children, to live in the traditional nuclear, biologically related family (Bureau of Census 1994a). These differences are not so dramatic if we focus on children in two-parent homes. Of those children, 72 percent of white children, 62 percent of Black children, and 59 percent of Hispanic children live in a traditional two-parent household (Bureau of Census 1994a:3). In other words, the rate of children living in two-parent families varies significantly by race. Of those who live in two-parent families, the proportion of "traditional" two-parent families versus two-parent "blended" families exhibits less of a racial divide.

These longitudinal studies indicate that fatherhood is often not continuous and singular, but is serial or multiple. Men may be present in many households as social fathers even when they are not legal or marital fathers. Frank Furstenberg and Kathleen Mullan Harris describe serial fatherhood as being defined by a changing marriage system, linked to the coresidency of men and children, and created by marriage or a marital-type relationship.

> The responsibilities of fathers are carried from one household to the next as [men] migrate from one marriage to the next. Some men who become stepparents or surrogate parents in a new household often transfer their loyalties to their new family. Relations with their biological children become largely symbolic if they survive at all. . . .
> Many men are biological fathers and sociological fathers, but a growing proportion are not both at the same time. (Furstenberg and Harris 1993:217)

The strong link between social fathering and marriage connects nurturing by men to an institution in decline, given the declining rate of marriage and the high rate of divorce. Male parenting thereby parallels the episodic, serial character of men's adult pairings. Ever since 1975, the first marriage rate has declined, the divorce rate has risen, and the remarriage rate rose but then declined to a rate similar to the first marriage rate. The change in family structures was profound. "Most young women in the 1950s got married by the time they were 20 and quickly had two or three children. Almost 80 percent of all U.S. households were married couples in 1950. . . . During the 1950s, the marriage rate went up, people began marrying earlier in their lives, and the divorce rate dropped sharply" (Coltrane 1996:40). Women were full-time mothers, especially those with young children; men were breadwinner fathers largely absent from the daily lives of their children (Coltrane 1996:41–42). The decline in married households since the 1950s has been significant: by the year 2000, married couple households will constitute only about half of all U.S. households. Currently, many households are composed of single individuals, or single-parent families. Marriage occurs later in life and does not last as long. Half of all marriages end in divorce, although remarriage is also frequent. Children are born later in their parents' lives, and families have fewer children (Coltrane 1996:209–210).

In 1995, 63 percent of men were married, 8 percent were divorced, and 27 percent were never married. The rate of marriage increases steadily as men age, from 45 percent between the ages of twenty-five and twenty-nine, to 79 percent between forty-five and fifty-four. Of all marriages, 40 percent are remarriages for one or both parties, and the divorce rate for remarriage is about the same as for first-time marriages, although it occurs sooner. The median duration of a marriage is 7.2 years, with an average of one child per divorce (Bureau of Census 1998b).

Marriage occurs later in life. In 1994, the median age at a first marriage was 26.7 years for men and 24.5 years for women. There is a correlation between divorce and age. The older a person is at marriage, the more likely the marriage is to last. Delayed first marriage is associated with women's increased education and work experience, which also relates to delayed and lower fertility (Bureau of Census 1995d:1).

While rates of marriage have fallen and divorce has risen, cohabitation has increased significantly. The number of male-female pairs has remained stable since 1980, but more of those pairs are cohabiting than marrying. Social fathering is strongly linked to marital-type relationships, although cohabitation relationships are even less stable over time than marriage. Unmarried couple households have increased seven times since 1970 (Bureau of Census 1996e:1). Proportionately, there were seven unmarried couples for every one hundred married couples in 1994. Approximately one-third of those couples had children under fifteen (Bureau of Census 1996e:2; Bureau of Census 1996f:1–2). Of all nonmarital births, about a quarter are to cohabiting couples, with only two-thirds of those relationships converting to marriages (Hetherington and Henderson 1997:213).

Cohabitation is increasing both before first marriage and remarriage, and as a substitute for remarriage. Half of all marriages after 1985 began as cohabiting relationships (Bianchi and Spain 1997:10). Of single-parent families, one in seven includes a cohabiting couple (Bianchi and Spain 1997:11). Many stepfamilies cohabited for one year prior to remarriage (Hetherington and Henderson 1997: 214). The children present in cohabiting pairs are often from a former marriage or nonmarital union. In 1992, two-thirds of all cohabiting couples included one divorced partner.

Marriage patterns are significantly racially differentiated. In the Black community, marriage is correlated with economic opportunity and success:

> In the same period of time that joblessness among black men was rising, blacks also experienced an explosive rise in female-headed households, increases in out-of-wedlock birth, and declining marriage rates. The confluence of these trends raises important questions about the possible relationship between black males' declining economic power and their declining presence in the home. ("Keeping Pace with Change" 1993:11).

Both joblessness and single-parent family rates doubled for Blacks from 1960 to 1992. The proportion of never-married adults increased by 80 percent. According to one study, less than three out of four Black women marry, as compared to nine out of ten white women. The rate of unwed fatherhood is 25 percent for Black men aged twenty-three to thirty-one in 1988, 9 percent for Hispanic men, and 2 percent for white men. The rate of unwed fatherhood among Black men is ten times greater than that of whites and two and a half times greater than that of Hispanics ("Keeping Pace with Change" 1993:13).

Marriage and cohabitation are significant to fatherhood because fatherhood is so strongly tied to men's relationships with women.

Men's serial partnering commonly translates into serial fathering. Social fathering is connected with the other dominant pattern of fatherhood, namely, the split between highly involved and secondary, even disengaged, fathers. The link in these patterns is the importance for most fathers of their relationships with mothers. Just as significant, however, is men's relationship to wage work.

EMPLOYMENT

Employment is often seen as the defining characteristic of fatherhood, since a father is classically defined as being first and foremost a breadwinner. Overall, 75 percent of adult men are in the labor force as compared to 60 percent of adult women. In the prime working ages of twenty-five to fifty-four, 92 percent of adult men are in the labor force as compared to 76 percent of adult women (Bianchi and Spain 1997:18–19). The gap between working married men and women remains significant: 96 percent of married men aged thirty-five to forty-four were working as compared to 77 percent of married women (Bianchi and Spain 1997:31–32).

All employees work longer hours in wage work than they did in 1980. The increase in hours of wage work for women was nearly twice the increase for men, but women began from a lower base. Fathers with children under the age of eighteen work longer hours than other men, while mothers with children under eighteen work fewer hours ("Employment Characteristics of Families in 1997" 1998:8). Many employees are allowed time off during the day to attend to family matters. But only half of employed parents can take a few days off from work to care for a sick child without job consequences like loss of pay, use of vacation time, or the risk of discipline for fabricating an excuse to remain home. The proportion of workers with flexible schedules which permit them to begin or end work at different times is less than a third ("Employment Characteristics of Families in 1997" 1998:2).

Most men have seen a decline in their real wages by approximately 10 percent since 1970 (Kimbrell 1995:109). Men nevertheless still earn more than women, although younger men have less of a gender advantage (Costello and Krimgold 1996:63). The increasing contribution of women to family income has permitted most families to stabilize their income, but not significantly to increase it (Bureau of

Census 1992c). The proportion of families in which both parents work increased by one-half between 1970 and 1990, from 40 to 60 percent (Bureau of Census 1992c). Another factor which has helped families remain economically stable has been a decrease in the number of children per family (Bureau of Census 1992c). Nevertheless, the poverty rate for families with children increased one-third, to over 15 percent (Bureau of Census 1992c).

Despite the differences in work patterns between men and women in general, the mean household incomes of fathers and mothers were nearly the same in 1992, at about $45,000 (Costello and Krimgold 1996:86). The high incidence of single parenthood keeps the mean down for mothers, while the incidence of a nonworking spouse keeps it down for men (Costello and Krimgold 1996:86). But in terms of income distribution, a much higher proportion of mothers live in households in the lowest fifth of wage-earner households, 27 percent as compared to 17 percent of employed fathers (Costello and Krimgold 1996:86).

There are significant differences in the work that men and women do. Women are concentrated in a narrow range of jobs. They continue to be viewed by many as "choosing" certain jobs, hours, and lack of advancement as a trade-off for involvement with their children (*EEOC v. Sears, Roebuck and Company* 1988; Schultz 1990). Men's employment patterns are significantly different. Approximately 30 percent of men work in construction or manufacturing, whereas only 10 percent of women work in those areas. Nearly 40 percent of men and more than 40 percent of women work in retail trade and services (Costello and Krimgold 1996:60).

The level of gender segregation has changed. In 1970, two-thirds of the female labor force would have had to change occupations in order to have the same work patterns as men. By 1990, only one-half would have to do so (Bianchi and Spain 1997:20). The decline in job segregation has been partially attributed to "structural shift," as the rate of growth in some male-dominated occupations has been slower than in female-dominated ones (Bianchi and Spain 1997:23).

Men focus on their roles as providers in their selection of work, while women give greater consideration to family responsibilities. Men select fringe benefits, opportunities, and advancement over control of work schedules (Costello and Krimgold 1996:91). Men do less part-time work than women: 11 percent of all males versus 28 percent

of all females. Men who work part-time are often young and employed at entry-level jobs. They earn less per hour than women working part-time, who tend to be between the ages of twenty-five and
fifty-four (Costello and Krimgold 1996:70). Of all employed parents,
79 percent have permanent, full-time wage work, while 21 percent are
contingent workers (part-time, seasonal, or temporary). Fathers are
much less likely to be contingent workers than mothers: 13 percent as
compared to 29 percent. Mothers are six times more likely to work
part-time. Four-fifths (80 percent) of them do so by choice (Costello
and Krimgold 1996:83). Fathers and mothers both feel that their respective supervisors are more sympathetic than the general workplace
to family responsibilities, and both feel they have made career sacrifices for their families.

Wage work is thus another key factor in the maldistribution of
family work between men and women, and the differences in fathering and mothering practices. Limited opportunities for women, a rigid
structure for men, and the economic as well as cultural pressure on
men to disproportionately engage in wage work all undermine men's
nurture of their children and cooperative shared parenting with an
adult partner. The symbiosis between men's wage work and their
relationships with mothers are key factors in men's social fathering
patterns.

HISTORICAL PERSPECTIVE

How do contemporary fatherhood patterns fit within a historical perspective? The cultural and historical images of fatherhood are of authority figures: the King, the Elder, and Father in heaven (Burgess
1997). "Fathers in our culture are to be patriarchs. The literal meaning
of patriarch is father and ruler, and for us the two ideas are so completely identified that it takes a leap of imagination to grasp that there
are societies in which father does not mean ruler" (Burgess 1997:4).
The association between fatherhood and God, and the placement of
fathers at the apex of the hierarchy, permeates Christian theology
and was historically reflected in legal and social understandings of
fathers. "Fathers, in all their aspects, were relegated to Heaven, elevated or reduced (depending on your point of view) to one-dimen-
sional lawgivers, in the image of whom earthly fathers were to make

themselves. . . . The classic family image after Rousseau shows a seated (submissive) mother, with a standing (dominant) father, raising his child up before him in acknowledgment of paternity" (Burgess 1997:11–12). Fathers were also shown as heroes and leaders: they "held the reins," "navigated the ship" or were "shepherds of the flock" (Burgess 1997:13). Ironic, and hauntingly contemporary, are the contrasts between the images used and those never or rarely represented. "What was missing were images of men with babies. . . . Over many centuries, the maternal bond has been visually represented, [but] only paternal power has been displayed" (Burgess 1997:13–14).

Preindustrial fathers spent a great deal more time with their children by simple proximity, and children were virtually totally dependent on their fathers, even as adults (Stearns 1991:29–31). Industrialization led to two changes: the separation of wage work from family and the declining significance of property (Stearns 1991:38). As fathers separated from their children, a new literature supported the exclusive role of mothers as children's caregivers (Stearns 1991:40). Men were to be breadwinners, and secondarily, disciplinarians.

Anthony Rotundo sees two major periods of fatherhood in America, namely, patriarchal fatherhood (from 1620 to 1800) and modern fatherhood (from 1800 to the present), and perhaps an emerging third period which he calls participant fatherhood (Rotundo 1993). Rotundo focuses on fathers' duties, their emotional relationships, and the social, intellectual, and economic factors that underlie fatherhood (Rotundo 1993:64). He sees economics as the strongest historical force undermining fatherhood, stronger even than divorce. Economic developments have made it difficult for men to be breadwinners, while the large-scale entry of women into the workforce has signaled the end of men's exclusive claim to breadwinning. Rotundo also notes that the emergence of highly involved fathers is part of a long-term shift from authoritarian ideals toward more participant fathering.

Robert Griswold also documents this shift in fatherhood ideals from a hierarchical focus on order and dominance to "mutuality, companionship and personal happiness" (Griswold 1993). Concepts of childhood have changed, from seeing children as evil ones needing to be tamed to innocents needing to be taught. Mothers' roles have become more important, while industrialization had a major impact on the household economy. All these factors, Griswold argues, weakened father-child connections. He traces the new fatherhood to the 1920s and the emergence of a "masculine domesticity."

Ralph LaRossa, in his work on this era, describes the new image of father as "economic provider, pal, and male role model all rolled into one" (LaRossa 1997). Central to this era was the rise and fall of "daddyhood" or "men as pals" and, at the same time, men's fall and then rise in child-rearing status. "Daddyhood" meant that men would be companions to their children, more engaged in their care and the household, although with no commitment to gender equality (LaRossa 1997). In the 1930s the emphasis shifted in favor of the father as a role model. A study of popular magazines from the twentieth century shows the shift back and forth between two visions of fathers, one as providers and the other as nurturers (Atkinson and Blackwelder 1993).

Another historian of the late nineteenth and early twentieth centuries has emphasized the racial construction of masculinity. Gail Bederman exposes the intersection of race and sex in defining manliness and, implicitly, fatherhood (Bederman 1995). Manliness was clearly and quite explicitly constructed as white at the turn of the century, marginalizing all women and men of color. The best man was white; whiteness was the qualifying factor to be a real man. So, by definition, nonwhites could not be men. She demonstrates this by examining the rhetoric around the 1910 fight between Jack Johnson and Jim Jeffries.

> The Jack Johnson controversy . . . was only one of a multitude of ways middle class Americans found to explain male supremacy in terms of white racial dominance and, conversely, to explain white supremacy in terms of male power. . . . [Between 1890 and 1917] as white middle-class men actively worked to reinforce male power, their race became a factor which was crucial to their gender. . . . Jack Johnson's racial and sexual challenge so upset the ideology of middle-class manhood that both the white press and the United States government were willing to take extraordinary measures in order to completely and utterly annihilate him. (Bederman 1995:4–5)

Bederman convincingly demonstrates that the term "civilization" became a code word for whiteness. The civilized man was white, and the only good man was white.

Although the Great Depression raised significant concerns for men, World War II restored men's breadwinner status as well as their role as protectors of democracy. "The war became not only a war against fascism but . . . a war in defense of the American home and its traditional division of labor" (Griswold 1993:162). At the same time, there was concern about the absence of so many fathers from home, especially for boys, and the danger of the inordinate influence of women, or "momism" (Griswold 1993:164–170). The baby boom following the war was a demonstration of manhood. "To reject marriage invited doubt about a man's masculinity and sparked suspicions that the poor man suffered some infantile neurosis, some pitiful and hopeless attachment to his mother. At best, such men were escapist; at worst, homosexual" (Griswold 1993:189). But within several decades, that connection was severed. "What ended . . . was the equation of fatherhood and manhood. . . . [B]y the end of the 1970s, adult manhood was no longer burdened with the automatic expectation of marriage and breadwinning. Men had broken free. What was once quixotic had become acceptable, even respectable" (Griswold 1993:221).

At the same time as this freedom was won, the definition of fatherhood and manhood dramatically shifted. The greatest challenge to male breadwinning and male privilege came from the increasing number of women doing wage work. "Survey evidence suggests that American men [with working wives] have had a difficult time coping with the employment of their wives and tend to be unhappier and have higher rates of mental distress than those whose wives do not work outside the home. The reason, according to the experts, ultimately lay with men's sense of adequacy as providers" (Griswold 1993:220). The other trend since the 1960s has been simply less time spent as fathers.

> Because of later marriage, declining fertility, and soaring divorce rates, the overall time men spent in family environments with children present dropped significantly. . . . Thus, at the same time that increased attention is being given to the role of fathering, it seems likely that men, on average, are spending less time in living arrangements where there is an opportunity to occupy the role of father. (Griswold 1993:221)

In the twentieth century, the exclusivity of the breadwinner function shifted toward widespread acceptance of women's contribution to family income or an acceptance of women's roles as sole breadwinners. Burgess sees the 1990s model of fatherhood as one where fathers are imagined to be performing the *same* nurturing role as mothers; men are told they can still be men and retain their gender identity, though they cannot claim an exclusive or unique role. But the cultural messages have been historically grounded in *difference*.

In a whole range of ways, writers on fatherhood over the past century, in attempting to justify the father's role, have hung their hats on the notion of fathering as a distinct, "gendered" activity. Fathers have been said to be of value not simply because they are individuals or even because they are men, but because the things they do when they are with their children and the way that they do them are "different." (Burgess 1997:185)

In sum, several things seem to be clear from the historical record. First, the Industrial Revolution did more to change fatherhood than any other single historical event. The ongoing consequences of that fundamental economic shift continue to affect both fatherhood and motherhood. The physical separation of family and work, coupled with the sexual division of work, have reinforced gender segregation in ways that we have yet to unravel. Second, race plays a vital factor in constructs of masculinity and fatherhood, more blatantly in the past but not so subtly even now. Third, fathers are not appreciably more involved with their children than they have been in the past, nor does past reality bear out the myth of the perfect family. Fourth, many contemporary concerns about fatherhood have echoes in the past, and are often strongly connected to fears about overfeminizing boys, as well as a presumption about the rightness of strict gender roles and gender hierarchy.

Fatherhood and patriarchy have historically been intertwined, and men's dominance and male-female differences have been taken for granted (Griswold 1993). The role of father has been seen as essential and unique. The most enduring historical definition of a father has been as breadwinner, and the emotional or companionate side of fatherhood has been distinctly secondary. Although greater interest in fatherhood has been characteristic of the twentieth century, at the same time fathers have had less actual involvement with children, and have avoided household and child care tasks.

The perception that social problems in the early twentieth century were grounded in fathers' roles and families' patterns sounds quite contemporary. Concerns about the absence of fathers, the importance of fathers, convincing men to parent, and men's inability to father all sound familiar. But advocates for progressive visions of fathering did not, for most of the century, see this as inconsistent with presuming a defined domestic role for women. In effect, then, they had a very limited definition of fatherhood that in no way replicated motherhood.

One final historical footnote. Father's Day did not become an official holiday until 1972 and was originally seen as a response to the creation of Mother's Day (Griswold 1993:175; Schmidt 1995:275–76). Sonora Smart Dodd had organized a movement through the Protestant churches in Spokane, Washington, as she wanted recognition for the nurturing her father did, raising six children after his wife died. The religious organizations taking up the cause valorized a more muscular version of fatherhood. The holiday was often viewed as humorous, even ridiculous, a telling comment on the discomfort of seeing men as nurturers. Only when retailers promoted Father's Day did it become a national holiday.

CHAPTER 2

Fathers in Practice: The Conduct of Fatherhood

How do men parent? When they nurture children, do they do something unique and essential? In this chapter I explore what we know about fathers' nurture. I look at contemporary ideologies and realities of men's parenting. Although we know considerably more about fathers' nurture now than we did in the 1970s, there is much that we still do not know. This makes any analysis necessarily provisional, and exposes the degree to which judgments about fathers have been social and cultural rather than grounded on real data. The strongest cultural and ideological belief about fathers is that they are different. The clearest reality about fathers is that they are important, but not because they are different.

IDEOLOGIES AND REALITIES

Fathering is not a static practice. It changes in relation to the age and development of the parent, as well as in relation to the number, age, gender, and developmental stage of the child (Larson and Richards 1994; Shulman and Collins 1993; Shulman and Seiffge-Krenke 1997). In general, fathering and mothering are not that different (Starrels 1994). However, even when the fathering is comparable to mothering, the conduct may be experienced differently, or have different consequences for children. Fathering intersects and interacts with differences in male and female socialization as well as with the changing developmental tasks of children at different stages (De Luccie and Davis 1991; Larson and Richards 1994).

Fathering also varies in response to the changing expectations and constructions of fatherhood. Forty years ago virtually no men were present at the birth of their children. Today, almost 75 percent of fathers are present during the birth of their children, giving support to their spouses (Snarey 1993, 33). In 1974, the American College of Obstetricians and Gynecologists endorsed the presence of fathers at childbirth. The practice of including fathers spread rapidly in American hospitals. The current expectation—that fathers will be present, that they will have attended classes in order to be educated about the birth, and that they will provide support during childbirth—is testament to a major transformation in the conception of fatherhood in a relatively short period of time. The presence of fathers at childbirth creates a new connection between fathers, mothers, and children. Nevertheless, at childbirth many fathers experience a strong sense of difference from mothers. Biology can easily be viewed as a gender-specific, differentiated, separate destiny. Childbirth then marks the beginning of the sharply gender-differentiated patterns of fathers' and mothers' involvement with their children (Berman and Petersen 1987; Marsiglio 1997; Shapiro, Diamond, and Greenberg 1995).

Gender differentiation is also characteristic of men's role in conception and pregnancy. One can argue that the definition of fathering starts at conception. Men's sense of fatherhood is reflected in the way conception and prebirth caretaking is undertaken (or not) by fathers. Procreative activity, sexual activity, childbirth, and men's involvement with their children are related (Krampe and Fairweather 1993; Marsiglio 1997; Volling and Belsky 1991). Until the 1980s, men's perceived secondary role was reflected in their exclusion from family planning strategies to reduce teenage pregnancy. Other trends that have diminished men's reproductive roles include the development of reproductive technologies that separate procreation from sexuality, men's declining responsibility for the financial support of their children, and the rise in men's parenting of children to whom they are not biologically connected (Marsiglio 1997).

Once children are born, contemporary ideology supports men's active nurturing. What that means is not always clear. Fatherhood research shows that there is no clear model for fatherhood. Men are still creating and constructing something "new," a role different from that of their fathers and grandfathers, but one that is ambiguous and unstable (Cath, Gunsberg, and Gurwitt Gunsberg 1989; Daly 1993; McBride and Darragh 1995). Some researchers identify the role as mothering; others use a less loaded, more gender-neutral term like generativity, nurturing, or caregiving. This new model of fatherhood is always contrasted with the image of fathers as breadwinners or economic providers with no other dimensions.

While the rhetoric of a "new" fatherhood is strong, the reality is that the practice of fathering has not changed tremendously (Messner 1992). Michael Lamb identifies the factors relevant to fathers' involvement with their children as motivation, skills, self-confidence, social support, and institutional practices (the need for economic support and the barriers imposed by the workplace). He sees little change in the actual work of fathering, measured as engagement or interaction, accessibility, and responsibility. The greatest increase is in the area of fathers' engagement, especially in play time. The least increase is in the area of responsibility (Lamb 1987).

Joseph Pleck's work on paternal involvement confirms that contemporary fathering is characterized by greater involvement, but not significantly greater in absolute terms (Pleck 1995). Men are more involved in parenting younger children rather than adolescents, parenting sons rather than daughters, parenting biological children rather than stepchildren. Fathers who participate most, work at lower white-collar and professional jobs, while fathers in blue-collar and middle or high management positions and self-employed fathers participate the least. Fathers' participation is consistently higher when mothers work and when men become fathers at an older age. Greater paternal involvement can exact some short-term costs in the workplace, in marital relationships, and in self-esteem as measured against traditional roles. In the long term, greater involvement yields benefits such as career success and individual self-development (Pleck 1995).

GENERATIVE FATHERING

Why and how the men who *do* nurture do so, has been studied from both adult- and child-centered perspectives. John Snarey's fascinating longitudinal work explores fatherhood from an adult developmental perspective (Snarey 1993). Snarey chronicles men who were interviewed as boys in the late 1930s, and were followed through adulthood until their own children were on the verge of becoming parents (Snarey 1993). Snarey focuses on the degree to which these men practiced "good" fathering, which he defines as "generative fathering" (Snarey 1993:1–2). Generativity is an adult developmental stage identified by Erik Erikson, and is a concept utilized by several scholars to focus on the benefits and importance of fatherhood for men. Snarey defines paternal generativity as "the ways good fathers constructively care for their daughters and sons in childhood and adolescence and promote their children's social-emotional, intellectual-academic, and physical-athletic development" (Snarey 1993:1). Such fathering is a moral commitment and experience (Snarey 1993:357). "Parental generativity . . . requires the 'significant sacrifices' of love and the generative 'commitment to take care of [what] one has learned to care for'" (Snarey 1993:22, quoting Kotre 1984).

The core thesis of Snarey and others who focus on generativity is that fatherhood, or some form of care for others, is good for men and critical to social generativity, defined as giving back to the community and society at large."The degree to which a man's external life is characterized by mature love (caring for others) and mature work (creativity, productivity) tends to be critically correlated with the maturity level of his psychological development" (Snarey 1993:91).

The factors that contribute to generativity are connected to men's families of origin and their families of procreation. Snarey notes the centrality of women in both families: the status of men's own mothers, but even more significant, the employment and educational status of their wives. High father involvement was strongly correlated with strong marital commitment (Snarey 1993:337). At the same time, men's fathers are a significant factor in men's own child-rearing practice, either as a model to be replicated or as an example to be reworked or rejected (Snarey 1993:323).

Snarey's analysis emphasizes the complexity of fathering, in the sense that the determinants of involved fathering are grounded in individual personality and family history, social patterning and social-ization, and external structures, especially the workplace. His research also stresses the fluidity of fathering concepts. Fathering is a practice that can change in a generation, even in an individual's lifetime.

Snarey's work connects more involved fatherhood with marital re-lationships, women's work, and economics. He suggests that to in-crease father involvement requires emphasizing women's employ-ment opportunities and education. The implications of that strategy plus the economic necessity for two earners, he argues, will recast fa-therhood. He points to restructuring the workplace as the key to bringing about change in fathering. For Snarey, the value of father-hood lies particularly in its social consequences. Not only is it good for individuals and children, but it is also good for society.

Other researchers who have embraced the concept of generative fa-thering emphasize the psychological dynamic and benefit of more in-volved fathering (Hawkins et al. 1993). Rather than social benefits, they focus on individual benefits. The transformative potential of par-enting and its contribution to gender equality are captured by Dorothy Dinnerstein: "[T]he process of nurturing life is the most pro-foundly transforming experience in the range of human possibilities. Because women have this experience and men generally don't, we live and think and love across a great gap of understanding" (Hawkins et al. 1993:549, quoting Dinnerstein). Fathering may contribute to men's development of emotional skills, and rejection or compensation for the learned responses of anger, avoidance, and lack of communication (Levant 1995a). In this sense, fathering is a means of recasting mas-culinity by developing skills that overcome the negative characteris-tics of traditional masculinity. John Ross also argues that involved fa-thers attain and express "sublimated mothering" that has its roots in the development of gender identity in childhood. Ross's thesis is that boys have womb envy: not a fear of masculinity, but rather a desire to give birth. That desire is ultimately channeled into fatherhood. Nur-turing fathers create a model of parents as partners, mutually engaged in family.

[A] man does not come to fatherhood in a vacuum. His paternal identity, expressed in fathering his children, is embedded in a life-historical, intra-psychic, and interpersonal context. . . . In childhood are discovered the pre-stages of paternity, the successive parental identifications that accrue to the self-representation, preparing the way for the active nurturance and generativity of the adult man.

[Achieving nurturing fatherhood as an adult is] crucial to the positive identity of a man. . . . Fatherhood attests to one's manhood while it allows for a transcendence of the limits inherent in a single gender identity. (Ross 1994:63)

CHILD DEVELOPMENT

While the generative fathering model emphasizes adult development and social benefit, other psychological research has focused on the impact of fathers to child development. This work has evaluated the role of fathers in intact two-parent marital families, as well as the impact of a father's absence in single-parent families. In both respects, whether they matter to children and whether fathers matter because they do something unique and essential have been primary research questions. Predictably, these volatile questions provoke strong views that sometimes skew the research or the interpretation of research outcomes. Both the question of fathers' impact and their uniqueness are often discussed as *differences* between fathers and mothers.

One of the most recent and most comprehensive examinations of the impact of fathers on child development and the claim of a distinctive role, is Ross Parke's study of fatherhood (Parke 1996). Parke concludes that fathers have a significant role in child development in terms of their positive impact on children. This impact—plus men's behavior—is different enough from that of mothers to suggest that fathers play their parenting role differently. They are not, as Margaret Mead described them, biological necessities but social accidents. Parke sees fathers as having both a direct and an indirect impact on children, either by nurturing their children themselves or by supporting the mother's nurturing role. He recognizes the cultural message encouraging fathers to be more nurturing, but agrees that change has been much more evolutionary than revolutionary. He does not claim that men's differences are biological. Instead, he sees them as cultural. Parke sees those differences played out in gender roles, the father's relationship with the mother, cultural scripts, and the lack of institutional support.

The gender-specific practice of fathers, according to Parke, operates in at least two ways. First, there are well-documented differences in the way fathers involve themselves with their children from the way mothers do. Parke also tends to include wage work—the traditional breadwinner role—as part of fathering. But at the same time, by so doing, he expands the scope of motherhood and acknowledges the greater contribution by women to the care of their children.

Second, Parke's work shows that the conduct of fathers has a different impact on male and female children. His work suggests that if fathers are more involved, girls will experience a greater degree of the more traditional gender role models. Boys seem to benefit most by a father's presence, but that presence can reinforce traditional masculinity along with intellectual and other forms of development. Thus, a strong claim remains for the difference fathers make, but not for biological essentialism; their cultural and social roles are extremely powerful. Indeed, many researchers note that fathers parent sons more than they do daughters, and that they frequently do so differently from mothers (Starrels 1994). A separate literature exists on father-son and father-daughter relationships, with far more research devoted to father-son relationships. The tie between father and son is still most critical and may even be a potentially dangerous factor (Real 1995; Segell 1995). Yet, one researcher who has reviewed the literature argues that the available studies fail to support the assumption that parents nurture the children of opposite sexes differently (Russell 1997).

Michael Lamb's overview of the research on fathers and child development emphasizes the multiplicity of ways in which fathers affect children, and carefully distinguishes the way men have fathered from any claim that fathers inherently parent differently than mothers (Lamb 1997). Lamb identifies several ways that fathers influence children, emphasizing the importance of indirect as well as direct patterns of influence. Breadwinning remains the first and foremost role for men. Second, fathers support other family caretakers, normally the mother. Third, fathers provide direct support by doing housework and childcare. Fourth, fathers affect family dynamics by their relationships with partners and children. Fifth, fathers' conduct varies in different cultural settings.

Lamb sees the research as supporting the view that gender matters little in nurture. The more critical factors are parental warmth, nurturance, and closeness. Individual characteristics are less important than relational ones; the quantity of time is less important than how that time is spent. Finally, it is the family context that is critical and not the father-child relationship in isolation. The cultural context as well may vary the impact of paternal relationships. The multiple levels at which fathers affect their children suggest that men do not play a gendered role as much as they do that of a secondary caretaker, which is the most common parenting practice of men.

Brenda Geiger also concludes that fathers nurture like mothers, based on her examination of the more uncommon situation of primary caregiver fathers (Geiger 1996; Radin 1994). According to Geiger, the role of caregiver, not gender, controls behavior. Fathers perform the role of nurturing essentially the same way as mothers, except for different play behavior (Geiger 1996). Men are most likely to act as primary caregivers when functioning in an egalitarian relationship, and their caregiving contributes to creating such a relationship.

Geiger's study focuses on the care of children under age two, when parents either swap traditional roles or work in tandem. Geiger points to the influence of Freudian and attachment theory in emphasizing the role of mothers. She also notes that much of the literature emphasizing the differences between the behavior of fathers and mothers compares *traditional* fathers to mothers, but few have looked at nontraditional fathers. In her study, the behavior of primary caregiving fathers resembled that of primary caregiving mothers, with the exception of greater father participation in rough-and-tumble play. Another notable difference was the use of paid baby-sitters by the fathers, since most worked at least part-time, as compared to primary caregiver mothers who usually did not do wage work and only used sitters several times a month. She also notes that even secondary caregiving fathers were considerably involved, and hardly fit the stereotype of the breadwinner disengaged from the care of his children. She concludes that gender differences in parenting are minimal and result from differences in the parents' involvement (Geiger 1996:95). This would argue for an androgynous model of parenting rather than a gender-specific one, while pursuing a gender-specific strategy to increase fathers' involvement (Geiger 1996:105).

Another issue hotly debated by child development scholars is the significance and impact of a father's absence. Some researchers claim that a father's presence or absence makes minimal or no difference to children (Crockett, Eggebeen, and Hawkins 1993). Others claim that fathers play an important role in development (Biller 1993). A review of the literature can support both propositions—that fathers are important and that they do not matter (Amato 1994). The literature is oriented toward the assumption that a father's absence is detrimental; very little has been done on a father's presence and its association with negative developmental outcomes related to the distinctive roles of fathers in the home (Phares and Compas 1992).

Probably the most outspoken proponents of the importance, distinctiveness, and necessity of fathers are David Popenoe and David Blankenhorn. Popenoe argues for the value of fatherhood and marriage based on biological difference, the importance of gender differences, and outcomes connected to a father's presence, and rejects social constructionism. He argues for the value of a revitalized marriage model, changing the cultural message, and modifying the patriarchal and paternal models. His fatherhood image is of a nurturing (but still different) father (Popenoe 1996). Blankenhorn argues for the essential and distinctive role of fathers based on the literature on absent fathers, and the importance of fatherhood and marriage for civilizing and taming men (Blankenhorn 1995). The claim is also made by many that fathers are essential role models for young boys, and affect educational, sexual, and delinquency outcomes for boys and girls (Horn 1997; Thevenin 1993).

In my view, the importance of difference and the uniqueness of fatherhood is political and cultural, not developmental, at least for the child. Even Blankenhorn's work suggests it may be a developmental need for the adult only, as a kind of cultural subterfuge. The pattern and experience of fathering is clearly of value to children but it is not essential. Fathers' value ultimately rests not on their uniqueness but on the value of their nurture to children. It is also clear that a significant structural block to men's nurture is the workplace. In the next chapter, I return for a closer look at men's work and family relationships.

CHAPTER 3

Fatherhood, Work, and Family

The patterns of fathers and their fathering practices point to the importance of work-family connections. Men's perceptions and feelings about fatherhood reflect a desire for involvement and significant stress concerning parenting. A survey taken for CNN in 1995 found that 77 percent of fathers, across age and demographic groups, think it is harder to be a father today than in their fathers' generation ("National Men's Health Week Survey" 1995). Overwhelmingly, men identified spending quality time with their children as the most important characteristic of good fathering, as well as being a strong male role model for children. Men felt that being a good father and spouse was more important than career success or being the sole provider. Two-thirds felt that balancing work and family was difficult, and nearly half cited the stress of job security as a factor in work-family stress. More than half the men experienced stress on a daily basis, and the most common reaction was simply to keep it to themselves.

According to a major report issued by the Families and Work Institute in 1997, the work and family experiences of men and women have moved toward convergence (*National Study of the Changing Work-force* 1997). The proportion of dual-earner families has increased, mothers' time in household work has declined while that of fathers has increased, and mothers' child care has remained constant while that of fathers has increased. Men still spend more time doing wage work and women still spend more time doing family work, but the patterns are converging. What has been lost most is individual time.

A whopping 85 percent of wage and salaried workers live with family and have daily family responsibilities, with family defined as relations by blood, marriage, adoption, or partners. Most significantly for an examination of fathers, 46 percent of workers are parents with children under 18 who live with them at least half the time (*National Study of the Changing Workforce* 1997:5). Of these employed parents, one in five is single; of those, 27 percent are men. So, looking at the half of the workforce who are parents and have children in the household at least half the time, we see mostly two-parent parents (although this does not tell us how many are men and how many women); of the one-fifth who are single parents, about three in seven are men. Most married fathers have a working spouse: two-thirds of married employees with children under eighteen have partners who work ("Employment Characteristics of Families in 1997" 1998). How visible or invisible does that make fathers? It depends a lot, of course, on the gender composition of the workforce and where these parents are distributed in the workplace.

It is fascinating to see the impact of parenting at any one specific moment in the workplace. In 1990 the Institute for Women's Policy Research evaluated the impact of the lack of family and medical leave in the context of congressional consideration of the Family and Medical Leave Act (Spalter-Roth and Hartmann 1990). That study demonstrated the gender and race consequences of becoming a parent, based on the position of parents in the workforce before their child's birth and their ability to return to the workforce and recoup lost earnings and opportunities after the birth. Black men's position in the labor market after the birth of children worsened. The earnings gap between Black and white men increased, and the rate of unemployment increased for Black fathers as compared to the rate for white fathers. There was less of a gender difference between Black men and women, and more of one between white men and women (Spalter-Roth and Hartmann 1990:19). In addition, the distribution of household work, which includes both housework and child care, became maldistributed, the gap widening between fathers and mothers. This unevenness affects future income and ultimately lifetime earnings and pension/retirement benefits. The differences were more extreme for whites than for Blacks (Spalter-Roth and Hartmann 1990:20). Thus, parenting involved not only a short-term loss of income, but also had a long-term impact on employment with lifelong consequences that varied by gender and race.

It is equally fascinating to see the shifts in fathers' work-family relationships from a more extended historical perspective. In 1830, 70 percent of American children lived in two-parent farm families. A century later, less than 30 percent did so. The configuration of a breadwinner father and a homemaker mother rose from 15 to 55 percent in the same period (U.S. Department of Health and Human Services 1996a). A significant proportion of fathers shifted from being a presence in the lives of their children to being absent. The physical location of income-earning shifted dramatically for men, while the nature of household work shifted for women. Of course, the comparable modern shift has been the shift of women out of the home to do wage work. For children, particularly preschool children, this has led to a dramatic transformation in their relationship to their parents.

Family work has changed considerably in the past twenty years. Men's time with their children has increased substantially, to an average of 2.3 hours per workday. Mothers spend an hour more per day than fathers spend, which is virtually unchanged over the past twenty years. Men's time on housework has increased by one hour per day, while women's has declined by slightly over half an hour. Women still spend more total time on chores than do men (Bianchi and Spain 1997:32; "Employment Characteristics of Families in 1997" 1998:5–6).

Several fascinating studies flesh out work-family patterns of two-parent biological families. These studies highlight the nature of fathering within the context in which the greatest proportion of men do the most nurturing. Kathleen Gerson, who has combined a review of the work-family literature with an in-depth study of fathers, grouped the fathers in her study into breadwinner fathers, autonomous fathers, and involved fathers (Gerson 1993). Each group accounted for about one-third of the total. Of the involved fathers, roughly one-third were highly involved, coequal partners; the rest viewed themselves as mothers' "helpers" (Gerson 1993:181). Highly involved egalitarian fathering or primary fathering was "fragile and rare" (Gerson 1993:234). The group of highly involved fathers was not so much pulled by a new model of fathering as they were disenchanted with the workplace. Blue-collar men in dead-end jobs saw work as a means of generating an income and turned to the family for their value in life. White-collar men were more disillusioned with the price of success and opted to leave the fast track. Fathering was often seen as a loss, or a giving up, of some privileges and opportunities. Involved fathers were more often than not coupled with career-focused mothers with good job opportunities and above average pay.

Diane Ehrensaft's earlier work with a group of forty families stresses the difficulty of accomplishing shared parenting, and the differences experienced by men and women in achieving that goal (Ehrensaft 1987). "The majority of intact families today have two working parents. But, unfortunately, the reverse is not true: the majority of these families do not have two workers parenting" (Ehrensaft 1987:7). Although Ehrensaft describes the sharing of nurturing and care as dual mothering, psychologically and culturally, the experience of mothering is very different for fathers and mothers. Gender-neutral tasks are experienced in distinctly gender-differentiated ways. The factors that influence the ability to achieve shared parenting are the structure of the workplace, societal norms and culture, and the connections between fathers and mothers. Again, the workplace status and opportunities of mothers significantly affected whether parenting would be shared.

Women in Ehrensaft's study perceived motherhood as an expected primary role and felt they had to explain any departure from that role. They often felt guilty when they crafted a different relationship between work and family. Men, on the other hand, had to explain why they were involved in "motherhood" or child rearing and what had permitted them to depart from the breadwinner role. At the first moment of sharing, mothers and fathers confront an immediate challenge to egalitarian goals by virtue of their physically different places at childbirth, differences imposed by breast-feeding and assumptions of women's innate superiority as parents. In addition to these biological justifications for less than coequal parenting, Ehrensaft notes that the other common considerations were career expectations and financial needs.

Ehrensaft explains that fathers and mothers reacted in very gender-specific, separate but equal ways, to parenting. Examples included dressing and worrying about children, and the higher rate of spillover between family and work for women than for men. She also notes that the path to shared parenting involved a rejection of traditional gender roles. Women were conflicted about those roles while men felt alienated from masculine roles. Both women and men seemed to accept that there are gender differences in the way men and women parent, in that men's parenting is best characterized as "doing" and women's parenting as "being." Consistent with Carol Gilligan's argument that women are socialized to emphasize connectedness to others while men are socialized to emphasize and develop autonomy, Ehrensaft sees men as having clearer boundaries as "mothers" than do women, for women have permeable boundaries and the very essence of their being is tied to parenthood.

Ehrensaft's fascinating study suggests that men and women nurture in similar and different ways at the same time. Men roughhouse and physically play with their children more while women communicate and nurture their children's emotional connections more. But even when fathers and mothers are doing the same things—such as dressing their children, or buying them clothes, or worrying, or planning for them—they feel differently as they do them. The differences are connected to different socialization and development patterns. This suggests, and the child development literature confirms, that men can mother or nurture as well as women while the ways in which they nuture and experience parenthood will vary across some continuum. Fathers come to parenthood with profoundly different socialization and societal supports than do women.

Another fascinating area of difference explored by Ehrensaft is the experience of the parent-child bond for fathers and mothers. Fathers were often surprised by the intense feelings they had for their children, and expressed themselves as "falling in love" with them. Men linked their feelings to intimacy; women linked theirs to nurture. Ehrensaft speculates that fathering permits men to develop close emotional relationships that American culture and socialization often deny them. The father-child relationship may be safer and less conflicted than men's intimacy with women. Men feel a sense of "opening up" while women often feel a need to balance a strong sense of connectedness with a sense of self. She suggests that for men shared parenting is a "compensatory . . . corrective emotional experience that could restructure men's relational abilities, spilling over from parenting to other arenas of life" (Ehrensaft 1987:159).

Ehrensaft found that the impact of shared parenting on children was strongly positive. Contrary to fears of "overparenting," children were strengthened by their bond with two adults, not conflicted or confused. Shared parenting also affected children's gender development, especially for boys. Yet boys express this at their peril. Ehrensaft describes a class assignment for a group of seven- and eight-year-olds who were asked to write a poem on the theme "if I were a boy or if I were a girl." Each child was to write from the perspective of the opposite sex. Ehrensaft notes that even in a school environment emphasizing nonsexist education, girl-hating was a dominant theme in the boys' papers. No parallel was evident in the girls' papers (Ehrensaft 1987:234). Girls typically listed being a "mommy" as one of the things they wanted to be when they grew up while the boys frequently made no mention of being a "daddy," because they had more important things on their list.

The complex links between fatherhood, gender roles and gender equity, and household work are reaffirmed in the work of Scott Coltrane (Coltrane 1996). Coltrane's work mirrors the findings of Gerson and Ehrensaft: a shift toward more father involvement but the persistence of gender inequality and a pattern of gender difference despite greater sharing of child care and housework. Coltrane links the broad patterns of demographics and large-scale research to in-depth interviews with two sets of coparenting dual-earner couples. He concludes that involved fatherhood is linked to internal relationship negotiation, and external pressures and ideology. Women's wage work, greater income, and longer hours all press toward more sharing of child care. The timing of children, particularly if they come later in life, contributes to more sharing. The necessity of dual incomes to maintain family income, the benefits of nurturing parenting, ideological commitment to equality, and the long-term dynamics of women's wage work, all contribute toward shared parenting. Men can mother as well as women, yet they continue to do less child care and housework. "[T]he underlying equation of men with work and women with home has been surprisingly impervious to the labor market changes that have occurred over the past few decades" (Coltrane 1996:26). The sexual division of labor, inside and outside the home, has been stubbornly persistent.

Coltrane found that housework, even more than child care, has remained strongly gendered. Studies in the 1970s and 1980s showed that women did two-thirds of all the household work and that tasks were allocated by gender (Coltrane 1996:46). With more women working, men did more household work and women did less, which created a twofold effect on the ratio. By the late 1980s, men had more than doubled their contributions, and the most recent surveys show the gap closing even more, with men doing as much as 30 to 35 percent of housework (Hochschild and Machung 1992; Levine and Pittinsky 1998; Pleck 1993).

Child care has seen an even more dramatic change in fathers' activities, although a gender gap remains, and men and women in general differ in the care they do. Men now contribute close to one-third of the child care hours in dual-income homes (Coltrane 1996:55). Like Ehrensaft, Coltrane found that couples struggled to create and sustain shared parenting. He also found differences in the way work is shared and in the impact of work patterns on family roles. He divided the families in his study into those with a main provider and those with coproviders. In main-provider families, sharing was less equal and more gender differentiated. In coproviding families, the wives' employment was more valued and men's family contributions were greater. "One of the power dynamics that appeared to undergird the household division of labor . . . was the relative earning power of each spouse, though this was modified by occupational prestige, provider role status, and personal preferences" (Coltrane 1996:111).

Complex factors link fathers to greater sharing of child care and housework, as men do more

> when women have careers and identify strongly with their work, but also when they put in long hours at relatively menial working-class jobs. Men also do more if their wives earn more of the total household income, especially if they are defined as economic co-providers. More sharing is evident when wives negotiate for change, delegate responsibility for various chores, and relinquish total control over managing home and children. Sharing of family work is also common when husbands' and wives' attitudes and ideology support gender equity. When husbands are employed fewer hours and value family time over rapid career advancement, they do a greater proportion of the housework and child care. Finally, more tasks are shared when fa-

thers get involved in infant care, take responsibility for the mundane aspects of parenting, and move beyond the role of household helper. Social and demographic factors associated with more sharing [include] . . . when the couple has a more cosmopolitan and less dense social network . . . delay the transition to parenthood until their late twenties or thirties . . . [delay remarriage] . . . [and have] fewer and older children. (Coltrane 1996:200)

Coltrane identifies ten predictors of greater father involvement: wives' employment, wives' earnings, wives' initiative and home management, ideology, husbands' employment, fathers' attachment to parenting, social networks, delayed parenting, divorce and remarriage, family size and age of children (Coltrane 1996:223–28). The more involved fathers are in child care, the less misogynist men are and the more social and political power women have (Coltrane 1996:193). Coltrane concludes that the key is gender cooperation rather than gender differentiation. Shared parenting is, then, critical to achieving gender equality.

James Levine's recent work on men's work-family relationships confirms many of Coltrane's findings, although Levine interprets the data a bit more optimistically. He notes that the level of work-family conflict is nearly as great for fathers as it is for mothers (Levine and Pittinsky 1998). In 1993, in both company-specific and cross-sectional surveys, the level of conflict between work and family was nearly the same for fathers and mothers. Two-thirds of fathers and mothers experienced conflict between work and family (Levine and Pittinsky 1998:15–16). Levine also notes that for a majority of men, the family was a greater source of satisfaction than was wage work (Levine and Pittinsky 1998:17). Levine does not see this as a shift in men's priorities in the sense of less commitment to work and more to family, but rather as a high level of commitment to both. He suggests that this ideal is strongly supported socially, although it coexists with continuing support for primary male breadwinning. He cites survey evidence of such dual commitments and egalitarian caretaking, while at the same time continuing to see breadwinning as more strongly a male responsibility (Levine and Pittinsky 1998:19).

Men's stronger family commitments and ideals serve as explanation, Levine argues, for the equal level of work and family conflict, because in fact, not only in aspiration, men are doing more. Levine contends that the gap between fathers and mothers is not nearly as dramatic as Coltrane and others suggest, for several reasons. First, pointing to the work of Joseph Pleck critiquing the data which served as the basis of Hochschild's conclusions, he argues that the calculations used were simply incomplete. In fact, he contends, men spent three times the minutes attributed to them for daily household work, reducing the imbalance to 2.5:1 from 8:1. Pleck reviewed the Szali data used by Hochschild to compare parents' time on housework and child care and found that some data were excluded. Notably, Hochschild's calculation excluded weekend time and activities, including "shopping, administrative services, repairs, and waiting in line" (Levine and Pittinsky 1998:24–25). More significantly, Levine would redefine the scope of work and family not only to include time omitted from earlier calculations, but also to include time spent in paid work and commuting (Levine and Pittinsky 1998:25). He points out that the differential in work done in the home has dropped dramatically over the past thirty years. Adding the higher average time spent by fathers in wage work and commuting makes the combined time spent on wage work and family work roughly equal for fathers and mothers, even if fathers do more wage work and mothers more family work (Levine and Pittinsky 1998:26).

While the gap between men and women still exists, it is narrowing and the consequences are remarkably similar for men and women. Conflict with wage work increases as men do more family work. Because family work is devalued and associated with women, Levine believes that men's conflicts are more hidden (Levine and Pittinsky 1998; Snarey 1993). Men must struggle with the fear that their commitment to family not only threatens their commitment to work, but also that it means they are not sufficiently masculine (Pleck and Pleck 1997; Willinger 1993).

Coltrane's and Levine's work reflect the ongoing importance of the relationship between work and family responsibilities and relationships for men, their intersections with women, and the continuing gendered character of both work and family that confounds fathering just as it does mothering. A significant amount of the literature on fathers points to workplace structures and culture as critical barriers to more involved fathering (Andrews and Bailyn 1993; Hood 1993; Riley 1990). Women's work patterns have drawn fathers into more parenting, but the workplace resists that role for men while continuing to expect women to perform family work (Brayfield 1995; Frankel 1993;

Moorehouse 1993; Tuttle 1994). The gap between an egalitarian ideology and a sharply gendered reality remains (Marsiglio 1997; Messner 1992; Pleck 1993). It is undeniable that fatherhood as a practice of nurture rather than of breadwinning continues to be rejected in the workplace. Structurally, culturally, and economically that rejection still undermines fathering in a more profound and different way than the workplace structures which place barriers before mothers. The continuing sexual division of labor in work and family, as well as the ongoing racial hierarchy superimposed on that division, powerfully contribute to the skewed pattern and limited definition of fatherhood.

CHAPTER 4

Subgroups of Fathers

In this chapter I review the research on several subgroups of fathers: divorced fathers, Black fathers, and gay fathers. Modifying "father" with these terms exposes the norms of fatherhood: married, white, and heterosexual. Assumptions of deviance abound in much of the older literature on these three groups. More recent research tells rich stories of accomplishment and pluralistic approaches to fathering, suggesting positive models from these subgroups of fathers.

DIVORCED FATHERS

Much of the debate over the essential and unique nature of fathers is grounded in the realities of divorce and the absence of many fathers from the lives of their children. Paralleling this trend is the high rate of remarriage and the common occurrence of a stepfather in the lives of many children of divorce. The dynamic of fatherhood in divorced families reflects many of the same interconnections as it does in intact families. Yet the emotional, power-related, and geographic realities are so different as to produce an entirely different context of fatherhood. The rhythm and challenges of stepfatherhood, just recently beginning to be examined, are yet another distinct, though increasingly common, context of fathering—social fatherhood, uncoupled from biology, and frequently practiced without the legal formalities of marriage or adoption.

The postdivorce pattern of fathers' relationships with their children is bleak and disheartening for both fathers and children. Roughly half of all first marriages end in divorce, and the rate is even higher, nearly two-thirds, for remarriages (Arendell 1995:78). As many as two out of three children spend some time in a single-parent household before reaching age eighteen (Dowd 1997a:5; Fox and Blanton 1995:259). This rate varies significantly by race. The divorce rate for African-Americans is higher than for whites. African-Americans are more likely to separate without divorcing, to have a lengthy separation, and less likely to remarry. Nearly 40 percent of white children experience one divorce; 75 percent of Black children do. One out of every ten children goes through two divorces with their primary parent before they reach age sixteen. With the high cohabitation rate, one of seven divorced parents lives with a different partner between marriages (Hetherington and Stanley-Hagan 1997:192).

A high proportion of divorces include children. Most children remain with their mother, as mother custody remains at nearly 90 percent. Just as women can expect to spend some of their adult lives as single mothers with custody of their children, men are highly likely to be noncustodial fathers living apart from their children (Fox and Blanton 1995). Studies disagree as to whether contested custody awards are mother- or father-biased (Arendell 1995:78). Whether custody is legally or physically joint, or primary custody with one parent, mothers normally remain the primary parent. Coequal parenting is rare, as is father custody, although both are increasing. This picture follows from the parenting patterns established during marriage. Men parent disproportionately less than women during marriage, and the gap is even wider for men who do not marry the mother of their child. The disconnection long accepted for unmarried fathers is beginning to be accepted for once-married fathers.

The determinants of the high mother-custody pattern after divorce are unclear. Eleanor Maccoby and Robert Mnookin's 1992 study indicated that in 80 percent of the cases, parents did not make conflicting requests for custody and mothers requested it more frequently. Conflict was more common when mothers requested sole custody and fathers requested joint custody; 67 percent of the cases ended in sole custody to the mother. Seltzer's study of cases in the mid-1980s found that joint custody was more likely when the father's income was higher and the divorce was more recent (Fox and Blanton 1995:261). Greer Fox and Joan Kelly identified the following factors as increasing the likelihood of father custody: having a son as the eldest or only child, having older children, the inclusion of a guardian's report, and the father's role as plaintiff. In each study, legal process and socioeconomic and family composition affected custody outcomes (Fox and Blanton 1995).

The visitation patterns of divorced fathers without custody are uneven, and contact is infrequent and diminishes rapidly over time (Greif 1995a; Kruk 1994; McKenry et al. 1992; Parke 1995). Twenty-five percent of children see their fathers at least once a week. Sadly, over a third see their fathers only a few times a year or do not see them at all (Hetherington and Stanley-Hagan 1997:192). Parke also identifies several factors that discourage parenting after divorce: geographic distance, a hostile relationship with the former spouse, and the impact of remarriage and stepfatherhood. Fathers who have weekly contact are a distinct minority, as are those who have monthly contact. In one study, half the fathers had not visited their children in the past year, and ten years after divorce only 10 percent of the children had weekly contact with their fathers, while almost two-thirds had no contact in the prior year (Furstenberg and Cherlin 1991). While more recent studies show some improvement, nearly a third of divorced fathers had no contact, and only a third saw their children once a month or more. Visitation problems are frequent (Fox and Blanton 1995; Wolchik 1996). A very strong factor affecting visitation, noted across several studies, is the nature of the father's relationship with his former wife (Fox and Blanton 1995).

Although the assumption is that more contact is important, the empirical data to support this are thin or nonexistent (Fox and Blanton 1995). Visitation or the lack of it does not make a difference to the child's future; child support does (King 1994a and 1994b). Ironically, the greater significance of child support and the inconsequential role of visitation seem to reinforce economic parenthood. These factors most likely also reflect the limited resources and opportunities of many women, together with the continuation of preexisting parenting patterns. To the extent that child support was ever paid, as contact declines so does the support. Only about half the women who were divorced in 1990 received support awards, and only half of those received full payment. Nonpayment or partial payment is common (Parke 1995). Some fathers cannot pay, but clearly a significant portion simply do not do so, particularly those fathers who do not stay in touch with their children.

How does this affect children? Joan Kelly's review of the literature suggests that divorce has a clear impact on children, but not of a magnitude that we might imagine (Kelly 1993). The children of divorced parents, especially boys, have more adjustment problems and more difficulty with intellectual and academic endeavors, but the size of the difference is not great. The age of the child at the time of the divorce is significant, there being more problems when the children are younger. The children do not differ significantly on issues of self-esteem and depression. The majority of children of divorced parents, according to Kelly, function within normal limits. Other work reviewed by Kelly indicates that there is such a range of outcomes that one cannot talk about the children of divorce as a homogeneous group. Often negative outcomes are traceable to predivorce issues, not to the divorce itself. Parental conflict is a key factor in children's outcomes, whether in the marital family or in the ongoing postdivorce family. Also critical is the psychological adjustment of the custodial parent. On the other hand, the findings are mixed or inconclusive regarding the impact of the noncustodial parent, usually the father. "The impact of paternal access after divorce must be seen in relation to the child's age and sex, the closeness of the father-child relationship prior to divorce, marital conflict, maternal and paternal adjustment, and mother's hostility after separation" (Kelly 1993:39).

Joint physical custody, although still a minority arrangement, works well for children when the parents are cooperative and maintain the father-child relationship to a much greater degree (Kelly 1993). On the other hand, a review of the studies on joint custody shows few differences in the adjustment of children to varying types of custody arrangements. A trend exists of self selection of a workable arrangement and a drifting away from joint custody to mother custody (Johnston 1995). What matters most is the stability and quality of the parent-child relationship, not the structure of custody or visitation (Johnston 1995):

> Overall, the evidence suggests that when children begin the divorce experience in good psychological shape, with close or loving relationships with both parents, their adjustment will be maintained by continuing their relationships with both parents on a meaningful basis. There will be gender and age difference within this framework. Parents will maintain their children's positive adjustment by reducing their conflict or working their disputed issues out in a mediative or counseling forum and avoid placing their children in the middle of their struggles. (Kelly 1993:45; see also Johnston 1995)

Divorce creates "opportunities for men and women to deal in new ways with the issues of autonomy, connectedness and power" (Fox and Blanton 1995:272). After divorce, noncustodial fathers lose much of their power over wives and children. They also lose their relationship with their spouse, which often connected them to and facilitated their relationship with their children in the first place. They are thrust into situations which are unfamiliar and in which they lack experience and skills. Furthermore, their socialization pushes them toward negative strategies, including the refusal to seek help and support. The decline in connection with their children is thus tied to feelings of powerlessness and the experience of conflict. While women experience economic stresses, men experience emotional and relationship stresses linked to their socialization and face these issues with little cultural or social support (Fox and Blanton 1995:277).

Terry Arendell's study of divorced fathers divides them into traditionalists, neotraditionalists, and nurturing fathers. The first two groups are linked by their critical connection to their former wife, while the nurturers see their primary relationship as being with their children. In addition to collecting existing data on divorce, Arendell conducted in-depth interviews with seventy-five men. "Divorce brought, or pulled more sharply, into questioning notions of their own manhood—assumptions about self and place in the family and the world" (Arendell 1995:13). The traditionalists frequently blame the legal system and women for their disconnection with their children, although Arendell finds loss of power and control in their discourse and experience (Arendell 1995). Ironically, it is the nurturing fathers who are poorly supported by the legal structure, and often socially viewed as unmanly by their peers. Among divorced fathers, disconnection from children is seen as a viable choice. Connection requires a cooperative relationship with the mother and a new focus on the children away from the prior intimate relationship. It is clear from this work how crucial the mother-father relationship is for any post-divorce fathering relationship to flourish, and how much that relationship is tied to gender norms and stereotypes.

Most of the men saw themselves as victimized, divorce as a war between the sexes, their families as broken, and their role as fathers marginalized (Arendell 1995:13). "Broadly outlined, the story shared by a large majority of these divorced fathers was one of perceived injustice and discrimination, resistance, and frustration and discontent" (Arendell 1995:16). Much of this negative feeling was direced at the legal system (Arendell 1995:73). The second tale, less common than the first, was one of growth, adjustment, and adaptation. The approach of these men was child-centered (Arendell 1995:17).

Arendell's portrait of nurturing men contrasts sharply with the conflicted, frustrated, and oppositional fathers that dominate her study. The nurturing fathers were partners with their former spouses, engaged in extensive, ongoing cooperation, and closely involved with their children. Much of this occurred by circumventing, rather than utilizing, the legal system. Interestingly, the cooperative relationship worked best when neither parent remarried. However, these men viewed themselves, and believed they would be viewed by others, as deviant because of their relationship with their former spouse—a revealing view of what the norm of divorce is perceived to be. They also saw their parenting style as atypical for men. Arendell calls them "gender subversives" (Arendell 1995:250).

This portrait of the unusual nurturing father is borne out by other researchers who have focused on primary caretaking fathers. This is also an atypical role that presents logistical and emotional challenges. According to Geoffrey Greif, who has studied single fathers, although some of the adjustments are becoming easier, the long-term prospects are not encouraging:

> [P]ublic opinion of these men is [not] any more accepting that it had been, . . . is [not] changing swiftly . . . [and] conditions at work are [not] any more responsive. While parenting for fathers in the 1990s may be easier in terms of dealing with the children and with the court systems, continued difficulty at work and the lack of social satisfaction . . . tend to balance things out. This is not to say that fathers

cannot or should not parent alone. It is to caution that broad changes in the community to accommodate fathers are not likely to be forthcoming. (Greif 1990:224; see also Eggebeen, Snyder, and Manning 1996)

The disconnection of noncustodial fathers is heightened by the fact that many men become stepfathers. An estimated 75 percent of women and 80 percent of men remarry after divorce (Parke 1995). As noted earlier, approximately 40 percent of children spend some time with a stepparent before reaching age eighteen (Parke 1995). Many of those stepparents are men, given the dominant form of custody of children with their mothers. The most common remarried family structure is that of one spouse with children from a previous marriage, 86 percent of these families being composed of a biological mother and a stepfather (Hetherington and Henderson 1997:214). Other possibilities include a stepfather who has his own nonresident biological children, a blended family in which both spouses bring children from previous marriages, or the addition of biological children to the simple stepfamily. Of course, former spouses or partners from prior relationships may also remarry, extending the familial structure.

The presence of a stepfather can ease economic stress, but it may also discourage contact with the biological father, or create conflict between the biological father and the stepfather. The relationship with the stepchild is an uneasy one, one that has only recently begun to be studied (Bloom, Conrad, and Miller 1996; Bray and Berger 1990; Cooksey and Fondell 1996; Pasley and Ihinger-Tallman 1994). Alongside the high remarriage rate is the higher divorce rate for second marriages than for first marriages. For children and men, the relationship of social father may well be limited in time and difficult in space. "Despite the diversity among step families, all share the tasks of incorporating outsiders in an established family system or blending two family systems, of simultaneously establishing close marital bonds and functional parent-child relationships, and of adapting relationships with family members outside of the household" (Hetherington and Henderson 1997:214).

Divorced fathers' practice of fathering separates into two sharply divergent patterns that highlight the complexity of redefining fatherhood. One group is highly engaged, sometimes more engaged than during their marriage. The second group is disengaged, even totally disconnected from their children. Both sets of divorced fathers may coparent with stepfathers, and/or become stepfathers themselves. Many engage in serial parenting. Some parent all the children in their lives even if in multiple families. Divorced fathers are thus emblematic of some of the most connected and creative parenting, as well as some of the most distant and hostile relationships with children and former spouses. They expose the model of fathering within marriage and the lack of a model for postdivorce fathering. Divorced fathers perhaps most sharply pose the choice between fatherhood based on status or conduct. An exclusive focus on divorced fathers, however, emphasizes the fatherhood dilemmas of white middle-class men, and excludes fathers marginalized on the basis of race or sexual orientation.

BLACK FATHERS

Most of the literature on fathers focuses on white middle-class fathers. As with mothers of color, fathers of color especially African-American fathers, are stigmatized and denigrated. While white fathers may fight the image of the financially capable deadbeat dad or the uninvolved, distant father, Black fathers are seen as little more than irresponsible, and generally as undesirable and incapable. The discourse of inferiority masks the realities of economic disempowerment that not only make it difficult to fullfil traditional breadwinner father roles, but also prevent that role from being recast in a more nurturing direction. Rethinking fatherhood seems like a luxury when fatherhood, as the culture has defined it, is so difficult to attain.

However, the actual patterns of fatherhood by men of color suggest not only a context of disadvantage but also the existence of alternative models based in different contexts. Hispanic fathers are stigmatized in a different way, as hypermasculine and hyperpaternalistic under a presumed understanding of *machismo*. Again, educational and economic barriers, as well as structural discrimination, are ignored in favor of negative cultural and racial assumptions of inferiority. Finally, yet another way of understanding the explanations and negativity surrounding fathers of color is to acknowledge the success of fathers or mothers under these conditions. This approach would challenge not only the presumption of inferiority but also the security of an ongoing racial and gender hierarchy. The reality for men of color, after all, is the dominance of families where fathers are not present, together with a more privileged, albeit insufficient, economic position for women of color. Translated into white racial and gender realities, it is a world of female superiority both in the home and in the wage workplace. Fatherhood for men of color, therefore, reflects the very same fears that may be raised for white men when they shift their definition of fatherhood.

To the extent that racial differences between fathers have been studied, they have most commonly been studied for Black fathers. There is a smaller body of scholarship on Hispanic fathers. The limited study of Black men has to be placed within the context of the limited study of fathers in general. Thus the comparison is not to a richly developed scholarly tradition, but rather to one still developing.

Most of the extant scholarship on Black fathers comes from a deficit, pathological perspective, emphasizing an absence from the home and an inability or unwillingness to fulfill the traditional role of father. This negative view reflects popular and academic stereotypes about Black families in general and Black fathers in particular. "[B]lack males are stereotypically perceived as residents of poor inner-city neighborhoods, hyper masculine, financially irresponsible, and uninvolved in their children's lives" (Taylor, Jackson, and Chatters 1997:249; see also Cochran 1997; Gadsen and Smith 1994; Taylor et al. 1992; Wade 1994). Regardless of whether the causes are seen as individual, cultural, or the consequences of racism the focus has been on the negatives, on the fathers who have failed. The failure of Black fathers is linked to a range of problems disproportionately experienced by Black children, especially males. Social patterns are linked to individual failings. Mirroring the denigration of Black women as mothers, there is little positive association between Black fathers and their children in the literature. The dominant frameworks are matriarchal models of Black families laying blame for perceived negative characteristics of Black children on the deviation of Black families from white middle-class norms. The matriarchal model sees female-headed families as deviant, and as indicative of inability or unwillingness of Black men to provide for their families (Cochran 1997).

The literature on minority families commonly views racial and ethnic families as deviant or defective (Mirande 1988 and 1991). The Anglocentric ideal of an egalitarian, democratic family structure is the norm, and racial and ethnic minorities' families are presumed not to fit this mold. Asian and Hispanic fathers are viewed as patriarchal, dictatorial, and authoritarian. Black and Native American fathers are characterized as absent, uninvolved, and ineffectual. Racial identity is used to generalize family conformity to a cultural norm identified and described by an outside dominant culture. More recent research has challenged these general assumptions and also revealed the diversity in racial and ethnic families (Mirande 1988). For example, researchers have noted the different ways in which fathers function inside and outside the home. In their dealings with the "outside" world, fathers serve as the head of a united unit, while "inside" the home mothers often have considerable authority alongside fathers. Moreover, minority cultures are in constant flux. The interactions of minority fathers with minority and majority culture are only beginning to be explored (Mirande 1991).

Only recently, beginning in the late 1970s and early 1980s, has scholarship begun to explore the positive attributes of Black fathers, including the distinctive patterns of successful fathers (Cochran 1997). This scholarship rests on Afrocentric models that view African-American families in light of their origin and adaptation of African family traditions, as well as on ecological approaches that view families in context and in light of the value structure of their indigenous culture (Cochran 1997).

Black fathers must be viewed within the context of their being Black males. As a group they are described by some as being on the verge of extinction, an extremely high-risk population. "They experience higher rates of unemployment, poverty, morbidity, and imprisonment and have shorter life expectancy, less access to health care, and less education than their white counterparts" (Cochran 1997:342). Within this group, young Black men are particularly at risk.

Black fathers and their children must also be seen against the backdrop of the demographics of Black families. Female-headed single-parent families are the dominant family form. In 1994, nearly three-quarters of the births to Black women were to unmarried mothers, as compared to a quarter of the births to white women (Taylor et al. 1997:40). Black women are less likely to marry if pregnant, and in general the Black marriage rate has been declining. Two-thirds of Black children live in single-parent households. Only a third live with both parents, as compared to three-quarters of white children and two-thirds of Hispanic children (Taylor et al. 1997:15).

Few of the single-parent households are headed by men. Four percent of Black children live with their fathers rather than their mothers; this is comparable to the figure of white children living with single fathers. Children who do live with single Black fathers are much more likely to have a father who was never married to the mother, unlike single white fathers who are either divorced or separated from the mother (Taylor et al. 1997:47). Most Black fathers do not parent alone. They live in a subfamily, cohabiting or living with a related adult. Black children are also more likely to live with a grandparent than are white or Hispanic children. Approximately 12 percent of all Black children live with grandparents; usually the household includes one parent and one grandparent (Taylor et al. 1997:16). Finally, Black children are more likely than white or Hispanic children to live with neither biological parent.

The history of Black families continues to affect the role of fathers, the marital relationship, and parent-child relationships. Family structure was valued to an incredible degree during slavery, and after emancipation an estimated 70 to 90 percent of Black fathers were present in the home (McAdoo 1988). Although Black families suffered during the twentieth century as the result of northward migration, more than two-thirds of Black fathers lived with their families in 1970 (McAdoo 1988).

From 1880 to 1925, two-parent families were the dominant family form in poor Black communities. During the Great Migration, however, families often split apart due to urbanization and industrialization. They were also affected by the switch to skilled labor (Wade 1994). One researcher described families as having three configurations, all tied to economic patterns: matriarchal-matricentric, middle-class egalitarian two-parent families, and patriarchal affluent families. "In other words, the family's socioeconomic status affects its structure and the role of the father" (Wade 1994:564). Thus, economic stability increases fathers' participation in their families; economic affluence, however, correlates with a decline in participation.

The poverty statistics for all children are alarmingly high, but for Black and Hispanic children the figures are catastrophic. More than 40 percent of all Black and Hispanic children are poor, compared to 16 percent of white children (Taylor et al. 1997:17). By one estimate, if comparable work and family patterns existed among the families of Black and white children, the poverty rate for Black children would drop by half. This projection demonstrates the impact of economic disadvantage on Black children and their families. Not only are they poor, but they remain poor for longer periods. Poverty is connected to the disadvantaged position of women heading households, as well as the inability of fathers to contribute to the household. Black men have twice the rate of unemployment, earn less than 60 percent as much as their white counterparts, and suffer from both under- and unemployment (McAdoo 1993; Mincy 1989). Black children are overrepresented in the population of the abused and are exposed to a disproportionate amount of violence outside the home as well.

Fatherhood for Black men is more common at an early age, is non-marital, and often involves fathers' living apart from their children (Taylor et al. 1997:31). When fatherhood occurs earlier in life it means the challenges of parenting are greater and makes the implications of involved parenting more severe in terms of the impact on the father's work life. It also signals the consequences of blocked opportunity, which make having a child seem more desirable and a way to achieve adulthood (Cochran 1997). Nevertheless, fatherhood at a young age is usually unplanned. The father is unprepared and ignorant about his role, is relatively uninformed about child development, and is at risk for unemployment and dropping out of school. Even though most young fathers do not live with their children, they often wish to remain involved with them (Cochran 1997). The level of their involvement is tied to self-image and self-esteem (Christmon 1990).

> The transition from adolescence to adulthood is a special developmental domain during which society assumes that certain social and psychological maturations have occurred. For African American males and fathers, the developmental and transitional issues are exacerbated by public perception and limited opportunity and reward structures. . . . Their transition is typically from adolescence to fatherhood, void of the temporal space to deconstruct adolescent myths, play out adolescent fantasies or realities, develop intellectual competencies, or construct notions of parenting and responsibility for self or others. (Gadsen and Smith 1994:645)

At a policy level, not only are these developmental issues and transitional perspectives critical, but so is recognizing the complexity of the factors that influence young fathers' involvement: families of origin, the social and cultural construction of fatherhood roles, the ability to be a provider, and lack of knowledge about parenting (Gadsen and Smith 1994).

The research on teenage pregnancy has focused almost exclusively on young women, both in terms of pregnancy prevention and child rearing. Fathers have been presumed to be irresponsible. Yet much of the more recent scholarship indicates that although this is a difficult developmental time for young men to take on parenting responsibilities, many want to be involved and do have a positive effect on their children (Allen and Doherty 1996). The literature about fathers suggests that young fathers have a significant emotional and psychological desire for a connection with their children. If fostered, this interest would result in involved parenting over the long haul. When asked how he felt about being a father, one young man responded as follows:

> It kinda gives you, it's a . . . it's an unexplainable feeling. Like when I was in the delivery room and he came, and he was there, you know, and he looked at me . . . it was like, you're in awe. That's the best way I can say it, you're in awe! You're like wow! He looks at you and your body like tingles. . . . [I]t's almost like catching the Holy Ghost or something! (Allen and Doherty 1996:152)

Overall, white children have more contact with their fathers, but among nonresident fathers, Black fathers have higher levels of visitation. Research on Black families shows that Black fathers, especially middle-class ones, remain involved with their families to a greater degree than white fathers. Their style is authoritative, but not authoritarian (Erickson and Gecas 1991). A study comparing Mexican, white, Puerto Rican, and Black fathers found that Mexican and white fathers were closest to the traditional view of fathering, marrying and being economic providers (Stier and Tienda 1993). All fathers participated in economic support based on their economic and labor market status, but interestingly, Black fathers were more likely to continue contact and noneconomic support. This is significantly different from white fathers, who link economic support with contact. When unable to provide economic support Black fathers still offer other forms of support (in services or in kind) and maintain contact (Stier and Tienda 1993). In another study, researchers found that Black men did more household work, including tasks typecast as feminine, than did white men. The amount of household work correlated positively with employment, not unemployment. A contrasting pattern exists for white men:

they do less household work when employment increases (Shelton and John 1993). In sum, the research suggests a more egalitarian pattern in Black households (McAdoo 1993).

It is significant that 60 percent of Black children whose father was not in the home nevertheless had a functional father figure in their lives. This person was likely to be their own biological father or another relative, whereas for white children he was more likely to be a new spouse or partner (Taylor et al. 1997:31–32). Recent research on single-parent families indicates that when children raised in female-headed single-parent households do well, they may do so because their fathers, although living outside the household, maintained a relationship with them (Zimmerman, Salem, and Maton 1995). One study found that adolescents in single-mother households received more parental support than those in other familial structures. In addition, many of those children spent time with their fathers or saw them as their male role models. The authors of the study suggest this indicates that parental support and connection may be more significant than family structure (Zimmerman, Salem, and Maton 1995). This indicates the viability of the nonresidential fatherhood paradigm, and argues against a shared physical household being critical to involved fatherhood. Nevertheless, geographic closeness may still be critical, which closeness is more likely in the still highly concentrated housing patterns of many minority communities. It also implies, as the authors note, that an orientation of research (or policy) around the traditional nuclear family may simply make no sense for communities in which such families are not the norm or which function in a different way. Family structure is less important than adult-child connections, which may or may not be dependent on sharing a physical household.

Extended family structure has consistently been cited as a major strength of Black families. This may or may not include the coresidence of other family members. These networks are not all the same, and some may operate less strongly or positively than others. But in general the extended family provides significant support for children and parents (Wilson 1992).

The strongest and most consistent finding among recent research on Black fathers is their difficulty or inability fulfilling the economic provider role, which is connected to the worsening economic position of Black men in a postindustrial economy (Bowman and Forman 1997; Cochran 1997). At the same time as single-parent female-headed families increased from 21 to 47 percent, the rate of employed Black men fell from 75 to 55 percent (Davis 1989:80). Most scholars attribute this to structural changes in capitalism. This problem, of course, calls for radical change in order to be effectively addressed (Davis 1989:88).

Economic problems result in significant role strain for Black fathers (Bowman 1992). The response to this can be adaptive or maladaptive, that is, the resources of the community and culture may provide additional support to perform the fatherhood role well or may instead, exacerbate the strain. Some argue that role strain explains the declining marriage rate among Black Americans (Testa et al. 1989). William Julius Wilson has linked the strain to changing residential patterns that separate middle-class Blacks from poorer Blacks, so that the neighborhoods concentrated around a single disadvantaged class, in a way that affects housing and education as well as employment and income (Testa et al. 1989:221).

The consequences of an inability to provide economically are social as well as economic, and are reflected in other races and classes in periods of high unemployment. Adult development is threatened by this discouraging barrier, as one develops the feeling of failure (Testa et al. 1989:222). "So many African-American men die knowing their journey was derailed, upset, sabotaged, and scuttled by the society into which they were born. And they understand . . . their complicity in that tragic circumstance" (Pate 1994:76). It is critical to see Black fathers within this ecological context, that is, the ecology of racism and economic disadvantage (McAdoo 1993). Economic stability strongly affects father involvement and role perception (Cochran 1997; Fagan 1996). Economic circumstances and self-esteem play a stronger role in fathers' involvement than residential arrangements. As noted earlier, Black fathers may remain very involved with their children although not sharing a household with them. But if the father is not doing well economically or suffers from low self-esteem, he is less likely to be involved.

These economic patterns parallel those of white men. The patterns of Black men are not unique, only the magnitude is (Gadsen and Smith 1994:645). It is nevertheless amazing to see connections maintained under adverse conditions. In Elliot Liebow's classic study of streetcorner men, the most common relationship—when paternity was acknowledged—was intermittent financial or other support, and minimal ongoing contact. Some men in the study, however, maintained close contact with their children despite their inability to provide economic support and their failure to share a household with them (Liebow 1967).

The irony of this is the potential for the argument that Black fathers need to be supported in achieving the traditional provider role, even at the expense of reinforcing patriarchal privilege (McAdoo 1993). On the one hand, one recognizes the importance of the provider role. On the other hand, accepting it uncritically without analysis of its implications for mothers, is not helpful. The challenge, then, to borrow an expression used by African-American women, is to "lift as we climb," that is, to empower men and women equally and gain ground for the benefit of all (Davis 1989). Noel Cazenave points out that masculinity is not something you *have* but rather something you must constantly *prove*. The double bind for Black men, he observes, is that they must prove themselves but are blocked from doing so by structural and societal racism.

The most critical way of proving one's masculinity is by being an economic provider, and it is precisely in that respect that Black men are denied the means to be men in traditional terms. Indeed, photos of civil rights protests during the 1960s show placards carried by Black men inscribed, "I Am a Man." Cazenave argues that "adequate economic provision is essential for *all* modes of male familial involvement, especially the more multifaced and expressive modalities" (Cazenave 1981:183). The greatest risk of noninvolvement, then, is connected to class factors; conversely, Cazenave sees the greatest potential for increased male involvement in the family among economically secure middle-class Black fathers. At the core, it is the provider role, and the difficulty of fulfilling it, that is critical (Bowman and Forman 1997:237). An expansion or reorientation of traditional fatherhood roles may be particularly helpful to Black fathers. But attention to structural changes in the economy and to opportunity structures that so disproportionately affect Black men is equally important. Cultural and community orientations counter the negative effects of economics. "Protective cultural resources . . . such as the flexibility of family roles, cohesive multi-generational kinship bonds, para-kin friendships, racial consciousness, and strong spiritual beliefs" are all among those resources (Bowman and Forman 1997:244). Black fathers experience a significant array of positive resources and demonstrate remarkable resilience amidst severe and significant problems. Despite these challenges, their conduct is not significantly different from that of other fathers (Bright and Williams 1996; Taylor et al. 1997). More specifically, Black men who are economically secure and fulfill the traditional provider role, parent much the same manner as other fathers of their social class (Cochran 1997; McAdoo 1993; Wade 1994).

Other men of color face similar problems of stereotyping. Researchers have noted the negative stereotypes associated with Hispanic fathers, tied particularly to stigmatized notions of *machismo*, paternal power or headship, and *la familia* (Bronstein 1984; Mayo 1997; Vega 1992). Recent research focuses on the adaptive strategies of Hispanic families, while also examining the actual workings of those families. As with Black fathers, Hispanic families display a positive model and context, especially the strong role of the extended family and community. Among Hispanic fathers, the traditional fatherhood role and family context are admittedly patriarchal, but hardly the harsh, authoritarian, abusive stereotype. The issue is whether this gentler form of patriarchy can be separated from the extended family model. The patriarchal connection is cultural, internal to Hispanics, as compared to the inability to achieve an external standard of masculinity. By this I mean that fatherhood is defined within a cultural context that includes powerful familial support premised upon a system of roles that includes the presumption of male headship.

On the other hand, research into the actual workings of Hispanic families demonstrates a far more egalitarian structure than this cultural image would suggest. This might indicate that the cultural construction of *la familia* as well as *machismo* is changing fundamentally in a way that will reframe or discard paternal power as traditionally known. Finally, it must be noted that neither Hispanic culture nor the identifiable Hispanic subgroups are culturally monolithic. Hispanic culture is affected by immigration, a factor not significantly present for Black fathers. Similar issues arise with respect to Asian fathers and the affirmative model of family in Asian culture, where fathers function within a similar cultural environment (Shon and Ja 1992).

As in many other areas of society and culture, race is a significant factor in the construction of fatherhood. It operates both positively and negatively. Positively, "race" is a shorthand for cultural and social patterns and resources, as well as socialization, that suggests important alternatives to dominant cultural definitions of fatherhood, both in theory and in practice. In particular, nurturant fathering by non-custodial fathers and significant involvement by extended family and community in general, are distinctive characteristics more likely to be found among Black fathers than others. Negatively, the high proportion of Black fathers not resident in the child's home reflect severe economic discrimination that translates into the inability to achieve the traditional economic provider role. This role has been the core definition of fatherhood for majority white culture.

It is critical to keep the perspective of Black fathers in view, then, for several reasons. First and foremost, the economic issues of fatherhood must be resolved in a way that reduces, rather than further exacerbates, the economic divide between Black and white children. Furthermore, for Black fathers economic issues precede the noneconomic issues, which drive the priorities of more advantaged groups of fathers. The challenge is how to increase economic resources and decrease discrimination, without reinstating economic patriarchy as a precondition for racial equality. By paying attention to race, then, we must confront the issues of class, which benefits the children of all races. Second, by focusing specifically on Black fathers we are reminded of the role of culture or, more accurately, of cultures in the redefinition of fatherhood, both in terms of the range of contributions and the range of outcomes. These are affirmative models of resistance to the destructive structural and cultural context of the dominant culture.

GAY FATHERS

"The central heterosexist assumption that everyone is or ought to be heterosexual is nowhere more prevalent than in the area of parent-child relationships" (Patterson 1995:255). Many would see gay fathers as a contradictory and impossible phenomenon. "The man who is both a homosexual and a father is an enigma in our society. The term *gay father* is contradictory in nature ... as *gay* has the connotation of homosexuality while *father* implies heterosexuality" (Bigner and Bozett 1989:155). Gay fathers face a powerful stigma and blatant bias not encountered by other groups of fathers, or at least not to this degree:

> Lesbian and gay families with children are less likely than heterosexual families to enjoy legal recognition for their family relationships, equal access to medical care, or freedom from harassment, bigotry,

and hate crimes. The quality of life for lesbian and gay parents would be greatly enhanced if they could be confident that their sexual orientation would not be held against them as they pursue parenthood, bring up their children, or seek custody of their children after a partner's death or the breakup of an intimate relationship between parents. Like the offspring of heterosexual parents, children of lesbian and gay parents would feel more secure if their relationships with parents were protected by law. (Patterson 1995:270)

At best, we can only estimate the number of gay and lesbian parents, based on assumptions of the base rate of homosexuality in the population. The estimates for lesbian mothers range from 1 to 5 million, and for gay fathers from 1 to 3 million (Patterson 1995:256). The estimated number of children with gay and lesbian parents ranges from 6 to 14 million. Kinsey estimates that 10 percent of the population is homosexual; others believe that 10 percent of gay men and 20 percent of lesbians had children while in heterosexual marriages that ended in divorce (Patterson 1995:256; Patterson and Chan 1997:246). Other figures suggest the base rate of 10 percent is too high, or that the rate of parenthood may be higher (Patterson 1995). One recent estimate puts at five thousand to ten thousand the numbers of lesbians who have become parents after coming out; no similar estimates are available for gay men who have become parents through surrogacy or adoption (Patterson 1995). These figures do not include partners of lesbians and gay men, who may or may not act as either social parents or, in states which formally provide a means to do so, as adoptive parents.

Only a minority of gay men are fathers. One estimate is that between 20 to 25 percent of self-identified gay men are fathers (Bigner and Bozett 1989). They are a small group within gay male culture, which focuses on single males and couples. "It is not uncommon for the gay father to experience discrimination and rejection from other gays who are not fathers because of these restrictions to freedom and the lack of understanding if not devaluation of the place of children in one's life" (Bigner and Bozett 1989:159). This is not because gay men cannot form intimate relationships, since an estimated 40 to 60 percent are in steady relationships (Stein 1996:38). It would be expected, however, that those relationships reflect a more masculine style, and men in general have higher degrees of autonomy, separateness, competition, and aggression than women (Stein 1996). While these characteristics are not by definition incompatible with nurture or a nurturing partnership, they may make one more difficult. Certainly the sense is that gay fathers are at the margins of both fatherhood and gay male culture (Bigner and Bozett 1989; Bigner and Jacobsen 1989). They are not strongly identified or supported in either.

Most gay fathers become fathers through heterosexual marriage, and then come out to their partners and children. The majority of gay men who became fathers in this way are noncustodial parents postdivorce. A major concern for them is the reaction of their children to their coming out. Most children are able to accept their father's homosexuality (Bigner and Bozett 1989).

A much smaller group of gay fathers become parents as gay men by choice, through surrogacy or adoption. This raises legal and financial barriers and challenges. Adoption by homosexuals is barred only in Florida, although the ACLU filed a class action lawsuit in 1999 challenging the statutory ban (Yanez 1999). New Hampshire, the only other state with a statutory prohibition, repealed its statute in 1999. Some twenty states allow same-sex couples to adopt (Altimari and Daly 1999). But even in states in which it is allowed, regulations or informal barriers may deter or prevent adoption by homosexuals. Only in 1997 did a New Jersey gay male couple successfully challenge regulations preventing their adoption of children as a couple, although permitting it individually. The couple completed the adoption of their two children two years later. Surrogacy is another option, but expensive and legally more risky even in states where it is permitted (Elovitz 1995; Golombok and Tasker 1994).

Scholarship on gay fathers' parenting primarily compares them to straight fathers and lesbian mothers (Allen and Burrell 1996; Bozett 1993; Golombok and Tasker 1994; Patterson 1995). There are more studies on lesbians than on gay men (Green and Bozett 1993; Perrin and Kulkin 1997). The questions around which most of the literature focuses are whether gay or lesbian parents parent differently from straight parents, and whether gay and lesbian parents determine their children's sexual orientation, with anything other than heterosexuality being presumed to be harmful. The consensus of the research is that they do not parent differently from straight parents, and that sexual orientation is not "passed on" or taught by a parent's nurture (Allen and Burrell 1996; Bozett 1993; Golombok and Tasker 1994; Patterson 1995). Gay and lesbian parents do not adversely affect the gender development of their children (Bigner and Jacobsen 1989; Bozett 1989 and 1993; Cameron and Cameron 1996; Golombok and Tasker 1994; Green and Bozett 1993; Patterson 1995; Patterson and Chan 1997; Strader 1993). Not only do they pose no risks, but they pose no barriers to gender development either. Children learn their gender roles without two sexes or a same-sex model present in their household (Casper, Schultz, and Wickens 1992).

The literature also supports the conclusion that, contrary to stereotypes, gay men do not pose a risk of incest or child abuse. "Gay parents and their lovers are involved in virtually no reported cases of child sexual abuse" (Robinson and Barret 1994:161). This research has been crucial to the fight by gay men and lesbians for custody or visitation in the face of a strong mythology about homosexuals.

The intriguing possibility presented by the experiences of gay fathers is their parenting styles might offer insights into what male parenting might be like outside conventional gender scripts. First, gay men may have a different concept of masculinity, or be less controlled by the limits on behavior set by the dominant standard of masculinity. Second, gay men's relationships with their same-sex partners may less likely fit the heterosexual partners patterns of inequality, and the gendered interaction of fathers and mothers, characterized by the strong impact of mothers on men's fathering. Both these assumptions reflect the further assumption that homosexuality is not simply about the sex of one's desired partner, but that it involves a different construction both of self and partnership which challenges conventional gender roles.

Of course, countervailing assumptions are possible. First, because of the powerful myths and stigma attached to homosexuality, gay fathers may compensate by staying within conventional definitions and understandings of fatherhood, to prove that they are "just as good" at fathering as heterosexual dads. The limiting effect of homophobia and heterosexism may constrain their relationships. Second, given that homosexuals are usually raised by heterosexuals, their modeling of partnership and fatherhood is based on the heterosexual model.

Very little of the limited research on gay fathers explores the quality of gay fatherhood in this sense. Most existing research, focused on debunking myths of difference, emphasizes only that gay fathers parent similarly to, and with similar effects as, straight fathers (Bozett

1993). Researchers are only beginning to focus on affirmative differences, from a perspective that values diverse family forms and the broad range of fathers. In terms of benefits to children, one researcher sees four possible benefits accruing from gay fathering: respect for diversity; experiencing different interpretations of gendered behavior and more egalitarian roles; understanding that families are not simply biological, but are also based on love and choice; and experiencing support for their families in the context of visible gay culture and community (Allen 1997). There is some evidence that gay fathers put more energy into creating stable positive relationships with their children, that they make a concerted effort to provide them with opposite sex role models, that their perspective on parenting emphasizes nurture and is less traditional in terms of paternal attitudes, that paternal roles have more significance for them, and that they assess themselves more positively as fathers (Bigner and Bozett 1989; Bozett 1993).

Openly gay fathers are "less authoritative, use less corporal punishment, and experience stronger desires to rear children with nonsexist, egalitarian standards" than closeted gay fathers (Bigner and Jacobsen 1989). One study that compared gay and nongay fathers found gay fathers demonstrated greater responsiveness, guidance, and limit setting, and demonstrated comparable levels of involvement and intimacy (Bigner and Jacobsen 1989). Other researchers confirm these characteristics and note that gay fathers' nurturant styles are closer to mothers' parenting styles that to those of nongay fathers (Allen and Burrell 1996; Bigner and Jacobsen 1989; Bozett 1989; Patterson 1995). The suggestion of difference is limited to small samples, and researchers caution against generalizations based on limited data.

Gay fathers face more serious legal obstacles to parenting than other groups of fathers. Until the early 1960s, the sexual acts of homosexuals were criminalized in all jurisdictions (Rivera 1991). Many of those laws have now been withdrawn or declared unconstitutional, or are rarely enforced. In some jurisdictions, however, their mere existence affects courts' custody and visitation awards. In addition, gay fathers continue to contend with widespread myths and concerns beyond the issue of whether they are engaging in criminal conduct. These myths include the belief that they are child molesters and represent a danger to the children in their care, that they will influence their children's sexual orientation toward homosexuality, that their sexual orientation will result in stigma and ridicule for their children and that custody should therefore be avoided, and most fundamentally, that their conduct is morally reprehensible and renders them unfit to be parents (Bigner and Bozett 1989; Golombok and Tasker 1994; Patterson 1995; Rivera 1991). In addition, gay fathers' ability to demonstrate that they are financially responsible parents may be hampered by discrimination in employment, which goes unsanctioned in federal employment discrimination law, and is illegal in only a handful of states.

The primary legal issues for gay fathers are to be recognized and treated equally with straight fathers, while at the same time being appreciated for their differences. The parallels with other marginalized fathers are clear. The uniqueness of gay fathers is the core issue of identity: acceptance of them as fathers and as parents, including the choice of nurturing children as gay males.

Looking at gay fathers it is evident that heterosexism and sexism strongly pervade the current definitions of fatherhood. Gay fathers are overwhelmingly noncustodial parents. In part, their opportunity to parent and their ability to connect their parenting to gay community and culture are limited. Stigma also translates into less research and therefore little information about the potential for alternative models based on the lives of gay fathers.

CHAPTER 5

Summary

What do the context and practice of fathering, to the extent that we know them, tell us? First, virtually all scholars emphasize how little we know, and therefore how provisional any data must be. We have neither the demographic data nor the tested correlations for fathers that we have for mothers. This factor alone is enormously indicative of our assumptions about fathers. Even more important, it demands that any definition or policy with respect to fathers be provisional.

Nevertheless, the data we do have indicate that most men, at some point in their lives, become biological fathers. This normally occurs when a man is between his mid-twenties and mid-thirties. Men's social fathering falls into one of five categories. First, are are nurturing fathers who parent their children as mothers do in terms of time, mental and physical energy, and tasks. This group includes sole-custody fathers, primary-custody fathers, and some fathers in joint custody or marital relationships.

Second, there are nurturing fathers in stepfamilies, blended families, or in families with cohabiting adults. Some of these overlap with

the first category, but most significantly their fathering is characterized by strong engagement with children without there necessarily
being a biological or adoptive tie.

Third, there are the less engaged fathers who are backup or minimal nurturers plus breadwinners, to some degree. Many of them live
in "traditional" two-parent families and in "coequal" two-earner families. They are also found in nonmarital or divorced families where the
parents do not share a household. Some are in step- and blended families where the father plays a distinctly secondary role to the mother,
and may or may not include an involved former spouse or biological
dad. Disengagement is tied to economic roles and/or to separate
households. It seems particularly apparent that many men cannot envision, or have difficulty maintaining, a relationship with their children when the children no longer reside in their household or when
the men no longer have a relationship with the mother of their children. In other instances, the inability to contribute to the economic
support of their children results in disengagement. On the other hand,
it is not uncommon that men who cannot provide economic support
are nurturant nevertheless or contribute in noneconomic ways to the
household in which their children live.

Fourth, there are disengaged fathers, some of whom play an economic role. These are almost exclusively biological fathers, some of
whom never married the mother of their children, some of whom are
former husbands who relatively quickly adopted a posture of noninvolvement in the lives of the children. Within two years of birth in the
case of nonmarital children, and in about the same time after divorce,
fathers frequently minimize or abandon the nurture of their children.

A final or fifth category encompasses fathers who have never engaged with their children and have no connection of any sort with
them. This includes sperm donors and men who voluntarily relin-
quished their parental rights in order to place a child for adoption. This
category also includes men who do not know they are fathers, and
men who abandon their children emotionally and economically but
rationalize their decision on other grounds.

The combination of fertility rates, nonmarital births, high divorce
rates, and high remarriage rates suggests that many men may connect
with more than one of these patterns, and may experience fatherhood
as a series of relationships, or as multiple relationships carried on simultaneously. A serial pattern is a succession of fathering experiences

in which children are nutured only when they are part of the man's household. A multiple pattern, that is, the nurturing of biological, step-, adopted, and unrelated children who may or may not be physically present in one's own household, appears to be less common. The determinants in men's fathering patterns are households and women. There is a strong connection between fathering and marriage, or a marital-type relationship, and the presence of children in the father's household. The fluidity of family structures for children plus the predominance of women as children's primary parent means that for children, the mother is the constant parent, whereas the father may be either a constant or one in a succession or group of men who parent them.

The distinctiveness of men's and women's parenting is clearly evident not only in terms of household composition, but in other ways as well. Although the household and child care patterns of men and women are converging, women still do more than men. Women and men do different things, particularly with respect to the care of children. Finally, often the way in which women and men do the same things is different. However, when men parent to the extent typical of women, their parenting is remarkably similar to mothering. It is not distinctively "male." When men nurture children, they do so just as well as women, even if as a group they do less. Their conduct is not the same, but the differences seem to be related to men's socialization and acculturation rather than to something inherent in men.

Certainly, fathering and mothering are distinctive experiences. Nowhere is this more apparent than in the configuration of single-parent families. Although the number of single-parent fathers has grown significantly, mothers nevertheless predominate as the caregiving parent. Custody is dominantly vested in mothers; fathers' visitation diminishes rapidly, if it was ever present; and even joint-custody families often shift to sole or mother-dominant custody. Gender neutrality is hardly reflected in this pattern. The explanation for this varies, and includes the view that it simply reflects caretaking practices. Opposing this is the view that judicial bias—oddly enough by a still male-dominated judiciary—is responsible for the skewed gender pattern of single-parent custody and actual care.

Fathering differs sharply by race and, to a lesser extent, by class although sometimes they parallel each other, reflecting the economic disadvantage of race. Compared to white men, men of color, especially

African-American men, become fathers at a younger age, are less likely to marry the mothers of their children, and are less likely to contribute economically to their children or, if they do, to contribute less. White fathers, especially middle-class and upper-class ones, are more likely to be purely economic fathers. This compares or contrasts to lower-income males, disproportionately men of color, who are more likely to maintain a connection with their children even without a marital or household link. The family form most closely correlated with success for children, namely, dual-parent marital families of biologically related parents and children, is least common in communities of color. At the same time, the success rate among single-parent families, the dominant family form in communities of color, is greatest where the experience and acceptance of those families is high. Cultural stigma, attached to *both* mothers and fathers of color although for different reasons, attributes patterns of fathering and children's outcomes to failings of the race, which plays into racial stereotypes and stigma. The needs of fathers have been dominantly identified and articulated by middle-class white men.

A necessary question for any consideration of fatherhood is what is its impact along race and class lines given what we know of those patterns. Futhermore, fathers who have succeeded despite the social and institutional negatives have been largely ignored. While most of what we know about fathers is provisional, we know even less about a father who is not white, middle-class, or heterosexual.

Children's economic welfare is strongly tied to the presence or absence of fathers, reflecting the greater ability of most men to be better economic providers than women. The disconnection of many fathers from the lives of their children is reflected in the alarming rate of child poverty, which is increasing from one in five children under the age of eighteen to one in four. Child support continues to be viewed as an option rather than as a necessary obligation. A significant number of children are still without support orders, and nonpayment or less than full payment of support when orders are ordered is common. Although some nonpayment is connected to an inability to pay, it is more frequenlty connected to a refusal to do so. It is also frequently related to a corresponding lack of contact with children. Fathering is tied to economic obligations, but those obligations are denied when marriage, household connection, or physical contact breaks down. As for fathers entitled to support, awards are rare, and when made the nonpayment picture is similar to that of mothers. Child support represents a lower proportion of a father's income than a mother's, which is connected to both lower amounts predicated on women's lower incomes and to men's greater incomes. We should recognize, however, that a significant proportion of men work at or below the poverty line, and that men's wages in general have stagnated or declined in the 1980s and 1990s.

Children's psychological and intellectual welfare is a more complex picture. The mere presence of a father does not correlate with better outcomes, especially when children in homes with biological fathers married to their mothers are compared to children in stepfamilies. The differential in fathering biological and step or unrelated children appears to be quite significant, but not yet clearly understood. The general outcomes of children are about the same for single-parent and stepparent homes, although it is not always clear whether those single-parent homes have a sole adult in the household, or a social father figure even if not a legal stepparent or adoptive parent.

Stepparenting, whether legally or socially, is an extremely common form of fatherhood in America. The data on stepfamilies indicate that these families do not do well, and that we lack a good understanding of their dynamics or a healthy vision of how they should function. Not only is the relationship between the two adults and children different, but it is further complicated by the potential for several fathers (and mothers). Just as common as a family without a father figure or adult male in the household is one in which two or more fathers are associated with the children in the household.

Other distinct categories of fathers include single-parent and gay fathers. Single-parent fathers are a fairly discrete, identifiable group about whom some information exists. They are remarkably similar to single-parent mothers in their parenting styles and in their stresses, but dissimilar in that they are a small, fairly unique group. Most parent with a woman in the household, rather than alone. Gay fathers remain largely hidden and unidentified. The impact of sexual orientation on parenting remains largely unexplored. We do know that sexual orientation does not have a negative impact on children, but we do not know if gay men father differently. At least some data suggest that parenting is less integral to gay culture, perhaps making it more difficult to sustain gay fatherhood.

Clearly fathers are more engaged in the care of children than before, whether we are looking at child care for very young children, men who have primary or sole custody, or at the aspirations and ideals of most men as parents. Nevertheless, father care remains rooted in the assumption that the mother will be the primary caregiver. Fathers provide care out of economic necessity, providing more care at lower incomes, when engaged in shift and part-time work, and less as income rises. Men still "help" or assist with children rather than taking on an equal share and responsibility. How men parent, and the role they play in relation to mothers, is also significantly affected by the age and gender of the children. Sons continue to receive more of their fathers' attention, and fathers' involvement varies significantly by age (as does mothers').

These patterns suggest the complexity of the context of fatherhood. We must keep in mind the actual context of fatherhood when we consider redefining and changing legal and social policy. Particularly striking is the asymmetry of mothering and fathering practices and the degree to which fatherhood is tied not to biology but to the household and to connections with mothers. The distribution of fathers among caretaking, breadwinning, and disengaged fathers are patterns that any definition must either acknowledge or ignore at its peril. Contrary to ideals of gender neutrality and gender equality, fathers neither act nor are treated as equal to mothers. Children become poorer and poorer as men limit their responsibilities as fathers to the children residing in their household and increasingly spend less time connected to one intimate relationship.

The interconnections with gender are not limited solely to demographics or sociological studies of conduct. Two intersections that are particularly critical are the cultural concept of masculinity within the general definition of men's gender role, and fatherhood in relation to, even if not in connection to, motherhood. These two intersections are explored in Part Three. In Part Two I examine the law as it currently operates on the context and practice of fatherhood.

PART II · FATHERS IN LAW

CHAPTER 6

Constitutional Fathers

In this section I describe the theory and operation of legal doctrines that most directly define and impact on fatherhood. This broad overview presents a general picture of where fathers fit into our conceptions about families, and how the law impacts on their lives. Placed against the context and practice of fathering, the law has had a significant and increasing impact on fathers, especially because of the shift in the obligations and rights of unmarried fathers, as well as the heightened concern for the economic support of children after divorce.

I begin with the constitutional cases that articulate core values and definitions of fatherhood. I then sketch the basic structures of areas of law that assume or explicitly describe fatherhood in the chapters that follow. I argue that law has defined fatherhood constitutionally, at common law, and in modern state statutes and caselaw in biological and economic terms largely within a marital framework. This results in a minimalistic, status-oriented definition, granting rights on the basis of biology, or biology plus marriage, or some other sign of commitment to care, while at the same time

imposing (and only supporting) a limited scope of familial obligation, largely confined to economic support. In the chapter on biological fatherhood I examine paternity, adoption, and reproductive
rights. The chapter on economic fatherhood discusses child custody,
visitation, and child support, as well as benefits and tax law.

I intend to look at these areas as fathers do, that is, to take the
vantage point of fathers in assessing how they are viewed and
treated by the legal system. This focus should not obscure the fact
that other actors, especially mothers and children, may identify the
same problems as blocking support for parenting, while viewing the
operation of the legal system very differently. What comes across
strongly from fathers in the research literature and anecdotal accounts is the overwhelming sense that the legal system is biased
against them *as men*. This seems especially ironic since most of the
decision makers in the system are male. Thus, male judges, in the
perception of many fathers, are biased against them as fathers, dis-
advantaging them particularly with respect to custody and visitation, whether after divorce or when they have never married the
mothers of their children.

Despite the legal system's clear patriarchal origin, men see the legal
system as not protecting their interests in nurture, or as imposing obligations which are either unwanted, unfair, or unjustified. First, in the
area of reproductive rights, men see themselves as significantly disadvantaged if they want to become fathers, but advantaged if they want
to avoid fatherhood. Contraception remains a woman's responsibility
and most methods preventing reproduction are controlled by women.
The abortion decision is also legally solely a woman's decision. If an
unmarried woman has a child and the father's paternity is not established, the father has no responsibility whatsoever for the child. On
the other hand, once the child is born, if the father wants custody he
will face an uphill battle, whether the mother decides to raise the child
or place the child for adoption. Termination of the mother's rights
does not guarantee custody to the father or his ability to block an
adoption. If the mother wants to raise the child, he will have a difficult
time gaining custody. He will have an easier time obtaining visitation
rights, but they are subject to a best interests standard. He will be required to pay child support even if he has no contact or limited contact
with the child. If he wants an ongoing relationship with a child, he is
best advised to marry the mother and stay married.

A father can obtain some protection of his right to establish a relationship with his newborn or newly adopted child by exercising his right to parental leave. Of course he can only do this if he is working and if his workplace is covered by the statute. The legal system will not, however, provide him much protection if he is discriminated against on the job for exercising his right to such leave or once he returns. In addition, if his work and family obligations conflict, he has no legal recourse beyond the family leave period. If he does marry, and the marriage (as nearly half of all marriages do), ends in divorce he will face an uphill struggle for custody although he is likely to succeed in gaining significant visitation and joint legal (decision-making) custody. However, the legal system requires him to spend considerable time and money if he is unable to get along with his former wife and she blocks his contact with his children. If he stepparents, no matter how close his relationship with his stepchild, most likely it will not be legally recognized during marriage. If the stepfather's relationship with the mother ends, his parental relationship will not be legally protected except as a nonparent third party seeking ongoing contact. If he diminishes his contact with his biological or adopted children, he may face a request from a stepfather to relinquish his rights and allow the stepfather to adopt his children. State laws contain no provision to allow both to remain legal fathers.

Given all this, it is not surprising that fathers feel that women and the legal system are their enemies, not their supporters, in their quest to become nurturing fathers. Fathers sense that what is demanded of them is economic support and their desire to be fathers in any other respect may be tolerated but will not be strongly promoted. The disproportionate pattern of mother custody seems to confirm their allegations of bias, although the success of fathers in contested cases contradicts that view. The bleak pattern of men's visitation also suggests that the desire to nurture may be more ideological than real for a significant number of fathers.

If we are committed to redefining fatherhood, we must go beyond tinkering with the present system. If we do not, we will fail to meaningfully change the legal support of nurturing fatherhood. Nevertheless, if tinkering is the farthest we will go—or go now—then we must clearly think through the way the existing system works, in what direction we want to travel, and how even minimal reforms might support more nurture by some fathers.

COMMON LAW ANTECEDENTS

Before examining the current legal situation of fatherhood, we must review the common law backdrop against which constitutional, statutory, and case law function. Fatherhood and motherhood were highly gendered categories at common law. The historical focus of the common law was on *status*, from which conduct was presumed. The law's concern was on *being* a father, rather than *doing* parenting. The critical question was one of identification when genetic fatherhood was not self-evident. In Roman times, fatherhood was decided by the rite of *amphidromies*:

> In this rite, the father picked up the infant and walked around the house three times before witnesses. Children gained rights through the father's act as an expression of his will, not by simple biology. A citizen of Rome did not "have" a child, but "took" a child. . . . [T]he Roman father literally "raised" him. (Tripp-Reimer and Wilson 1991:7)

Under common law, fatherhood was primarily established not by such an act of affirmation, but by marriage. The law constructed fatherhood through the doctrine of legitimacy, giving legal sanction to real or fictitious genetic ties, while obliterating nonmarital genetic relationships.

> For the child to have a father *means* that it is "from one blood," the father's and conversely to be a father *is* to produce the substance, semen, through which blood is passed on to one's successors. . . . Now case two, illegitimate descent. This presents a quite different biology: the child under these circumstances is from the *body* of the mother alone; it is "spurious" . . . because "the ancients called the female genitals the *spurium*." So, while the legitimate child is from the froth of the father, the illegitimate child seems to come solely from factual flesh, from the seed of the mother's genitals, as if the father did not exist. (Laqueur 1990:210, citing medieval encyclopedist Isidore of Seville)

Within marriage, fathers had strong rights as the patriarchal head of the household. "We are informed by the first elementary books we read that the authority of the father is superior to that of the mother. It is a doctrine of all civilized nations" (Jennison 1991:1185n15). Patriarchy was a reflection of the divine order. "By the laws of the land the claims of the father are superior to those of the mother . . . human laws cannot be very far out of the way when they are in accordance with the laws of God" (Roman, Haddad, and Manso 1978:197). Fathers were presumed to be in control, presumed to have economic responsibility, and, in the preindustrial period, presumed to be present in the daily lives of their children. They were viewed as teachers, disciplinarians, and moral leaders as well as providers. Their obligation to provide economic support only existed, however, within marriage; there was no obligation to support children conceived outside marriage.

The denial of legal and economic status to women reinforced the preservation of fathers' status, control, and economic power. Mothers did not have to be identified; there was no difficulty doing so because childbirth identified motherhood. Mothers were biologically defined, and their role as social nurturers was presumed from biology. The legal focus on their marital status was for the benefit of fathers, not for the benefit of themselves or their children (Collier 1995a; Dolgin 1997; Mason 1994).

Several shifts undermined, although they did not totally eliminate, the connection between fatherhood and the patriarchal family. First, family members progressively left the common household. As the economy changed from agricultural to industrial and to postindustrial fathers were separated from the household. Children left the household to attend school. Last to leave were mothers, who still remained at home more often than fathers to provide for the needs of children. Second, the importance of marital legitimacy declined sharply. The power and value that a father could confer by legitimation has been significantly diminished. The social stigma of unmarried parenthood has been largely removed while the economic consequences of illegitimacy may still be significant. Third, we have moved toward imposing economic obligations on fathers for nonmarital children that parallel those for marital children. The strongest reinforcement of fatherhood has been in the economic area, both for nonmarital and marital children. Economic fatherhood is now the primary concern of the law. This has moved us away from social responsibility for children, imposing both greater and fewer obligations on fathers. Fourth, we have empowered women economically, at least in theory. Yet we have not articulated complementary conceptions or expectations of fathers. This is most clearly evident in the lack of a legal obligation to provide nurture. Fathers have gained more "rights" to visitation and custody, but mothers and children did not gain corresponding rights to enforce fathers' nurturing obligations. Only economic obligations are enforceable and strongly supported. At the same time, the legal structure also continues to privilege marriage and maintain parenthood largely as an exclusive status, despite the demographic evidence that men and children frequently have multiple fatherhood relationships, either serially or simultaneously.

Most of these changes have occurred at the level of state law, some in response to constitutional cases, some ahead of a shift in constitutional doctrine. Nevertheless the commitment to common law conceptions persists in legal doctrine. Marriage and economic providing are the key factors in the common law backdrop.

CONSTITUTIONAL FATHERHOOD: FUNDAMENTAL RIGHTS AND EQUALITY PRINCIPLES

Constitutional doctrine has little to do with the everyday lives of fathers. But clearly it is significant to the discourse of fatherhood and affects the legal threshold of fatherhood which translates into a constitutional minimum that states must observe. Fatherhood is situated within constitutional doctrines regarding the fundamental individual rights of families, marriage, and parents, triggering both substantive and procedural due process protections. Secondarily, fatherhood has been analyzed under equal protection doctrine, both with respect to differential treatment between unwed and marital fathers, and gender-based differences in the treatment of fathers and mothers. There is a core set of cases involving unwed fathers. In addition there are cases on illegitimacy, welfare, and abortion that focus on fathers' rights.

The value of parent-child and family relationships is nowhere expressly stated in the Constitution, but has been acknowledged to be an assumed subtext or an overriding supertext to the Constitution. The value and protection of the family is a fundamental right, one which the Supreme Court has easily recognized and strongly defended from the intrusion of the state (*Meyer v. Nebraska* 1923; *Pierce v. Society of Sisters* 1925). The Court's support of family most often expressly or impliedly means the marital, heterosexual, nuclear family (*Bowers v. Hardwick* 1986). Indeed, marriage is accorded a high value, venerated as much as if not more than the family. "We deal with a right of privacy older than the Bill of Rights. . . . Marriage is a coming together for better or for worse, hopefully enduring, and intimate to the degree of being sacred. It is an association that promotes a way of life, not causes; a harmony in living, not political faiths; a bilateral loyalty, not commercial or social projects" (*Griswold v. Connecticut* 1965:486). "The freedom to marry has long been recognized as one of the vital personal rights essential to the orderly pursuit of happiness by free men. Marriage is one of the basic civil rights of man, fundamental to our very existence and survival" (*Loving v. Virginia* 1967:12).

On the other hand, the Court has not limited constitutional protection to marital families. The most liberal position on the family has been expressed in cases supporting the rights of so-called "nontraditional" families, including extended and foster families. *Smith v. Organization of Foster Families for Equality and Reform*, a procedural due process case brought by foster parents, reflects a more open, liberal definition of family that deemphasizes biological relationships. One of the key issues in *Smith* was whether the relation of foster parent and child fit within the definition of family, thereby entitling foster families to the high constitutional deference afforded to "family." Biological connections were acknowledged as important but not as essential, and the Court cited marriage and adoption as examples of important familial relationships defined nonbiologically. The Court saw the key role of family as emotional and political. "Thus the importance of the familial relationship, to the individuals involved and to the society, stems from the emotional attachments that derive from the intimacy of daily association, and from the role it plays in promoting a way of life through the instruction of children . . . as well as from the fact of blood relationship" (*Smith v. Organization of Foster Families for Equality and Reform* 1977:842).

The Court reasoned that foster families were distinctive because their origin derived from the state, rather than from a relationship that existed prior to the state. In valuing this type of family, the Court honored and valued relationships whose origin was distinct from or "above" the state. This view reflected natural law concepts that social and emotional bonds supersede any statute, common law, or constitution. *Smith* can be read as recognizing the biological connection but valuing psychological, emotional, and social relationships. It is worth noting that to have their greatest value, those relationships are presumed to occur in a physically shared household.

Moore v. City of East Cleveland, a substantive due process case, also reflects this understanding of the importance and role of family. "Our decisions establish that the Constitution protects the sanctity of the family precisely because the institution of the family is deeply rooted in this Nation's history and tradition. It is through the family that we inculcate and pass down many of our most cherished values, moral and cultural" (*Moore v. City of East Cleveland* 1977:503–504). *Moore*, like *Smith*, emphasizes a liberal definition of family, that in *Moore* included an extended family. "Ours is by no means a tradition limited to respect for the bonds uniting the members of the nuclear family. The tradition of uncles, aunts, cousins, and especially grandparents sharing a household along with parents and children has roots equally venerable and equally deserving of constitutional recognition" (*Moore v. City of East Cleveland* 1977:504). And as Justice Brennan points out in his concurrence in *Moore*, "nuclear family" may be translated in racial terms to reflect common patterns in white suburbia. As both race and class affect family structure, he points out any limited definition of family has those consequences.

In the family cases, it is clear that one basis for valuing family, especially marital family, and for valuing parental status has been natural law. These are relationships "older than the Bill of Rights" (*Griswold v. Connecticut* 1965:486). But the same natural law ideas also supported the Court's view of men and women as essentially different:

> [T]he civil law, as well as nature herself, has always recognized a wide difference in the respective spheres and destinies of man and woman. Man is, or should be, woman's protector and defender. The natural and proper timidity and delicacy which belongs to the female sex evidently unfits it for many of the occupations of civil life. The constitution of the family organization, which is founded in the divine ordinance, as well as in the nature of things, indicates the domestic sphere as that which properly belongs to the domain and functions of womanhood. (*Bradwell v. Illinois* 1873:141, concurrence of Justice Bradley)

At the time the core fatherhood cases were decided, gender analysis was in transition from this view of sex differences. To some extent, the core fatherhood cases arguably reflect older essentialist views of gender difference.

In addition to natural law theories, constitutional doctrine surrounding family is grounded in common law perspectives. Particularly within constitutional analysis that views interpretive issues from the perspective of history and tradition dating back to the time the Constitution was drafted, common law doctrine carries great weight. Furthermore, since family law is traditionally a matter of state concern, federalism encourages deference to state doctrines, many of which are grounded in common law concepts. Common law perspectives, like natural law perspectives, are rooted in a patriarchal view of the family. In addition, the context of the core fatherhood cases primarily involves unwed fathers. Not surprisingly, marriage is critical to the outcome and reasoning of the fatherhood cases, and therefore to the constitutional notion of fatherhood.

Gender analysis is a secondary theme in these cases. This is somewhat ironic since the fatherhood cases involve common law frameworks intended to protect men's rights against each other, to absolve men from responsibility for children outside the realm of marriage, and to contain women's sexuality while ensuring men's paternity by limiting sexuality and procreation to patriarchal marriage. An attack on this framework is an attack on the privileges and limitations of patriarchal fatherhood. In addition, some of the equal protection analysis has focused on the justification for marriage-based classifications, differentiating between unmarried and married men. More recently the analysis has focused on gender classifications. Gender bias equal protection doctrine is grounded especially in cases challenging male stereotypes (*Califano v. Jobst* 1977; *Weinberger v. Wiesenfeld* 1975; *Frontiero v. Richardson* 1973). The gender challenge is that men are not being treated the same as women; fathers are not being treated the same as mothers. But those challenges are structured so that we simply look at one aspect of being a mother, rather than examining the full range of rights and responsibilities of mothers and their presumed interrelationship with fathers.

The construction of constitutional fatherhood, then, rests within this context of a strong regard for traditional families and marriage, with some respect for a broader range of families and a reevaluation of gender stereotypes. Fatherhood cases can be loosely grouped in several ways: first, by marital status, with the bulk of explicit decisions on the definition and nature of fatherhood involving nonmarital fathers; second, by the area of law touched in the particular case, including adoption, paternity, welfare, child support, and immigration; and third, by the constitutional argument or provision invoked, which may include substantive and procedural due process, equal protection, and privacy.

THE CORE FATHERHOOD CASES

The largest group of constitutional cases on fatherhood focus on nonmarital fathers. In the context of adoption, paternity, legitimacy, and child support, and most recently, immigration, the Court has grounded its analysis on the importance of marriage and on the stigma of illegitimacy in deciding whether to accord the legal status of fatherhood to biological fathers. The lead cases where men have asserted their status as fathers are *Stanley v. Illinois, Quilloin v. Walcott, Caban v. Mohammed, Lehr v. Robertson,* and *Michael H. v. Gerald D.*

The principles that emerge from the core fatherhood cases are that: (1) biology plus something more, whether an intention to or demonstration of nurture, even if minimalistic, is necessary if one is to be recognized as a father; (2) marriage, or maybe legitimacy plus marriage, trumps biological and social fatherhood; (3) the disparate impact of facially neutral rules or their application is likely unchallengeable under equal protection analysis, because equal protection doctrines require either facial discrimination or strong evidence of an intent to discriminate; and (4) deference to families might also mean a reluctance to quantify or qualify the scope of parental rights as a means to support a claim for more support of a parental relationship. Finally, there is little on which to base an affirmative claim for children or parents, as opposed to a negative claim to keep the state out of the relationship.

The stories in these cases, as well as their outcomes, are important. They are at the core of any constitutional definition of fatherhood, both for what they say and for what they do not say. Because marital status is critical to the outcomes, they also suggest, by implication, a great deal about marital fatherhood.

In *Stanley,* the biological father, who lived with the mother off and on for eighteen years but never married her, sought to be heard on the issue of the custody of his three children after the mother died. The Court held that a conclusive presumption by the State of Illinois that an unwed father was unfit violated his due process rights under the Fourteenth Amendment Due Process Clause (*Stanley v. Illinois* 1972). The father was described as "impecunious," and the dissenting opinion notes with disdain that he turned the care of the children over to nonfamily members, and the state eventually commenced dependency proceedings when it became clear that no adult was legally responsible for them. During those proceedings the father was concerned with the loss of welfare payments if others were declared guardians of the children, and a footnote indicates that at one point during the mother's life when it was assumed that she and Stanley were husband and wife, a neglect petition was proved against him with respect to the oldest of the children. The relevant facts for the majority were Stanley's biological relationship and long running, even if inadequate, presence in the household. These established an interest deserving of protection under the Court's protection of family, even if this was a nonmarital family. Interestingly, the Court did not seem to dispute the generally low opinion of unwed fathers as likely unfit; it simply provided them the opportunity to prove otherwise. Both the majority and dissent exhibited a negative opinion of unwed fathers and characterized them as unlikely to be interested in their children and, by nature, less connected to their children.

In the second case, *Quilloin v. Walcott*, the Court considered the rights of an unwed father in a stepparent adoption case. The father had no contact with his son until the mother married and her new husband sought to adopt him (*Quilloin v. Walcott* 1978). The Court unanimously upheld the adoption and the use of the "best interests of the child" standard. The child was born in 1964, and the biological father was listed on the birth certificate. The parents never lived together nor married. In 1967 the mother married, and the child lived with his maternal grandmother until 1969, when he returned to live with his mother, stepfather, and a son born during the marriage. The biological father irregularly provided economic support, despite the fact that the mother never brought an action to enforce his statutory duty of support. He regularly visited with the child and had given him gifts. When the child was eleven years old, with the mother's consent, her current husband filed a petition to adopt the child. At about this time, the mother decided that the contacts of the biological father with his son were disruptive to the family. In the adoption proceeding the child expressed a desire to be adopted by his stepfather and take his name, but also expressed a wish to continue to have contact with his biological father. Under Georgia law at the time, the child could not both be adopted and continue visitation; he could only have one or the other. At no time prior to the adoption petition had the biological father attempted to legitimate his child. The biological father objected to the adoption, petitioned for legitimation, and sought visitation rights. A colloquy from the trial indicates that the biological father did not understand the legitimation process, and therefore his failure to legitimate his child appears to have been due to ignorance, not neglect. Nevertheless, the adoption was approved over his objection.

Under the Georgia statute, adoption procedures distinguished between the children of unmarried and married parents. Children of married parents could not be adopted without the consent of both parents; children of unmarried parents could be adopted with the sole consent of the mother. Thus a mother could block an adoption, but not a father. The Supreme Court considered this case under a due process challenge, rejecting a last-minute equal protection argument. Since the biological father had been afforded notice and an opportunity to be heard, the procedural issue was framed as whether deciding this issue under the "best interests of the child" standard was constitutional (versus the absolute bar to an adoption that could have been exercised by a married father). The Court acknowledged the strong protection of the parent-child relationship, but found it persuasive that the father never sought custody of the child, and that the adoption was for the purpose of legally recognizing a de facto family unit. Because of these factors, the use of the best interests test was deemed appropriate. The Court also rejected an equal protection argument comparing unmarried and married fathers, emphasizing again the lack of custody of the child and therefore the biological father's failure to provide "daily supervision, education, protection, or care of the child" (*Quilloin v. Walcott* 1978:256). The Court's decision was unanimous.

In the third case, *Caban v. Mohammed*, the Court again confronted the issue of fathers' rights in the context of a stepparent adoption, and held it violated the Equal Protection Clause to treat mothers and fathers differently in the context of adoption. As in *Stanley*, the biological father and mother had lived together for four years, and had two children together (*Caban v. Mohammed*

1979). During that time, the father was married but separated from another woman. He was listed on the birth certificate of each child and contributed to their support. At the end of this period, the mother left to live with another man, and shortly thereafter she married him. The father maintained contact with the children after the relationship ended. He had access to the children every weekend when their mother brought them to visit her mother, who lived in the same building as the father.

The children then moved with their grandmother to Puerto Rico. After one visit, the father brought the children back with him to New York to live with him and his second wife. When the mother learned of this, she initiated custody proceedings. The father responded with cross proceedings for custody. In this scenario, then, there were two married couples seeking to establish custody of the children. Both spouses of the biological parents also wished to adopt the children. Under the New York statute that controlled the adoption, the mother could block the adoption by refusing to provide consent; the father's consent was not similarly necessary. The Court rejected treating the biological parents, unwed at the time the children were born, as divorced parents with substantive due process to maintain their respective parental relationships. Thus, the petition for adoption was appropriate. The question then was whether the biological parents could be treated differently.

The Court found that a potential for different treatment at birth based on biological difference could not extend beyond birth when, as in this case, both parents had cared for the children and the parents had lived as a "natural family" for several years. The biological father's participation in the rearing of his children (plus biology) triggered his entitlement to equal treatment with the biological mother. Much of the disagreement among members of the Court in this case was over the appropriate weight to be given to the importance of removing the children's illegitimacy by enabling them to be adopted. The majority rejected the concept of gender distinctions in the process of adoption in this case, even though it acknowledged the value of placing children in "normal, two-parent" homes and, by virtue of adoption, erasing the stigma of illegitimacy (*Caban v. Mohammed* 1979:391). The dissenting opinion of Justice Stevens focused not only on legitimacy issues, but also on the differences between fathers and mothers—differences rooted in differing social roles and responsibilities although tied to biological differences through childbirth (*Caban v. Mohammed* 1979:405).

In the Court's fourth case, *Lehr v. Robertson*, the Court again addressed stepparent adoption. The distinguishing factor in this case was that the father had neither married the mother nor maintained a relationship with the child after her birth (*Lehr v. Robertson* 1983). Eight months after the child was born, the mother married, and when the child was two, filed an adoption petition so that she could be adopted by her stepfather. Her biological father was given no notice of the adoption. He had not registered on the state's putative fathers' registry. However, prior to the completion of the adoption proceeding, he filed a paternity action, requesting a paternity determination, order of support, and visitation privileges. In this case the Court made it clear that biology alone was not a sufficient basis to trigger constitutional protection, as in *Quilloin*.

> The significance of the biological connection is that it offers the natural father an opportunity that no other male possesses to develop a relationship with his offspring. If he grasps that opportunity and accepts some measure of responsibility for the child's future, he may enjoy the blessings of the parent-child relationship and make uniquely valuable contributions to the child's development. If he fails to do so, the Federal Constitution will not automatically compel a state to listen to his opinion of where the child's best interests lie. (*Lehr v. Robertson* 1983:261)

The Court clearly saw marriage as the best protection of the father's interest, and the failure to marry as significant. The nature of the relationship was described as "custodial, personal *or* financial" (*Lehr v. Robertson* 1983:267). The dissent argued that the trigger should be the biological link.

Finally, in *Michael H. v. Gerald D.*, the Court was faced with determining whether a biological father who had lived with the mother for some time and maintained a relationship with the child could claim visitation rights when the mother reconciled with her husband. The facts of this case actually involve three potential fathers. The mother engaged in an affair with a neighbor and the child, Victoria, was born. The husband was listed on the birth certificate and held Victoria out as his daughter. The mother continued a relationship with the biological father, lived with him briefly, and then lived with a third man. The mother moved between these three relationships while the biological father filed a filiation action to establish paternity and his right to visitation. Nearly two years after that action began, the mother finally and permanently reconciled with her husband. The husband intervened in the paternity action and asked for dismissal based on the statutory presumption that established him as the father and barred a paternity action to be filed by anyone other than the husband or the wife.

In this case, fatherhood sufficient under the *Stanley/Caban* standard was contraposed to marital fatherhood. California had a marital presumption that permitted the marital couple to control the establishment of paternity, and provided that paternity must be presumed during the existence of the marriage. The presumption blocked the biological father from proving paternity, even though paternity tests had established a 98.07 percent probability that he was the father. The Court upheld the presumption based on the value given to the marital relationship under its family cases. The Court rested its opinion on veneration for the marital family. "The family unit accorded traditional respect in our society, which we have referred to as the unitary family, is typified, of course, by the marital family, but also includes the household of unmarried parents and their children" (*Michael H. v. Gerald D.* 1989:124n3). The Court also cited the long tradition of concern over legitimacy. Legitimacy and respect for the marital relationship trumped the parental relationship of the biological father with his child. This was a very close decision, both with respect to the appropriate standard for evaluating fundamental rights and with respect to the strength of the biological father's claim, given the establishment of a social relationship strong enough for a guardian to recommend that visitation be granted.

From these core cases emerges the fundamental rule that biology alone does not confer procedural or substantive rights when the father is not married to the mother. Biology confers an opportunity to develop a relationship marked by social or economic nurture. Thus, biology plus nurture, with nurture defined in a fairly minimalistic way, is the definition of fatherhood, but only of nonmarital fatherhood. Biology plus marriage is the other alternative. That alternative is seen as particularly valuable because it legitimizes the child. Another consequence of marital fatherhood seems to be to shield the conduct of the father from analysis. The status of marriage confers strong rights and invokes the Court's decisions that protect and value the privacy of the family, in particular the traditional, marital, intact, two-parent, heterosexual family. The value attached to marital fatherhood is so strong that in a conflict between a marital and nonmarital father, where the nonmarital father arguably met the standard of legal fatherhood set by the Court, since he had lived with and nurtured the child, the Court nevertheless validated an evidentiary presumption that, in effect, excluded the biological father from being heard on a request for visitation.

In all but one of the lead cases, the facts involved stepparent adoption by the biological mother's new husband. Marital fatherhood, even when nonbiological, was clearly preferred by the Court, because it provided the child with what appeared to be an intact nuclear family. The factual circumstances of these cases represent a significant portion of the context of fathering. With the exception of *Stanley*, the Court's initial case, these are cases in which multiple parental figures were present, sometimes standing with both the biological parents who conceived the child. None of the adoption scenarios represented adoption by "strangers." Rather, all the adoptions occurred in the context of an ongoing marital relationship. In *Michael H.* the assertion of rights was also in the context of a marital relationship, albeit one reconnected over a long period of multiple intimate relationships involving the mother. Also with the exception of *Stanley* (and perhaps even including *Stanley*), the fathers in these cases were seeking to protect ongoing contact with their children, but were not seeking custody. It is not entirely clear whether they were also seeking to protect their right to the opportunity for a connection, or perhaps even blocking the assertion of what was deemed an exclusive status by another man.

The Court clearly did not think much of any of these fathers. Lacking the status of marriage, they were seen as reprehensible. When the countervailing option is of a mother now situated within a marital unit, providing the appearance of a "natural" family, the Court sees a strong state interest in supporting that family. Thus, where parent-child and marital family interests conflict, the Court tips the balance toward the marital family. In none of these opinions is the nature of the relationship between the stepfather and the child examined. And, most tellingly, in two cases (*Michael H.* and *Quilloin*) the Court ignored the wishes of the child to maintain a relationship with the biological father. By the time the Court decided *Lehr*, the relationship in

Quilloin was all but erased; it was only a potential relationship, one where the father had never seized his opportunity to be a "real father." On the other hand, these fathers did not have much of a relationship with their children. While they had maintained contact with their children, and had a relationship with them, in virtually all these cases (apart from *Stanley* and *Caban*) the children had never lived with their biological fathers, nor spent an appreciable time with them. Their fathers were present only at the margins of their lives.

The Court's cases reflect a dual definition of fatherhood that divides along marriage. Even if nonmarital fathers are recognized as having parental status, they do not necessarily have rights equivalent to marital fathers. So, for example, a nonmarital father may be heard at an adoption proceeding, but he would not automatically prevail on custody, since that might be decided on the basis of the best interests of the child. Similarly, a nonmarital father could be ordered to pay child support but would not be guaranteed liberal visitation equivalent to that of a divorcing marital father. And the Court's cases arguably require that unwed fathers cannot trigger constitutional protection unless they share a household for a considerable period of time with the mother and child, either because the Court is more comfortable with a marital-type relationship between the parents (Dolgin 1997), or requires the opportunity or presumed conduct of parental nurture of the children. The most frequent doctrinal concern in these cases is the Court's protection of family privacy from state intrusion as a fundamental right. Although the Court recognizes family forms beyond the marital nuclear family, it accords the latter the highest protection, as a natural right that precedes the Constitution itself.

Marital fathers have had little explicit attention other than in *Michael H.* The Court has upheld the right of a father to remarry, even if he has not paid his child support for his children of a previous marriage, deeming the right to a new family more important than support of his children (*Zablocki v. Redhail* 1978). The Court has also recognized the due process rights of divorced fathers, in a stepparent adoption case, in an opinion with markedly little discussion compared to the unwed fathers' cases (*Armstrong v. Manzo* 1965). The strong protection of marital fathers seems to be presumed in the protection of family privacy decisions that accord an especially high value to marriage, as well as the Court's decisions upholding parental rights against state intrusion.

OTHER RELEVANT CONSTITUTIONAL DOCTRINES: ILLEGITIMACY, WELFARE, ABORTION, AND GENDER BIAS

Several other lines of cases flesh out the core fatherhood cases. First, the Court's illegitimacy cases define the father-child relationship in terms of economic obligations, without a hint of other obligations or rights. The obligation to pay child support for nonmarital children is quite recent. The key case, *Gomez v. Perez*, was decided in 1973; some states did not implement the constitutional requirement until the 1980s (*Linda R.S. v. Richard D.* 1973; *Gomez v. Perez* 1973). *Gomez* was decided as an equal protection case. The Court found no logic in denying children support on the basis of whether their father had married their mother. The Court has not recognized a constitutional right of custody or visitation, although the practice in many states has moved in that direction either as concomitant to economic obligation or by virtue of eliminating the distinction between marital and non-maritial children.

The Court's illegitimacy cases eliminated many of the distinctions between legitimate and illegitimate children in terms of rights and benefits, predominantly the right to economic support from their established biological fathers, on the grounds that such children need just as much support as do legitimate children, and should not be punished for the sins of their parents (*United States v. Clark* 1983; *Lalli v. Lalli* 1978; *Trimble v. Gordon* 1977; *Mathews v. Lucas* 1976; *Norton v. Mathews* 1976; *Jimenez v. Weinberger* 1974, *Levy v. Louisiana* 1968; *Califano v. Jobst* 1977). Illegitimacy, however, can still be a basis for distinguishing between children, especially when it affects the parent rather than the child. For example, the Court upheld a statute under which an unwed father could not sue for the wrongful death of his child, because the distinction disadvantages the parent, not the child (*Parham v. Hughes* 1979). A related set of cases has evaluated the sufficiency of procedures designed to protect men *against* fatherhood in paternity proceedings (*Clark v. Jeter* 1988; *Rivera v. Minnich* 1987; *Pickett v. Brown* 1983; *Mills v. Habluetzel* 1982; *Little v. Streater* 1981).

In the legitimacy cases the Court strongly preserved the status while removing negative consequences for children. A constitutional challenge to the category itself would have a hard time if the Court continues to look to "tradition," since the stigma attached to an out-of-wedlock birth was well established when the Constitution was drafted. Furthermore, when forced to choose between valuing marriage and eliminating legitimacy, the Court has ample precedent to privilege marriage. On the other hand, the movement by states to eliminate many of, if not all, the distinctions of illegitimacy for children, even to eliminate the category entirely, might persuade the Court under an argument of deference to states in the area of family law.

The most recent legitimacy case was an immigration case (*Miller v. Albright* 1998). The Court basically upheld differential treatment of the children of unwed father citizens and unwed mother citizens on the basis of what it views as biological differences. The dissent argued that the differential treatment was based on gender stereotypes about the likelihood of paternal caretaking of a child. Unwed fathers have a more difficult time passing on immigration preferences and conferring citizenship on children born outside the country. In *Miller*, the differentiation was not limited to birth, but carried over postbirth, and therefore represented a set of assumptions about the relationship between the father and mother, most notably the assumption that the unwed mother, whether citizen or not, would most likely raise the child. One can view this core assumption as simply a reflection of the overwhelming reality of mother care, or as the perpetuation of a gender stereotype of paternal incapability (*Miller v. Albright* 1998).

In addition to the illegitimacy cases, the Court's welfare rights cases touch on the relative positions of social versus biological or legal fathers. These cases involve consideration of rules that assume that any man in a household receiving welfare may be an actual or potential breadwinner father, justifying denial of benefits or a presumption of contribution that might result in ineligibility. In *King v. Smith*, the Court held invalid a "substitute father" regulation that treated as a father any man who either cohabited with the mother seeking benefits, or who had an ongoing sexual relationship with her, even if not cohabiting with her. The mother in this case had four children, three of whom were the children of a man who had died, and a fourth who had been abandoned by a father no longer in the household (*King v. Smith* 1968). The mother's paramour was a married man with nine children. The Court found the state rule invalid under the statutory scheme designed to replace the income of an absent or deceased parent, since the man was not the legal parent of any of the children, and did not contribute any income that could be taken into account for eligibility purposes. The Court's opinion expressly acknowledged the gendered origin of the welfare system and the assumption that a father's primary role was that of breadwinner. At the same time, it rejected any broader definition of "parent" or "father" beyond marital or biological definitions. It thus protected men against unwarranted financial obligations while protecting women against loss of income based on financial assumptions rife with class and gender assumptions and disapproving race judgments.

In subsequent cases involving variations on this issue—the so-called "man in the house" regulations devised by the states—the Court continued to strike down any rule presuming parental support by a man not legally obligated to provide support (*Van Lare v. Hurley* 1975; *Lewis v. Martin* 1970). On the other hand, the Court has upheld the inclusion of child support payments in the calculation of benefits, despite impacting the parent a child lives with in a family's effort to maximize needed resources (*Bowen v. Gilliard* 1987). When welfare rules were reformed to permit payment in the event of unemployment in addition to parental absence, death, or disability, the Court struck down the provision that provided benefits to families with unemployed fathers but not unemployed mothers—a scheme predicated on the assumption that men were the sole or primary breadwinners—as impermissible sex stereotyping (*Califano v. Westcott* 1979).

The Court has also dealt with fathers in the context of abortion, in challenges to statutes requiring the consent of husbands or notice to them in order for a woman to have a legal abortion. In general, men have privacy interests in reproduction that are well recognized and protected (*Skinner v. Oklahoma* 1942). Based on that doctrine, biological fathers-to-be may have an important, even a significant, interest in a child conceived but not yet born.

> We are not unaware of the deep and proper concern and interest that a devoted and protective husband has in his wife's pregnancy and in the growth and development of the fetus she is carrying. . . . Moreover, we recognize that the decision whether to undergo or to forgo an abortion may have profound effects on the future of any marriage, effects that are both physical and mental, and possibly deleterious. (*Planned Parenthood of Central Missouri v. Danforth* 1976:69)

Since a father is not similarly situated to the biological mother, however, and since her interest in control of her body is fundamental, the Court has deemed the mother's right of choice preeminent (*Planned Parenthood of Central Missouri v. Danforth* 1976). Giving a husband veto power by virtue of a consent requirement is therefore unconstitutional. In addition, the Court has held unconstitutional spousal notification requirements as posing a substantial obstacle that significantly burdens the right of choice, in view of the prevalence of spousal abuse (*Planned Parenthood of Southeastern Pennsylvania v. Casey* 1992). The Court has not had occasion to consider consent or notice requirements for fathers generally, but given the solicitude for marriage the Court would be unlikely to treat unmarried fathers any differently.

Most cases about fatherhood before the Court are framed as issues of procedural or substantive (fundamental rights) due process, or individual privacy rights. However, in some cases, the parties focus on equal protection. In some of the core fatherhood cases, the equal protection argument has focused on distinctions between marital and nonmarital fathers, arguments which seemed to make some sense in view of the Court's doctrine regarding nontraditional families and its illegitimacy decisions. The powerful support of marriage and legitimacy, however, prevailed over those arguments. On the other hand, with the shift in the Court's gender discrimination analysis, gender bias arguments were raised in some cases, especially where states continued to use facial gender classifications.

In its application of gender analysis to fathers, on the one hand the Court shows a sensitivity to context; on the other hand, it plays to stereotypes and dominant gender roles. So, for example, what appears as a bias favoring mothers in the core fatherhood cases is justified in terms of the common life circumstances of unwed mothers, who are frequently abandoned by the father of their child. The Court accepts a stereotype of unwed fathers as uninvolved, immoral, and irresponsible. In the abortion cases, the Court views the sexes as not similarly situated, seeing husbands as understandably connected to their wives, but less so to their unborn children, and therefore justifying differential treatment. On the other hand, in a statutory case involving potential reproductive harm to both women and men, the Court viewed men and women's similarity as critical to a finding that a woman-only reproductive health policy constituted facial discrimination on the basis of sex, not justifiable classification on the basis of significant sex differences (*International Union, UAW v. Johnson Controls, Inc.* 1991). At the same time, the Court afforded no relief to the male plaintiff who claimed discrimination on account of the policy's failure to equally protect men from reproductive harm.

It is an interesting and ironic aspect of the development of heightened analysis of gender discrimination that the cases that elevated the standard of judicial scrutiny involve men discriminated against because they did not fit the presumed gender roles under which various government entitlement programs were structured. Resisting stereotypes was the basis of the Court's early gender jurisprudence ratcheting the upward analysis of gender classifications. For example, the Court rejected a statute with a presumption of dependency for women while men's dependency had to be established, since it countered the norm. Social Security, a system connected to employment, provides benefits to caretakers of children who have lost a working parent due to death. However, it was presumed the deceased parent would be a breadwinner father, and therefore denied benefits to a surviving father caring for his son upon the death of his wife (*Weinberger v. Wiesenfeld* 1975).

The Court has steadily increased its level of scrutiny of gender-based classifications. In two of its more recent opinions, *J.E.B. v. Alabama,* a paternity and child support case, and in the VMI case, *United States v. Virginia,* the Court seemingly increased its scrutiny a bit more. Some argue that the Court embraced strict scrutiny as its standard in *VMI* (Kovacic-Fleischer 1997). In *J.E.B.* the Court considered whether intentional discrimination on the basis of gender in the state's exercise of its peremptory challenges to remove all but one male from the jury pool, which resulted in an all-female jury, violated the Equal Protection clause of the Fourteenth Amendment (*J.E.B. v. Alabama* 1994). The Court decided this case in the context of an earlier decision that the exercise of peremptories on the basis of intentional racial discrimination violates equal protection, using the demanding standard of strict scrutiny. The state defended its conduct based on a generalized fear that the men would empathize with the defendant and argued that gender discrimination ought not be subject to the same standard of analysis as race discrimination. The Court rejected the notion of generalized gender differences as justification, finding that this amounted to little more than prohibited gender stereotyping and was therefore unconstitutional. "Intentional discrimination on the basis of gender by state actors violates the Equal Protection clause, particularly where, as here, the discrimination serves to ratify and perpetuate invidious, archaic, and overbroad stereotypes about the relative abilities of men and women" (*J.E.B. v. Alabama* 1994:130–131).

The Court's analysis of the issue emphasized the parallels in the treatment of women and African-Americans with respect to citizenship in general and exclusion from jury service in particular. While the Court stopped short of declaring the analytical standard to be the same, it nevertheless emphasized that gender classifications require "an exceedingly persuasive justification" (*J.E.B. v. Alabama* 1994: 136). Because the Court found no basis for the classification that furthered the goal of a fair and impartial jury, it reasoned that deciding the standard of review was unnecessary (*J.E.B. v. Alabama* 1994: 137n6). It did specifically reject the argument that gender is an appropriate consideration under an assertion that men and women perceive and react differently to trials. "We shall not accept as a defense to gender-based peremptory challenges the very stereotype the law condemns" (*J.E.B. v. Alabama* 1994:138, citing *Powers v. Ohio*). Even where stereotypes may reflect some empirical truth, they cannot be used, according to the Court.

In *VMI*, the Court considered whether the state could maintain a male-only military academy on the basis of the essential value of sex-segregated education. The Court held the scheme unconstitutional, applying a standard that required that any proffered justification be "exceedingly persuasive," with the burden of jus-tification "demanding" (*United States v. Virginia* 1996:533). The Court rejected the notion of gender differences permitting or even requiring segregation in education. "Generalizations about the way women are, estimates of what is appropriate for most women, no longer justify denying opportunity to women whose talent and capacity place them outside the average description" (*United States v. Virginia* 1996:550). These cases suggest that any facial classification of fathers would have to withstand searching scrutiny, although neutral classifications (like parental leave or the primary caregiver standard) could avoid such scrutiny unless other factors met the intentional discrimination standard.

In both these opinions, vigorous dissents pointed out the movement of the Court toward an analytical standard virtually indistinguishable from that used for racial discrimination, and the emphasis in the majority's analysis of the parallels between race and sex discrimination. What is perhaps most significant for fathers is to compare not only the facts of the cases to situations confronting fathers in dealing with the legal system, but also to insert "fathers" or "men" in the critical language of the Court's opinion. This suggests that, in claims of bias against the system, fathers could utilize a more searching standard of scrutiny that might well challenge the Court's own prior jurisprudence regarding fathers.

SUMMARY

Constitutional fatherhood is overwhelmingly marital fatherhood, reflecting the strong model of marital fatherhood in the common law. This means fatherhood grounded in a patriarchal and heterosexual tradition. Most of the case law on marital fathers can be understood as law protecting and supporting men over women and in relation to other men. When fatherhood is connected to marriage, responsibility is automatic; the man has no choice. At the same time, it is subject to very high protection against any other claims of parenthood, and until quite recently the marital father had supreme power in the family under a patriarchal understanding of family, including both the relationship between spouses and parent-child relationships. Economic fatherhood is presumed and need not be imposed. Social fatherhood exists within the sphere of privacy, which is protected for the marital family. Conversely, outside marriage, fatherhood has been protected and permitted only as long as it does not threaten the marriage of another man. An unmarried biological father whose paternity did not threaten a married man was permitted unlimited choice, and had no obligations as a parent if he did not acknowledge paternity or paternity was not established.

Especially in light of sharply changing demographic patterns, plus a standard of gender analysis that keeps inching toward strict scrutiny, some open constitutional questions regarding fathers remain, including: can biologically based obligations without rights be justified if imposed as a result of paternity but not maternity? In other words, can a state impose financial obligations without access? Can states justify the primary-parent tilt of the custody structure? And how should courts monitor or evaluate nurture without violating family privacy? If the trend toward eliminating distinctions between marital and non-marital fatherhood continues, it is questionable whether legitimacy can be maintained as a legal status. Also open to question is whether fathers' social relationships can be measured by the marital standard of biology alone, or the postdivorce standard of the best interests of the child, an implicit social fatherhood standard.

Fathers might look to constitutional case law for a variety of reasons: as a minimal framework for defining fatherhood, or as the protection for individual civil rights grounded in treasured relationships of parent-child, family, and self. Constitutional arguments might be used to challenge common law or statutory definitions or to question the application of those definitions. Fathers would find a patchwork of cases, focusing unevenly on different fathers at different phases in the cycle of their relationships with their children. A movement in the direction of seeing fathers as indistinguishable from mothers could potentially threaten mothers unless the current relationship between fathers and mothers and the broader social context of motherhood is taken into account. A movement in the direction of supporting social fathers might be challenged by biological fathers, and the question could be squarely raised as to whether biology triggers or should trigger parental status and rights.

Both these possibilities are explored in greater depth in Part III. The cases focus on the *status* of fatherhood, although in the process they describe the content and conduct of fatherhood. The conduct is far less than that presumed for mothers. It is critical to remember that this is a constitutional standard and it specifies only a minimal standard. Constitutional doctrine can be read as supporting social fatherhood, but it retains a strong connection to marriage.

CHAPTER 7

Biological Fathers

If constitutional fatherhood remains strongly linked to marriage, biological fatherhood is arguably becoming more dominant at the state level. The common law linkage of biology and marriage has given way to statutory impositions of responsibilities and a movement toward the establishment of rights which gives greater recognition to fatherhood based purely on biology. In contrast to the constitutional requirement of "biology plus some further connection" in order to trigger constitutional protection of unwed fathers, state statutes have moved toward recognizing biology alone as the basis for fatherhood responsibilities and rights comparable to those of married fathers at divorce. Biology, in this view, is a sufficient and "natural" basis for social fatherhood. This is primal fatherhood which insures the essential presence of a male parent. Most importantly, the biological nexus is viewed as insuring sexual responsibility while establishing economic obligation. Biological definitions are the most powerful at the beginning of children's lives, when it can be argued that little else can be the basis for determining fatherhood. Reproductive technologies challenge even that assertion, however, and suggest the alternatives of intent and prebirth conduct as the relevant bases for determining fatherhood.

The movement toward recognizing biological fatherhood as the core definition of fatherhood has not, however, been unambiguous. Accompanying the shift toward greater rights for biological fathers there has been a persistent limitation of rights for men whose claims rest solely on a genetic link to their children. The urge toward limitation is strongest when placed in opposition to marital fatherhood.

In this chapter I focus first on the legal concepts of paternity and legitimacy. Then I discuss the child support system which treats unwed fathers on a par with marital fathers (at least in theory), and increasingly includes them in the related entitlements to visitation and custody. A more limited recognition of biological fathers, however, is evident in recent changes in adoption law, reflecting the tension between individual and family rights. Finally, biological fathers as sperm donors are permitted to forfeit their rights and are largely barred from voiding their forfeiture. At the same end of the spectrum are biological fathers who cannot block the actions of mothers with respect to choosing to terminate their pregnancy, although they clearly have the right to make decisions about reproduction and contraception equivalent to those of mothers.

PATERNITY AND LEGITIMATION

In contrast to the common law concepts of legitimation and paternity which excluded most unmarried biological fathers from legal fatherhood, modern paternity structures provide for both voluntary and involuntary establishment of paternity, and once established, impose support obligations equivalent to those for marital children. Paternity determinations have been transformed by scientific evidence that makes them much more reliable. The Human Leukocyte Antigens (HLA) blood test looks for markers on white blood cells, and in combination with red blood cell tests, can exclude a defendant with more than a 97 percent accuracy rate. In addition, electrophoresis tests in combination with other tests can establish a 99 percent accuracy rate (Roberts 1993:1021). The most recent technique is DNA testing, which has an even higher probability of reliability both in terms of excluding men and of linking them affirmatively to their biological children. The availability of these techniques renders unnecessary many of the common law and statutory procedural and evidentiary protections designed to deal with this issue. In many states, scientific evidence now creates a rebuttable presumption of paternity if it exceeds a specified level of probability (See Fla. Stat. Ann. § 742.13 [3][1996]; N.Y. Civ. Prac. Law & Rules 4518 [d][1997]).

Traditionally, paternity actions were brought by the mother or by the state, in order to relieve the state of responsibility for supporting the child, and to assist the custodial parent, presumed to be the mother, in supporting the child. The child also benefited, not only by virtue of support paid, but also by acquiring rights to inheritance, medical support, wrongful death actions, workers' compensation dependent's allowances, and veterans' benefits (Dowd 1997a). Now an action can be brought on behalf of a child. Voluntary procedures allow fathers to establish or disprove paternity and therefore avoid an obligation of support. Federal welfare legislation encourages states to improve and streamline their paternity procedures, and requires welfare recipients to participate in paternity establishment unless they fit under a narrow good cause exception in cases of domestic violence (Temporary Assistance to Needy Families Program 1997; 42 U.S.C. § 654[29][1998]). Recipients face financial sanctions if they refuse to cooperate. States are rewarded for greater paternity establishment (42 USC § 603(a)(2)(1997). States are required to provide for genetic testing of all parties in contested paternity actions, or contested support cases involving a federal support enforcement agency. Since 1993, states have been required to establish simplified civil process for voluntary acknowledgment of paternity, particularly encouraging hospital-based programs. This process is designed to make voluntary establishment simpler and faster. These paternity acknowledgments have the force of a judicial finding within sixty days of signing (Legler 1996; Roberts 1997). A man who claims to be or is named as a biological father is a *putative* father; if the man does certain things short of marrying the mother, he may be a *presumed* father (like nurturing and holding the child out as his own, or filing with the paternity registry); and he will be an *adjudicated* father once paternity determination is decided and judgment entered.

While the rate of paternity establishment is improving, paternity is not established for two-thirds of nonmarital children. In states that continue to recognize the marital presumption, additional children are presumed to be the children of their mother's marital partner, though this may not actually be the case (Dowd 1997a). On the other hand, paternity establishment has increased considerably in the recent past as the result of incentives beginning in the early 1990s, increasing the annual rate of established paternity by 50 percent (Legler 1997, 8). Outside the welfare structure, mothers are not required to establish paternity, and for a variety of reasons many women do not. In this sense, men's biological fatherhood remains optional or voluntary, rather than being fatherhood as a matter of course. "Biology, in short, gives men options. An unwed biological father may establish a relationship with his biological child. . . . Alternatively, he may treat the biological relationship as irrelevant and not become a father at all" (Dolgin 1993:661). Even if biological paternity can be established and a declaration that a biological father is the legal father would divest the child of legitimacy, at least some courts have been unwilling to do so, by applying a best interests test (*Department of Health and Rehabilitative Services v. Privette* 1993; Burke 1997). The ability to designate paternity early is technologically feasible. However, legal standards for filling out birth certificates are still amazingly lax and the pace of paternity establishment slow. The consequences, or increasing consequences, once paternity is established may well be a part of the slow pace of increasing the rate of paternity establishment (Parness 1993).

Constitutional doctrine would appear to lean toward eliminating the distinction between legitimate and illegitimate children. Furthermore, the Uniform Parentage Act, promulgated in 1973 and approved by the American Bar Association in 1974, also rejects the concept of legitimacy, saying "[t]he parent and child relationship extends equally to every child and every parent, regardless of the marital status of the parents" (Uniform Parentage Act 1973). The act establishes presumptions of paternity in response to *Stanley* and has been adopted in whole or in part in many states. In addition, the Uniform Putative and Unknown Fathers Act sets out the rights of biological fathers in matters of adoption, custody, paternity, and the termination of parental rights. It was approved by the American Bar Association in 1989 (9B U.L.A 82 [Supp. 1997]). The act contains a section that lists fourteen factors to consider when determining whether a sufficient parent-child relationship exists to trigger constitutional protection. In addition, some states have putative father registries which fathers can utilize before or after the birth of the child to provide notice to biological fathers, particularly of adoption or termination of rights proceedings (Howe 1993).

Nevertheless, distinctions between marital and nonmarital children remain, as is evidenced both by the Supreme Court's decision in *Michael H.* and by the decisions of other courts holding that children born within a marriage will not be "delegitimated" by the recognition of a biological father (*Department of Health and Rehabilitative Services v. Privette* 1993). Furthermore, even if the marital distinction is irrelevant, the Court does not recognize biology alone as sufficient to establish fatherhood. For constitutional purposes, "biology plus" is required.

The interlocking system of child support, custody, and visitation related to divorce has begun to be extended to never-married families. This represents a significant shift from the common law view of unmarried biological fathers. Beginning with the extension of child support obligations, states have moved in the direction of triggering a social relationship in addition to the economic one. The effect is to treat unmarried fathers the same as married fathers, linking obligations and rights to biological status.

Only in 1973 did the United States Supreme Court, in *Gomez v. Perez*, hold that illegitimate children have the same right to child support as do legitimate children (See also *Mathews v. Lucas* 1976). This was the trigger to amend child support laws to include nonmarital children. The push from welfare reform to recover the state cost of supporting women with welfare benefits who were entitled to child support also led to the stronger enforcement of unwed fathers' child support obligations. Prior to this decision, establishing paternity often resulted in a financial obligation more in the nature of a penalty than full child support. Furthermore, because paternity laws gave the father no rights to establish a relationship with the child, custody and visitation were simply not an issue.

In theory, unwed dads now have the same obligations as marital dads. Due to the low rate of paternity establishment, however, in reality the obligations are quite different. Nevertheless, this is a significant change in theory, driven by concerns about economic support and the rise in nonmarital births. Simple biology is enough to entitle biological fathers to a voice in custody and visitation. Either by statute or case law, putative fathers or those with established paternity are entitled to visitation, most commonly under a best interests standard (Miller 1998). Visitation has been ordered even against the wishes of the mother, and even in the event that the mother has subsequently married (Miller 1998). This widespread support of visitation has been a remarkable new development during the past few decades, triggered both by the *Stanley* decision and by changing social attitudes toward unwed fathers.

Custody law has witnessed a similar shift, although slower and less complete, toward greater consideration of unwed fathers as custodians (Goger 1998). Historically, the mother was the sole custodian of a child born out of wedlock. Fathers' custodial rights were far secondary, and in some jurisdictions fathers' rights were not superior even if the mother surrendered the child or was declared unfit. Currently, however, jurisdictions are moving toward a view that once paternity is determined, unmarried fathers are entitled to consideration for custody, whether primary, joint legal, joint physical, or sole (see *Morey v. Peppin* 1985). This is not a right to custody, but rather a right to be heard on custody.

This view of unwed fathers represents a dramatic change from the common law. Rights to custody coequal to those of the mother, rather than inferior to them, in addition to now well-established rights to visitation, represent a significant change toward seeing unmarried fathers as legally equivalent to married fathers. Biology alone triggers the right to be heard, although the social relationship clearly affects visitation and custody decisions. On the other hand, the dominant model of fatherhood from which unmarried fathers now benefit is largely a model of economic fatherhood. Indeed, the economic definition may be further reinforced for fathers who lack an ongoing intimate relationship or shared household with the mother of the child, and who have no history of shared parenting on which to build.

A right to custody grounded on a biological nexus has parallels to the joint custody movement for postdivorce families. Both connect fatherhood to status rather than to relationship. Both disregard the relationship between the father and the mother. Some unmarried fathers maintain healthy and cooperative relationships with the mothers and the children, or even create a relationship in place of an initial transitory one. In other situations, however, the lack of a shared household or of an ongoing relationship, or the brevity of the intimate relationship may make the imposition of the father into the lives of the mother and child disruptive and not in the child's best interests. The range of circumstances must be taken into account—something that can be done under the best interests standard—but which may require a qualitatively different showing, since often the past or present existence of a relationship strongly affects the individual determination. Once a father-child relationship has been established, however, it should presumptively continue unless it is detrimental to the child and/or the primary caretaker.

We have moved from seeing unmarried fathers as having a choice of whether to parent, capable of "walking away" from a child they had conceived, to according unmarried fathers nearly the same obligations and rights as divorced fathers, regardless of the nature of their relationship with the mother or any desire or conduct in relation to the child. We are moving toward more aggressive paternity determination. These changes are creating a purely biological definition of fatherhood that imposes rights and responsibilities on the basis of genetic ties alone. The impetus to do so, however, is primarily economic, to assist the state rather than to support social and nurturing fatherhood.

In reality nonmarital fathers and nonmarital children, and their relationship with each other, continue to be treated quite differently. The experiences recounted by unwed fathers seeking custody or visitation suggest that the legal system does not see them as equivalent to divorced fathers who once had a relationship with their children within a marriage. Furthermore, if the mother marries, the courts are sympathetic to maintaining the integrity of the marriage and blended family against the intrusion of the biological father. Welfare rhetoric condemns fathers and mothers for creating families outside marriage. It calls this *irresponsible* reproduction (McClain 1996). In this perspective, welfare is wrong because it replaces the provider role of fathers, permitting and encouraging mothers to have children independent of fathers and marriage. Even worse, women fail to domesticate their sons, who may be even more difficult to tame because of the lack of male role models in their lives. "On the one hand, men outside that fatherhood role are irresponsible, antisocial, sexually predatory, and violent. On the other hand, a woman parenting without a father's presence produces a dangerous family form, particularly dangerous for boys" (McClain 1996:389). As McClain argues, focusing on irresponsibility avoids attending to structural issues and the inadequacies of the status quo. She sees a more viable alternative in collective responsibility and a sensitivity to both agency and constraint, and the interplay of male and female *irresponsibility* in reproductive conduct. Her analysis points to the complexity and difficulty of constructing responsible parenthood without reconstructing a system of dominance.

ADOPTION

In contrast to the significant shift toward biological fatherhood with respect to child support, custody, and visitation, a more qualified recognition of biological fatherhood has occurred with respect to adoption. On the one hand, the result of the Supreme Court cases on unwed fathers, many of which were litigated in the context of adoption, triggered statutory modifications to insure due process rights of notification and some opportunity to be heard, while recognizing the child's important need to establish a relationship with parents and a stable home. This has resulted in a range of adoption statutes that balance the biological father's right to notice, his ability to block the adoption, and his own right to an award of full custody to care for his child, against the child's right to stability and permanency. The basic trend has been to accord fathers procedural rights to be heard or to deny consent, but only for a limited period of time after the birth of the child. Beyond the limited time frame, the father's consent is not required to place a child for adoption. Refusal to consent in a timely proceeding can be overridden in some states on a best interests standard, while in others the standard is parental fitness (Elrod and Spector 1998).

The common law view of unwed fathers was that they were irrelevant to adoption; fathers were neither asked for their consent, nor could they be heard to prevent an adoption or to seek custody themselves (Wehner 1994). The underlying assumption was that fathers were not only disinterested, but also presumptively unfit as parents.

One change favoring fathers, like birthmothers, is open adoption and independent adoption. Until recently, birthfathers, like birthmothers, had no connection with their children after they terminated their parental rights. This has changed by virtue of the rise in independent adoptions, empowering birthparents to negotiate agreements, albeit often nonenforceable, with adoptive parents, and by virtue of adoption registries that enable connections between adopted children and their biological parents (Dowd 1994). With the exception of the most open model of adoption, this gives birthfathers only limited rights. At the same time, it represents movement away from the notion of adoption as a substitution of parents, who are then treated like "natural" parents by the reissuance of a birth certificate (Dowd 1994). Seeing fathers as not necessarily exclusive, if viewed from a generist, trusteeship perspective, means, in the adoption context, that both biological and adoptive fathers can maintain connections, and that biological fathers as well as mothers can act responsibly with respect to questions of surrender of rights and ongoing connections (Woodhouse 1994). The movement for rights to birthparents is grounded in a strong argument for the importance of biological connections.

The most pressing issues for fathers with respect to adoption, however, are the right to prevent placement of the child for adoption and the right to custody of the child as a matter of biological right if the mother wishes to place the child for adoption. This requires balancing the sometimes conflicting interests of fathers and their children. The arguments have to do with whether biological fatherhood should trigger custody rights, on the basis that fathers should not be treated any differently than mothers, and whether mothers should be heard on fathers' custody when they have signed a consent to adoption. The most common statutory pattern is to limit paternal rights by placing significant responsibility on the father within a limited time frame if he wants to be heard. To serve the child's best interests to have a permanent home, fathers are required to be attentive to the mother during her pregnancy or diligent once the child is born if they wish to assert their paternity (Elrod and Spector 1998). For fathers this can mean that, unless they remain in an ongoing relationship with the mother or are informed of the pregnancy, the law gives them very limited time to learn of, or to be notified of, the existence of their child before their rights are terminated. If fathers are present at the adoption proceeding and if the statute requires the father's consent, which many do, then the refusal to give consent will block the adoption, unless the father's rights can be terminated under a fitness standard. This does not require the father to seek custody. On the other hand, if a father wants custody, he stands in a disadvantaged position compared to the mother unless he reconciles with her, and is also disadvantaged with respect to the adoptive parents if he is unmarried and the adoption is evaluated under a best interests standard.

With regard to newborns, the adoption scenario brings into sharp focus the concepts of biological fatherhood, and particularly the importance of biological identity, a concept that the common law recognized only in the context of marriage (Maravel 1997). The question is whether biological connection should be sufficient, or whether a commitment to parenting connected to prebirth conduct and postbirth intentions should prevail. One approach is to focus on the perspective of the child, which, at birth, may be speculative at best (Maravel 1997). Mary Shanley would resolve this issue by following the constitutional rule of "biology plus" to define fathers' rights (Cashman 1997; Shanley 1995). She identifies the positions on this issue as "maternal autonomy" versus fathers' rights, or mothers' right to consent without permitting blocking by the father, or the fathers' automatic right to custody and fitness based on biology. Rejecting what she calls false gender neutrality, she supports recognition of the differences in the situations of mothers and fathers at the birth event which necessitates a differential basis on which to evaluate not only genetic relationships, but also the assumption of responsibility and provision of care. Thus, her solution attempts to walk a fine line between acknowledgment of differences and rejection of stereotyping, while holding both parents to a standard of responsibility and nurture. For the father, at the birth he would be judged by his prebirth conduct toward the mother and child. Shanley sees this as a relational definition of parenthood, rather than one that is status based. Furthermore, she argues for the relevance of the mother's testimony on the father should the father offer himself as a custodian, rather than treating a mother who would give consent to adoption as uncaring or unfeeling or no longer a mother, and therefore voiceless in a subsequent action involving the father.

Larry May similarly argues for a more demanding standard of nurturing conduct for fathers, grounded in a moral vision of fatherhood (May 1998). May suggests that biological fathers (and mothers) should be evaluated by the same standard as prospective adoptive parents with no biological links (May 1998:36). Caregiving should be demonstrated, not presumed.

The position that most reflects a concern for nurturing fatherhood would require a showing that the father desires and has made provision for custody, and has done everything that he possibly could during the pregnancy to care for the mother and therefore indirectly for the child (See *In re Adoption of Baby E.A.W.* 1995). This places a standard on fathers similar to that imposed on mothers, who are judged by their care during pregnancy. No biological link is enough to retain custody if they are judged unfit.

It is less easy to justify that the mother should be heard on the father's request for custody. Birthmothers commonly do not wish the child to be placed with the birthfather, but want the child placed with the adoptive parents. Adoption planning is a means for a mother to make the best possible nurturing decision for her child. It is not abandonment of children, but care. A balance of interests might permit the mother in an individual case an opportunity to be heard, but does not afford her a veto on the father's request for custody. Mothers' relinquishment of control over decision making should be predicated on men demonstrating clearly and convincingly their willingness and competence to nurture. Instead of reinforcing biological rights, adoption should extend the nascent concept of social fatherhood and set a stronger nurturing standard.

SPERM DONORS AND OTHER REPRODUCTIVE TECHNOLOGIES ISSUES

In the area of reproductive rights and technologies, fathers arguably have the least ability to assert biological fatherhood. We presume men's ability to dissociate from their reproductive capacity, given their potential for being a father without knowledge of fatherhood. We have never considered male reproductive responsibility as engaging in sex solely with the expectation and readiness for fatherhood.

The law gives the least regard to the biological status of sperm donors, seeing the act of donation as an expression of intent *not* to be a father. Artificial insemination by a donor was not employed on a wide scale basis until the 1930s and 1940s (Hill 1991). By statute, donors are accorded no status as fathers (see Cal. Fam. Code § 7613[b][1995]; Or. Rev. Stat. § 109.239[1][1996]; Bernstein 1996). This is largely viewed as unremarkable, in comparison to surrogacy which has raised a host of moral, ethical, and legal issues. Recent suggestions for the modification of sperm donation have come from children seeking information connected to their sense of identity, but rarely from donors themselves. The suggestion is that information similar to that now available to adoptive children could be made available to the children of sperm donors.

One could argue that sperm donors are given more power than many biological fathers, since they control whether they will be viewed as fathers at all. Their intention overrides their biology. In contrast, men who unknowingly or directly, contrary to their intentions, conceive a child through intercourse cannot exercise a "choice" not to be treated as a father short of the child being placed for adoption. On the other hand, sperm donors may not change their minds, even when they have been accorded some relationship with the child (Polikoff 1996). The one instance where a court arguably granted power of "choice" equivalent to that of a sperm donor was in the case of a divorcing husband who was empowered to prevent the use or donation of embryos fertilized with his sperm (*Davis v. Davis* 1992). The father's control of his procreative potential was treated as if it had remained in his own body, subject to his own will.

Sperm donation thus downplays genetic ties, in opposition to biological fatherhood. Ironically, the advent of sophisticated, and not so sophisticated, reproductive technologies presents the possibility of continuing the common law refusal to accord biology the status of fatherhood. Such technologies suggest that "mere" biology is insufficient to make a father, and indeed, that fathers in the strictly biological sense have no legal status or meaning.

According to Lisa Ikemoto, concerns about reproductive technologies can be read as "concern about maintaining the security of paternity, particularly for white fathers . . . [as well as] a more general concern about maintaining the primacy of the nuclear or marriage-based family as the most privileged family structure" (Ikemoto 1996:1026). Infertility is defined in terms of marriage and heterosexual couples although, by use of that definition, unmarried persons—gays and lesbians in particular—can be excluded. Gay men are especially excluded, and viewed as doubly disabled from parenthood both as men and as gays. Without connections to marriage and mothers, parenthood cannot be imagined. In contrast, it is easier to envision parenthood for lesbians.

Who should prevail in disputes over custody when reproductive technology yields multiple parents (genetic, gestational, and social) has been cast by many commentators as pitting biological definitions against issues of intent. An intent standard disconnects parenthood from biology completely, and defines a parent, at least at the birth of a child, as a state of mind or consciousness rather than a person with a genetic or gestational connection (see Ark. Stat. Ann. §9–10–201 [1997]). This is an interesting distinction from the conduct/nurturing standard that has emerged in the adoption context. By looking at consciousness or intent, certainly conduct can be a guide. But in such a view, reproduction is so intentional that nurture is assumed without having to be specifically demonstrated. The effort to reproduce, and inherently, the money spent, is the protected interest.

The protection of economic interests is a recurring theme in legal definitions of fatherhood. One other distinctive piece here is the comparison of mothers and fathers. The potential connections of mothers to children through gestation as well as genetics are treated as legally and analytically distinct from those of fathers, who have only a genetic connection. Intent standards seem to most benefit fathers, but also deny them any psychological or emotional connection outside a gestational context. Yet adoption cases reveal a different phenomenon: that parents and children can develop a deep emotional and psychological connection in the absence of a genetic link and not necessarily related to intent.

One argument made by those who favor resolving issues by the intent standard is that it accords with the common law view of fatherhood as not biological, but rather as determined by the man's relationship to the mother and child, specifically by marriage (Hill 1991). This nonbiological definition is perpetuated in the statutory law of paternity that recognizes assumptions tied to relationships rather than using established technology to designate paternity (Hill 1991). It is similarly perpetuated by donor insemination laws that protect the fatherhood of the intended parent over the biological parent (Hill 1991). Surrogacy laws in most states protect the surrogate's husband against the usual marital presumption in favor of the intended father.

The parallel to intent is the doctrine of consent. Legitimacy is conferred by the husband's consent to insemination (Dolgin 1994). The first statute to deal with artificial insemination using donor sperm was enacted in 1964, and about three-fifths of states statutorily regulate such insemination (Dolgin 1994). The goal of these statutes, much like the construction of adoption in traditional adoption statutes, is to replicate the traditional family. Beginning in the 1950s, cryopreservation presented new possibilities, including the possibility of genetic fatherhood after the death of the father, or after the divorce of a couple who intended to conceive. Courts seem inclined to decide such cases based on the intent of the sperm donor (Dolgin 1994).

Jane Dolgin sees the consequence of new reproductive technologies as changing definitions of family and fatherhood even as the courts try to fit new problems into a traditional structure (Dolgin 1993, 1994, and 1997). She demonstrates that a biological vision has given way to a more social concept tied to intent, and therefore, by its nature fluid and changeable. Fathers' roles in this changing vision are confusing. On the one hand, fatherhood continues to be defined relationally, with the critical relationship being the one with the mother and not the independent father-child relationship. This is consistent with the constitutional concept of fatherhood. On the other hand, child support presents a confounding perspective, for it takes an exclusively biological view of fatherhood as triggering obligation and, presumably, rights.

Dolgin views the relational definition of fatherhood as linked to definitional changes that can be traced to the Industrial Revolution. She sees earlier definitions of fatherhood as strongly biological as well as connected to marriage. With the advent of industrialization and fathers' lack of significant daily interaction with their children, their roles came to be defined by behavior, and therefore, she argues, to be chosen. Fatherhood was constructed and chosen, not the natural consequence of a biological tie (Dolgin 1997:96). The continuation of this mode of fatherhood reinforced traditional family forms. Alternative modes that encouraged father-child relationships irrespective of family undermined traditional family forms (Dolgin 1997:98). But both were linked by the notion of choice. Fathers chose to be fathers by their choice of a relationship (or not) with the mothers, or by exercising bioloigcally rooted choices to have relationship with their children without any connection to relationships with the mothers. A man could become a father only by what she calls "familial" acts, a definition that supports traditional definitions of family and links fatherhood to those traditions.

Thus, fatherhood and motherhood have been seen quite differently:

The father-child relationship, outside the larger context of the family as a social institution, has been accorded little significance during the last few hundred years. Society does not see social paternity to inhere in biological paternity. . . . [A] biological (genetic) link between a man and a child may be taken as evidence of the obligations (but not necessarily the rights) of parental ownership even though no familial relationship has been actualized socially. . . . In contrast, the mother-child relationship, more fully contained by the boundaries of home and hearth, and defined biologically, has been recognized as a *natural* unit, not necessarily dependent for legal recognition on the correlates of a larger family network. In short, since the nineteenth century, claims to maternity have invoked nature; claims to paternity have invoked culture. This continues to be the case. (Dolgin 1993:644)

Only child support cases define fatherhood as turning solely on biology. Yet Dolgin also argues that those cases impose obligations without recognizing "real" fatherhood (Dolgin 1993 and 1997:110). "No relationship *with the child* is assumed to flow from the man's biological paternity in these support cases. His responsibility for the child's support is in essence, even if not literally, a matter between the man (as autonomous, individual—not as family member) and the state" (emphasis in original; Dolgin 1997:110).

Dolgin concludes that the ideology of the traditional family valued families conceived as "holistic, hierarchical, social unities that endure in the face of, and as a defense against, the tensions and contingencies of everyday life" (Dolgin 1997:246). In contrast, surrogacy and new reproductive techniques bring money into the parent-child relationship, and also challenge the social consequences of biological parenthood (Dolgin 1997:250). Courts have tried to fit the new realities into the old definitions. In so doing, they have challenged the very definitions they are trying to preserve.

Radhika Rao similarly argues that reproductive technologies undermine traditional family models (Rao 1996). They expose the social construction of the family rather than the natural or biological construction. They remove the demarcation between family and market since the market is used to make families come into being. And they support private ordering and choice over stability and permanent relationships. These developments parallel changes in the definition of fathers: fatherhood likewise is exposed as constructed; the economic factor is apparent; and the valuing of choice over stability is also clear.

Finally, Dorothy Roberts reminds us that biological, genetic definitions serve not only gender but also race norms (Roberts 1995). In
contrast to the law of legitimacy, under slavery the genetic tie of a
child to a slave mother determined the child's status, while the genetic
tie between masters and their children born to slave mothers was
legally insignificant. Roberts argues for a different significance for genetic ties, "inspired by definitions of self, family, and community in
Black American culture, that recognizes genetic bonds without giving
them the power to devalue and exclude other types of relationships"
(Roberts 1995:211). The model of nonexclusivity is echoed by many
commentators in a wide variety of family situations. Roberts also
points to the importance in our culture of genetic ties as race determinants. Arguments about the importance of genetic ties, identity, and
cultural identification have to be read against the history of the racist
use of genetic ties to maintain white supremacy. Thus, for example,
the marital presumption had an exception: when a dark-skinned child
was born to a white woman, that child was not deemed the child of a
white husband (Roberts 1995:260). Similarly, in a California surrogacy case where the gestational mother was Black and the child was
white, Roberts sees the outcome of the case, which awarded custody to
the white parents, as overriding traditional presumptions of maternity
because of race (Roberts 1995:261).

Roberts argues that genetic ties have been less exclusive in the
Black community. Racial solidarity has been important, and nurture
and care have not necessarily been tied to blood relationships. She
notes the "radical potential of families consciously created out of
love and political commitment, rather than biological attachments"
(Roberts 1995:270). Along with consideration of the positive potential
of this model, she argues for careful vigilance regarding the racial implications of particular policies elevating the biological connection.
What she does not address entirely is the prevalence of nonmarital
families in the Black community, so that elimination of the tie between fatherhood and marriage is critical.

Roberts's perspective might equally well apply to the place of biology among gay and lesbian couples. Biological connections are a
primary link, essential to establishing legal parenthood by at least
one partner of the pair. At the same time, the heterosexist view of
the importance of both male and female linkages in the parental
pair (or male and female social parents) challenges the sufficiency of

the biological connection, or the completeness of the surrender of rights by sperm donors, egg donors, or surrogate mothers. From some lesbian couple cases where the semen donor subsequently filed a paternity action to establish or continue visitation, it is clear that failure to meet the requirements of the relevant state donor insemination statute means that an unmarried woman cannot have a child without risk of involvement by the donor (Polikoff 1996). Under the intent standard of parenthood, if the donor never intended to be a social father, and the mother never intended for him to play that role, then Polikoff suggests those intentions should control the custody and visitation issues.

SUMMARY

Both historically and currently, we think of biology as important and, in most cases, as defining of fatherhood. But it seems that the "paternal instinct" is understood very differently from the "maternal instinct." When we talk of a "paternal instinct," we do not envision a prebirth relationship with the child, but rather see something like a vested interest to stand first in line to create a relationship once the child is born. The creation of that relationship is still very closely tied to the nature of the father's relationship with the mother. Biological fatherhood is presumed to trigger social fatherhood, but a very different range of conduct is presumed than that for mothers. Economic providing is key.

For much of the history of the common law, paternity was not a certainty. Based on modern technology, it now is. Nevertheless we continue to have a very low rate of established paternity. If we established near universal paternity, what legal consequences should follow other than those of identification, health information, and the option to establish contact between child and father.

We are moving strongly in the direction of making biology a trigger for responsibility, and perhaps also for rights. Biology, then, would replace marriage or be a secondary test of fatherhood. We would do this either by recognizing and reinforcing the importance of genetic ties, viewing fatherhood as emanating from a "natural" blood/genetic connection, or alternatively, by emphasizing the importance of responsibility for the consequences of one's procreative/sexual activities. To the extent that responsibilities are defined as economic ones, without corresponding rights of social contact or custody, we have a very limited, gender-specific definition of parenthood. To the extent that we mean full-blown nurturing fatherhood, we are confronted with securing the rights and safety of the mother and the need to accept the presence of other father(s). If we limit biological fathers to economic fatherhood, then we separate fathers into different categories.

Another factor to be considered is the historical barrier to marriage for African-American fathers, and the current high rate of nonmarital fatherhood in that community, and therefore the consequences of any model that imposes economic obligations on either marriage or biology. On the one hand, it can be argued that a biological notion of fatherhood honors the genetic tie that was so horrifically ignored during slavery. On the other hand, it can be viewed as simply disproportionately intruding in the lives of women of color and poor women by mandating the identification of fathers, and also further stigmatizing men of color and poor men when the state imposes economic obligations that cannot be fulfilled under current social and economic conditions. The continued privileging and support of marital fathers has disproportionate racial consequences for fathers and their children, as does shifting to a biological model, if under either definition the structural discrimination against men of color and poor men goes unaddressed.

CHAPTER 8

Economic Fathers

Both biological and marital fatherhood focus on the status of fatherhood. Historically what fathers *did* included being patriarchs, teachers, moral leaders, disciplinarians, and economic providers. Currently, fathers are seen almost exclusively as breadwinners, though theoretically they are viewed as equally nurturing as mothers. The balance of their historic role has either changed, diminished, or simply no longer fits with contemporary conceptions of fatherhood. In this chapter I look at the legal doctrines and structures that define economic fatherhood, most notably the family law structure of child support, custody, and visitation. I also describe how this operates in conjunction with workplace legal regimes and tax policy to support the definition of fatherhood as breadwinner.

In a sense fatherhood is defined in reverse, much like marriage is, by divorce. Since marital fatherhood is preferred by the law, it defines fatherhood. Nonmarital fathers may be permitted the rights and responsibilities of this definition, but it is fatherhood within marriage that sets the standard. Until recently the law presumed sharply differentiated gender roles that defined fathers as bread-winners and mothers as the nurturers of children. The provider role of fathers was explicit, gender-defined, and limited to marriage. Fathers were the heads of households and had the right to the labor of all household members, as well as an obligation to provide for them. Children were clearly viewed as the property of the father. Until the nineteenth century, upon divorce fathers were granted custody of their children, retaining them as property with an obligation of support. During the nineteenth century, family law began to view mothers as the primary caretakers of children. Well into the 1960s family law presumed that mothers reared children, while fathers provided for them. Upon divorce, that pattern was continued, with fathers allowed to visit their children who were placed in the sole custody of mothers.

Richard Collier has analyzed the evolution of the law toward economic fatherhood in the context of the English system, which has strongly influenced and closely paralleled the American one (Collier 1995a). Collier shows that heterosexuality, sexuality, family, marriage, and breadwinning together crafted the dominant masculinity, which he calls the "family man." The "family man" was safely heterosexual, married, and connected to children but obligated to do wage work, which distanced him physically from and led to his marginal involvement in nurture. By making a father's absence a negative to be avoided, and his presence as critical to all members of the family—and simultaneously defining presence in economic terms as based on wage work—fathers came to be almost exclusively defined in economic terms. Collier's analysis shows the tricky place that we are in: masculinity has been reformulated in the twentieth century into a subtle form of father rights within a purportedly egalitarian regime. "The premise that men and women are now equal in marriage is deeply problematic. . . . The rhetoric of equality, bolstered by a belief in the new fatherhood and a reconstituted paternal masculinity, sits uneasily with the realities of the lives of many women and men" (Collier 1995a:179). The assertion of equality, along with claims to a desire for greater involvement, casts men as victims.

As Collier notes, and as I have discussed previously, biological fatherhood was never sufficient to establish fatherhood in the past. Marriage was the key status for defining fatherhood. Increasingly, however, marriage has become a less effective means of safeguarding legal fatherhood. Collier argues that what has taken its place is a naturalist argument that having a father is desirable, essential, and unique for all members of the family. Part of that essential role, very much defined by law, is an emphasis on men as economic providers. How central this economic role is to the construction of fatherhood is graphically illustrated by a 1985 case Collier cites, where a father wanted to live on social security in order to care for his four-year-old child. The judge stated that it would be "plainly wrong and silly if the father were to remain unemployed in order to look after one 4 year old boy. . . . I shall take a great deal of convincing that it is right that an adult male should be permanently unemployed in order to look after one small boy" (Collier 1995a:196, quoting from *B v. B* 1985). As Collier notes, "The familiar valorization of the masculinity/work relation negates the value of men's involvement in child care at the same time as promoting the ideal of breadwinner masculinity" (Collier 1995a:200).

From the perspective of many fathers, this is the reality under which the system continues to operate, despite the veneer of gender neutrality. What is most remarkable about economic fatherhood is that it is imposed within a system of gender equality and neutrality that operates from a set of assumptions about families rarely replicated in reality (Dowd 1997b). The outcomes from the system reflect strongly gendered patterns. At the same time, changes in the role of women and their expectations challenge the economic definition of fatherhood. Women's increased economic role undermines men's exclusive claim to the economic turf (Kimmel 1992).

CUSTODY

Half of the American children born after 1990 will be subject to custody laws at some point in their childhoods (Mason 1994). Under the statutory structures in place in most states, the physical custody of children will either be with a sole custodian or some version of joint custody. A father theoretically faces a custody structure that is gender neutral and committed to maintaining the parent-child relationships of both parents. Yet beneath that surface is a structure that leans toward a primary physical caretaker, and therefore unavoidably divides parents into primary and secondary care givers, with corresponding financial support obligations that give the appearance, although they do not necessarily constitute the reality, of a primary and a secondary financial parent. Most commonly, given fathering and work patterns, mothers have custody and fathers are obligated to pay the larger share of child support. Fathers interpret this as a strong antifather bias (Kidde 1997). At the same time, the system fails to provide adequate financial support to mothers, fails to insure that fathers are present in the lives of their children, and reacts negatively to mothers who depart from traditional gender roles. Therefore, mothers view the realities as reflecting a strong antimother bias. Thus those affected most by the family law structure experience it as strongly gender-biased. In addition, because the system is even more biased against nonmarital families (less support of fathers and fewer resources for mothers), and because marital versus nonmarital families are racially distributed, the system is strongly racially biased as well.

Custody in most states is decided on the basis of the "best interests of the child," a standard criticized for its indeterminacy, subjectivity, and vulnerability to judicial bias (Fitzgerald 1994). Even the alternative "primary caretaker" standard is stated in reference to a best interests standard (Cahn 1997). Until the 1970s, these determinations were made expressly to choose a sole custodian. Historically, until the nineteenth century, the sole custodian of the children was the father, as the sole parent under the common law was responsible for the support of the child. During the nineteenth century custody shifted to mothers, and by the twentieth century mother-custody was dominant and often expressed in a maternal preference or presumption, based on the notion that mothers were the "natural" or better caretakers of children, while fathers could be required to financially support both mothers and children. This view was especially captured in the tender years presumption, that very young children needed to be with their mothers. This presumption was often applied to older children as well and in the "all things being equal" standard, that if both parents were equally good caregivers, motherhood was the tipping factor in custody decisions (McNeely 1998).

Two significant changes in custody rules altered this view, at least in theory. First, a wave of custody reform in the 1970s removed gender preference, and made custody expressly gender neutral by statute or case law. Second, beginning in about 1980, states began to embrace joint custody as a preference. In theory, gender presumptions were removed from the custody structure and shared, coequal parenting became the postdivorce norm. The custody picture is not that simple, however. Joint custody can be either joint legal or joint physical custody. Joint legal custody varies sole or primary custody only to the extent of requiring that both parents be involved in major decision making. On the other hand, joint physical custody means that custody is shared between the parents, either equally or nearly equally. Joint physical custody might seem to require fifty-fifty custody, but in fact, nothing in the term requires more than sharing physical custody, which may or may not be on a strictly equal basis.

Currently, virtually all states permit courts to grant joint custody, and nearly a quarter assume this is in the child's best interests (Brinig and Buckley 1998; Elrod and Spector 1998). States may have a presumption for joint custody, requiring judges to order legal or physical joint custody unless a compelling reason exists not to do so. A weaker version of this position is a preference for joint custody, requiring courts to consider it as an option or declare their reasons for not awarding it. Finally, some states permit joint custody but do not have a presumption or a preference (Hutchison 1998). As one commentator notes, two potential benefits of joint custody are the creation or maintenance of a bond between the children and both parents, and the state's ability to monitor support and encourage more payment of support (Brinig and Buckley 1998).

Empirical studies suggest, however, that joint *legal* custody with physical custody to the mother is the most common arrangement (Maccoby and Mnookin 1992; Melli, Brown, and Cancian 1997). Since so much of joint custody is joint legal custody, the parenting time of the secondary parent does not increase. Rather, joint legal custody simply increases the amount of control the noncustodial parent has without increasing that parent's nurturing of the child (Singer and Reynolds 1988). One recent survey of judges indicated that joint legal custody was a clear judicial preference, despite a rebuttable presumption for joint physical custody (Stamps, Kunen, and Lawyer 1996).

With the exception of joint, coequal physical custody, all the custodial structures are variations on the theme of a sole or primary custodial parent, with the second parent playing a peripheral physical and social role in the life of the child. This diminished, secondary parental role is usually called visitation, although there are other names such as shared parenting, in order to diminish the notion that a parent visits his or her own child. Nevertheless, the second parent spends only occasional time with the child, often not including any overnight time. Variations include evening and weekend connections, school holidays and summer vacations, and other schedules that promote regular, but still limited, time with the child. The custody scheme arguably does not presume coequal parenting, given its tilt toward a single or primary parent structure, with the second parent playing at best a secondary role, or at worst an incidental one. That tilt also skews the child support obligation, since unequal residence requires that support be paid to the primary custodial parent. This structural predisposition is hidden by the terms "joint" or "shared" custody. Nevertheless, it is apparent in the actual distribution of postdivorce custody.

Custody is part of an overall view of marriage that is increasingly viewed as a coequal partnership. Interestingly, the custody structure, on its face, not just in operation, does not presume coequal parenting. Joint physical custody is not the preferred or expected norm, and is the least common form of actual custody. Primary custody is the norm and is a single-parent model. Theoretically, under gender-neutral principles, fathers could be the primary or sole custodial parent as frequently as mothers, or could be the dominant parent in a joint legal custody arrangement. Overlaid on marital caretaking practices, however, mother custody is dominant and fathers are commonly cast in a secondary parental role.

This legal structural bias may be reinforced by mental health professionals involved in evaluating children in custody determinations. According to some researchers, the best interests approach to custody rests on psychoanalytic and cognitive developmental theories that emphasize a child's continuity of relationship with primary figures, a goal best served by establishing one psychological parent under sole or primary custody arrangements (Wall and Amadio 1994). Alternatively, the family systems approach emphasizes the goal of arrangements least destructive to the entire interaction of family members, and therefore tries to maximize the maintenance of familial relationships and continued interaction even if the form of the family changes (Wall and Amadio 1994). While continuity is still a factor, supporting ongoing multiple relationships is equally important under this approach. The family systems approach would not necessarily favor coequal custody. Given what we know of marital caretaking practices, supporting ongoing relationships might still mean supporting a primary and secondary parent. This approach, however, would be consistent with both joint legal and physical custody arrangements, or with liberal visitation schemes that would maximize ongoing contact with any adult who has become part of the family (Wall and Amadio 1994).

That joint custody is not much more than a revamped primary custody system is evident from a recent study on the Wisconsin experience. "[J]oint legal custody with mother physical custody, has become the norm in Wisconsin, accounting for 81 percent of the cases . . . [with] significant differences in shared physical custody depending on whether the time shared is equal or unequal" (Melli, Brown, and Cancian 1997). Prior to 1970, the model was sole custody to a parent who was decision maker and residential parent. The sole custodian was usually the mother. Legal shifts since the 1970s ended the tender years presumption and increased the availability of joint custody. In the Wisconsin study, parents who spent 30 percent or more time with their children were considered shared custodians. Comparing 1990 with 1980, joint legal custody was found to have increased from 18 percent to 80 percent while sole and split custody had dropped considerably. Although physical custody with the mother dropped from 86 percent to 73 percent, it still predominated. The decline had not increased father custody but had increased shared custody. The more detailed the visitation scheme, the greater the time the secondary parent spent with the child in the year following divorce. The data show an increase in shared decision making, but no increase in any other form of caretaking. This seems to indicate that joint custody was not too far different from the old sole custody structure.

In these patterns the primary caretaker standard has clearly been operating at an informal level. David Chambers argued in 1984 that we do not have much empirical research to promote such a preference, or to the contrary, a preference for the secondary parent. All we know is that both parents are psychologically important to children, and that both can perform the caretaking role alone if need be (Chambers 1984). Chambers would support voluntary, but not mandatory, joint custody awards and sees only weak support for a primary caretaker standard. On the whole, commentators generally have been in agreement on not mandating joint custody (see Maccoby and Mnookin 1992; Singer and Reynolds 1988; Steinman 1983).

As Karen Czapanskiy has pointed out, the custody and visitation structure does not mandate visitation or shared parenting. Neither married nor unmarried fathers have a mandatory duty to nurture their children or maintain a relationship with them. While their support obligations have been strengthened and regularized, no corresponding duty of care has developed. This reflects the dominance of the breadwinner role, but also the construction of fatherhood as chosen and voluntary, not a matter of obligation and responsibility. Czapanskiy argues that a system that supports the continued maldistribution of care and ignores the withdrawal of fathers from their children is seriously flawed (Czapanskiy 1991). The support obligation is not, of course, limited to fathers; indeed, the accepted model is one of parents' coequal responsibility for their children. However, in reality, as it relates to the dominant primary caretaker or sole caretaker mode of custody, child support is overwhelmingly an obligation of the noncustodial parent, usually the father. Mothers contribute their share of support by providing the primary residence and bearing most of the costs of child rearing. As Czapanskiy points out, however, there is no corresponding enforceable obligation on the father to maintain relationships or to provide child care (Czapanskiy 1991). In response to the predictable objection that the law cannot mandate behavior, she argues that this is no more judicially problematic than control over parental moves, or other orders limiting parental autonomy such as restrictions on sexual or religious matters.

As Czapanskiy also points out, the move to more joint custody and to a shared model of parenting strengthens the position of the secondary parent but not the primary custodian, while it does not assure greater care and parental involvement for the child. Although the lack of visitation is sometimes due to some form of interference by the custodial parent (20 to 25 percent of the time), by far the greater reason for nonvisitation is that the visiting parent simply does not show up (Czapanskiy 1991:1449). The joint or shared model imposes increasing consequences for the custodial parent, but none for the parent who diminishes or fails to care for his child.

Czapanskiy suggests that parents ought to be reconceptualized in law as totalistic entities with comprehensive responsibilities, including cooperative relationships with the other parent(s):

> [A] parent is the person who, by procreation, conduct or adoption, enters into two commitments: First, a commitment to a dependent human being to provide all the nurturance, whether financial or

nonfinancial, of which the person is capable; and second, a commitment to deal respectfully and supportively with another person or persons who are in a parental relationship with the same child. The definition is premised on the notion that every parent has comprehensive responsibilities toward the child. Gone is the notion that one parent takes care of daily or repetitive nonfinancial tasks, while the main job of the other parent is to work for money. . . . The redefinition of parenthood is also premised on the notion that parental responsibility should be more significant than parental rights. (Czapanskiy 1991:1463–64)

This is significantly different from the joint or shared custody vision, which currently is premised upon a primary parent model that inexorably replicates and exacerbates a gendered division of labor with diminishing economic support and nurturing contact.

Another issue with respect to custody and visitation is the exclusivity of the scheme, permitting only two individuals to be identified and valued as parents. Katherine Bartlett's classic analysis critiques the value of this approach when the nuclear family has broken down (Bartlett 1984). As Bartlett sees it, exclusivity ends at divorce, since the child characteristically maintains relationships with both parents, and neither is able to act exclusively any more, even though no longer married. She is especially critical of the law's failure to acknowledge stepparents and the important relationships that they build with children. Similarly, unwed fathers are often placed outside the custody ambit. Adoption permits only two parents at a time, even symbolically replacing birthparents by reissuing a child's birth certificate when adoption is finalized. Bartlett argues for legal support of multiple parental figures, especially by a liberal use of visitation statutes, and favors rejecting a system that requires the child to give up one parental relationship in order to embrace another (see Holmes 1994; McConnell 1998).

Barbara Bennett Woodhouse argues for a more fluid sense of family by focusing on the combination of household and felt (rather than imposed) sense of obligation (Woodhouse 1996). She calls these *kinships of responsibility*. She is particularly concerned with promoting the welfare of dependent members of the household, as opposed to the "associations of choice" of independent, self-supporting adults.

Naomi Cahn argues that the custody process needs to be separated into two steps. The first step should focus on the identification of "parents" and the second on the needs of children, using the best interests standard (Cahn 1997). Cahn suggests that when multiple adults come forward as caretakers, we might want to consider them all rather than reducing them to two. Once all the parents are in the picture, we can evaluate what best serves children. To some extent the exclusivity problem has been mitigated by the enactment of third-party visitation statutes, although parenthood is still maintained as a limited status (Holmes 1994).

As previously noted, many fathers complain that custody awards are strongly biased against men, and that the relational rights of non-custodial parents are not enforced. The issue of bias in custody is hotly disputed, but in fact it seems that gender bias exists both with respect to men and women, but operates, not surprisingly, in different ways. Some argue that while women overwhelmingly have sole or primary custody, this represents voluntary settlements. Studies show that in contested custody cases men do as well as women in obtaining custody, and according to some studies, better. Fathers' success rates may reflect their real chances in the system, and therefore the absence of bias, or may reflect the fact that fathers only proceed when they have an extremely good argument *against* the mother as well as a strong argument *for* themselves.

The 1989 Massachusetts Gender Bias Study points out that when men seek custody in contested situations, 70 percent of the time they obtain it (McNeely 1998). It is also true, however, that in the period examined by the report, mothers received primary residential custody 93 percent of the time while fathers received it only between 2 and 3 percent of the time. Fathers received joint physical custody with mothers 4 percent of the time. Thus, fathers received primary or joint physical custody in less than 7 percent of the cases. When fathers sought custody, however, they won primary custody one third of the time, and joint physical custody almost half the time (McNeely 1998). These proportions are similar to national figures available for 1990. Men also claimed the courts were biased against them when structuring visitation and overnight residential stays.

On the other hand, fathers are not subjected to the same standards as mothers with respect to a need to balance work and family. When courts take into account relative economic resources, employment, traditional family values, and morality, women suffer disproportionately from stereotypes about appropriate women's roles that are not applied to fathers (Jacobs 1997). It is unimaginable to think of a court concerned that the number of hours a male breadwinner works will affect his ability to parent. By evaluating relative finances instead of considering the redistribution of resources, courts penalize women for a discriminatory opportunity structure, magnified by the barriers to parents succeeding in wage work. In addition, a morality standard, loosely applied, can sanction women for intimate relationships, but not men.

The claims of bias are significant and need to be further examined. If unsubstantiated, we need to ask why the myth of bias is so pervasive. Even without a bias issue, however, the system has been unsuccessful in fostering fathers' nurturing of their children or parenting cooperatively with mothers and other parent figures.

CHILD SUPPORT

Child support is the second part of this picture. Theoretically it is a means to insure that divorce does not cause a significant change in children's economic circumstances. The system reflects a norm of individual financial responsibility by legal parents for their children, a responsibility shared by both parents (Josephson 1997). Child support is also linked to concepts of dependency, as compared to entitlement or rights characteristic of benefits paid to wage workers (Josephson 1997). This is acceptable dependency because it links recipients to individuals as opposed to the state.

The current system of child support has become federalized largely through the enactment of federal welfare policy that conditions state receipt of funds on compliance with federal standards. Most significantly, beginning in the 1980s federal policy went from making highly discretionary decisions to setting guideline amounts intended to make support awards more universal and predictable (Josephson 1997). In addition, the federal government involved itself in the collection of child support through the welfare system and, for nonwelfare parents, through support orders.

On the other hand, a significant amount of child support still continues to be set and enforced privately through the courts. The trend, however, is to make child support more administrative and bureaucratic, handled through child support agencies at the local level rather than judicially by court-imposed orders, wage garnishments, or jail time when there is failure to pay. Child support enforcement includes the use of civil and criminal sanctions, including revocation or denial of driver's and occupational licenses, publication of the names of deadbeat parents, and other similar methods (Roper 1997). License revocation programs are in effect in nearly all states (Legler 1997).

Child support orders are far from universal, however. In 1992, only half of single-parent families with children had support orders (Roper 1997). Other studies put the proportion slightly higher, at six in ten eligible mothers (Garfinkel and McLanahan 1995). An even lower percentage of eligible men, 41 percent in 1991, have orders (Josephson 1997:49). Of those who have support orders, only about half actually receive the full amount of support. Nearly 75 percent of women receive some payment while 66 percent of men do (Josephson 1997:49). There is considerable state-by-state variation in the number of orders and in the rate of enforcement (Josephson 1997, 36-37). Nearly 40 percent of mothers and 25 percent of fathers do not receive support even if they have an award (Knitzer et al. 1997). An estimated 40 percent of divorced fathers do not pay child support (Roper 1997). Conservative estimates are that at least 60 percent of those required to pay but who do not are financially able to do so (Roberts 1997). Payment correlates with joint custody and visitation, with the rate of payment decreasing when fathers have less contact with their children.

Many fathers have difficulty paying child support because they are poor; others have difficulty because the child support represents such a significant proportion of their income. An estimated 15 to 25 percent of noncustodial fathers have extremely low annual incomes, defined as below $5,000, while only 10 to 15 percent have annual incomes above $40,000 (Knitzer et al. 1997:35). Poor fathers pay as much as two and a half times more support, expressed as a percentage of their incomes, than do richer fathers. Nevertheless, poor fathers pay about as often as richer fathers do (Knitzer et al. 1997:35). In general, the declining wages of men significantly affect their ability to pay their support obligations. At the same time, the differential in economic opportunity available to fathers as opposed to mothers, in general, continues to impose a greater burden for support on fathers due to discrimination in the market opportunity structure.

But perhaps the most serious problem with child support is its inadequacy. Because of that, even when child support is fully paid many children still remain insufficiently supported. Given widespread nonpayment and partial payment, the inadequacy problem is magnified. The support level is commonly no higher than the poverty standard and represents no more than one-third of the estimated normal expenses for children (Dowd 1997a:65). Not surprisingly, then, child support represents a fairly minor role in the income structure of single-parent families, despite its major role in public perception and in the family law structure (Dowd 1997a). Most experts agree that even if all those entitled to support orders had them and all support was paid, fully 75 percent of the poverty problem would remain (Garfinkel and Wong 1990:101). The effect of guidelines has been to assist middle-class women more than poor women who, even when supported, are paid an inadequate benefit (Josephson 1997).

The inadequacy of child support is grounded in the fact that it was never intended to insure adequate support. Rather, it was designed only as a partial contribution to a child's support. Much of this relates to its origins in the poor laws and bastardy law (Josephson 1997). The amount of support was discretionary, and often set low to avoid fathers' resistance to payment (Josephson 1997:31). In addition, awards were not automatically adjusted, so that over time their value declined in terms of real dollars (Josephson 1997). Deviations from guidelines are typically downward (Josephson 1997:99). Child support is commonly viewed as a proportionate share of parental income, not of children's needs. Proportionality means that parental resources may be adequate for needs but are not tapped, while, in other cases, parental resources are not adequate but not so inadequate as to trigger state support (Czapanskiy 1991; Josephson 1997).

Another potential source of income is spousal support, but permanent support is rarely awarded and temporary support is limited in time. Spousal support, now also called compensatory payments, theoretically could include a proportion of future income. Future income sharing could resolve the problem of a permanent loss of income as a consequence of mutual marital decisions to interrupt a career (Oldham 1997). To do so would be contrary to viewing property division as a "clean break." Under the conventional property settlement, marital assets are divided under an equal shares philosophy which values both unwaged work and waged work as presumptively equal contributions, and entitles both spouses to equal shares, but with no ongoing economic obligations. Alimony, designed originally to provide ongoing economic support to a spouse who was devoting herself to child care, or who had done so and was now unable to find waged work, has become an ever more marginal part of the economic picture. It is now designed primarily to provide temporary, "rehabilitative" support in order to insure that both partners are economically self-sufficient (Dowd 1997a).

Based on principles of gender neutrality and gender equality, in theory the family law structure increasingly embraces the notion of an equal partnership where work and family obligations are roughly equally shared, and therefore each partner remains self-sufficient within the marriage. At divorce, after dividing property equally, self-sufficiency is presumed to operate even when economies of scale are lost. To the extent one partner does more of the postdivorce child care than the other, that partner will be entitled to economic contribution in the form of child support. Technically this support is understood as an entitlement of the child, not of the custodial parent. Any inequality in child care, economic obligations, or parental role is presumed to be a matter of "choice" by the parties, reflecting either their choices during the marriage or at divorce.

The "clean break" model of divorce is one that facilitates individual, separate lives once parties decide the marriage has ended, and, increasingly, ends further obligations. Spousal support has moved in that direction. Some have argued that child support should move in the same direction and should do so explicitly. That is, in light of remarriage, child support obligations should be time limited, with the expectation that the state or a new spouse would take up the slack (Chambers 1984; Krause 1989). Nevertheless, legislative trends have gone in the opposite direction toward the federalization of child support, presumed uniformity by enforcement of guidelines, and increasing resources to insure payment. Since the 1970s, there has been nearly universal support both for centralizing payment and increasing enforcement efforts at the federal level (Elrod 1997; Josephson 1997).

The legal system seeks to increase child support awards and payment for both marital and nonmarital children. That is a radical change in theory, and an even more radical change in reality, within the span of only a few decades. On the other hand, the modern focus is consistent with the historic role of fathers as breadwinners. In the 1960s fathers could ignore support obligations after divorce and rarely be pursued for enforcement (Krause 1989:369). Paternity was rarely established for nonmarital children; support of those children was the mother's responsibility. Since the early- to mid-1970s, that has begun to change, certainly in theory. As a matter of public policy, we strongly favor biological and marital fathers supporting their children. The remnants of earlier thinking are nevertheless evident as consistent payment of child support continues to be seen as remarkable and praiseworthy, rather than ordinary (Dowd 1997a). At the same time, despite an ideological and social shift, and despite enormous resources devoted to child support administration, the reality of nonpayment, partial payment, and lack of awards, coupled with only slowly rising rates of paternity establishment, continues to be our context. Most significantly, the rate of child poverty shows little sign of abatement as sufficiency issues have been unaddressed while the focus has been on enforcement.

WELFARE

Although the child support structure is directed almost exclusively at fathers, historically the welfare structure has totally excluded them. The welfare system was never intended to benefit fathers. Fathers were presumed able to work and support their families under the breadwinner definition of fatherhood. The social welfare system for men was linked to work, to benefits that were seen as entitlements— unemployment, worker's compensation, and disability payments. In contrast, the social welfare system for women was linked to familial dependency (Josephson 1997:130). Welfare was for the "worthy" poor, a concept that limited benefits to certain women, initially to white women, and automatically excluded men. Since men have been presumed able to support themselves, their poverty is viewed as a personal failure, making them "unworthy" poor. In addition, supporting them as nurturers made no sense, as they were not viewed as caretakers of children. Women, on the other hand, may be poor because some man they had justifiably relied on no longer provided support. Women were most worthy if their husband had died. This entitled them to more favorable benefits under the social security system (Dowd 1997a). If, on the other hand, their poverty was due to "bad" behavior, they were stigmatized by the welfare system.

The American welfare system began explicitly as a system of support for widows. It was extended to mothers of dependent children, regardless of whether the absence of the father was due to death or some other reason. Although the language of entitlement became gender neutral, the assumption continued that benefits were paid to mothers on behalf of their children. In part that was due to the rise in the number of recipients who were never married. As of 1991, this accounted for just over half of AFDC recipients. In the 1990s children in never-married families were more likely to be living with their mothers. The second largest category, that of divorced or separated adults, is also dominated by mother custody. Divorced and separated families accounted for just over 30 percent of AFDC families in 1991. Only about 2 percent of families had a deceased father. The balance of families receiving benefits had fathers present who were either unemployed or incapacitated (Levesque 1993b:7n23). Other figures put the number of father-headed families or father recipients at 10 percent.

The number of families with fathers present and receiving benefits increased in the early 1990s as a result of legislation aimed at permitting two-parent families to receive benefits which eliminated the forced break up of families just to entitle them to benefits (Duncan and Caspary 1997; Wax 1996). In 1993, of the nearly 5 million cases per month, only about 360,000 were two-parent families (Committee on Ways and Means 1996:395). In 1993, 3.8 million mothers received AFDC as compared to 300,000 fathers (Bureau of the Census 1995c). Fathers qualified if they had a low enough income and were the single custodial parent of a child, or, if both parents were living together, if one of the two was incapacitated, or met other limited criteria. Since the program did not focus on men, it ignored many low-income men who did not fit its profile (Chambers 1995).

Fathers, therefore, have been largely excluded from welfare benefits, either because they are often not the caretakers of children, or because family resources could be best maximized by having benefits paid to the mother. Several welfare policies have worked to discourage the presence of fathers in the household as their presence disqualifies the family from obtaining benefits. The inability of a father to be an adequate breadwinner necessitated his physical absence, and often a withdrawal of his social relationship with his children, in order to meet the family's economic needs. Most notorious of these policies were the "man in the house" rules. Under these rules, recipients were disqualified if a man was living in the household, or, in some states, if he were engaged in an intimate relationship with the mother. More recently, "substitute father rules" have limited the consideration of the income of men in the recipient's household, when those men have no legal obligation to the recipient's children, unless one of the men is a stepfather or has taken on the role of a substitute father. The mere existence of a relationship with the mother is no longer sufficient to trigger an assumption of economic support (Zietlow 1996). Concerns about the perverse effect of driving fathers or father figures out of the household in order to qualify for benefits has led some states to experiment with different regulations under the most recent welfare reform (Knitzer et al. 1997).

The primary impact of the welfare structure on fathers, however, has been increased pressure to pay child support so as to reduce the burden of welfare on the state. Beginning in the 1970s and in response to the rising number of families on welfare in the 1960s, Congress began to focus on child support enforcement. In 1988 federal support guidelines were established and were to be implemented by the states along with increased paternity determinations and mandatory wage withholding. Child support continues to be the primary focus of welfare "reform" and is seen by some as a better alternative to public support, as a deterrent to irresponsible reproductive conduct, and as encouragement of fathers' noneconomic support of their children (Schoonmaker 1997).

This massive effort to increase child support has been disappointing and hardly cost effective (Josephson 1997; Knitzer et al. 1997). This is due in part to the targeting of fathers least able to pay; obtaining support from poor fathers is like trying to get the proverbial blood out of a turnip. Furthermore, even if fathers do pay, the amount paid is too insignificant to make a dent in the poverty of the caretaker and child, and therefore does little to reduce welfare expenditures. Another justification for child support enforcement has been to encourage stronger relationships between fathers and children. But as one commentator notes, unwed fathers frequently have no social relationship with their children; a mere biological relationship does not entitle them to full visitation and custody rights or consideration in many states. The relationship between mandatory child support and visitation has not been well developed under welfare law (Levesque 1993b).

Along with teenage mothers and "welfare queens," fathers have also become part of the "most unworthy" poor (Chambers 1995). The failure to pay support is, however, not gender specific; mothers also frequently fail to pay. Because so few mothers are ordered to pay support, the lack of payment is perceived as a problem exclusive to fathers (Chambers 1995). The race and gender impact of vigorous child support enforcement also disproportionally impacts men of color, and if it results in greater contact by fathers, it fosters greater disruption in the lives of women of color (Chambers 1995). I have argued elsewhere that the postdivorce structure merely reflects the patterns established during marriage, as well as the stance of the family law system to act negatively, rather than neutrally, toward single-parent families (Dowd 1997a). Because these are undesirable families, negative outcomes are justified as deterrents or simply as consequences of failed marriages or the inability to marry. Since those consequences are visited most directly on women, the outcomes accord with a gender ideology that puts the obligation and blame on women to make marriage work and to deal with the consequences of raising children. In addition, ongoing workplace discrimination, as well as benefit and tax structures, support a primary male breadwinner, not a nurturing father. The interaction of the family law structure with the work law structure reinforces the norm of economic fatherhood.

WORK-RELATED BENEFITS AND THE TAX STRUCTURE

Work-family responsibilities reinforce economic fatherhood. To the extent that workplace structures and law fail to insure gender equality, they work in tandem with family law structures to maintain economic fatherhood. Work law structures do this in two ways. First, existing law supports primary breadwinners as the ideal workers. The benefits and tax structure support the primary breadwinner model. Even more significantly, the lack of workplace supports for nurturing parenthood creates conflict and makes impossible demands on workers. In contrast to support for breadwinner parenthood, the only statutory structure supporting fathers' nurture is the Family and Medical Leave Act, which allows the breadwinner father to take unpaid leave in order to care for his newborn, newly adopted, or seriously ill child.

We tend to ignore the workplace legal structure, but it strongly limits fathers to economic roles. It builds on cultural messages that men are not interested in caring for children nor capable of doing so, and that society is uneasy about men's nurture (McNeely 1998).

> It is much more revolutionary to couple a man with his baby. In a world that loses constancy daily, we can accept a woman at the head of a conference table in an office with far more comfort than we can imagine her husband at home, holding the baby in his arms. . . . Even if the mother isn't there half the time, or doesn't enjoy mothering as much as work outside the home, and/or she isn't good at it, the nursery remains women's inviolate territory. If the baby responds to the father as lovingly and automatically as to her, then who is she, given the definition of womanliness . . . as caretaker? (Gatson 1997:277)

By comparison, historically there has been significant legal protection of women as mothers, even if it often operated as a barrier to opportunity, much like current reproductive harm policies (Gatson 1997). We continue to see women as "nurturing biologic actors" and men as "risk-taking economic actors" (Gatson 1997).

The mandatory employment benefits structure is oriented toward separation and support of the breadwinner (social security, unemployment, workers' compensation) with limited time away from work (sick leave, disability leave, limited paid holidays and vacations). Few employers provide child care benefits or paid parental leave; disability leave for pregnancy is by no means universal. To the extent families are considered, they are defined in very limited terms, without consideration for single parents, unmarried parents, and domestic partners of the same or opposite sex (Dowd 1989a).

Tax structures also continue to support the breadwinner ideal and sole wage earner, which, when added to the existing gendered configuration of work and family, reinforces the economic construction of fatherhood (Dowd 1997b). Edward McCaffery traces the core of this bias to tax rules created in the 1930s and 1940s (McCaffery 1997). The tax code disproportionately disadvantages secondary wage earners by adding their income to the primary earner's income and taxing the combined income at a higher rate. Since most secondary wage earners are women, this has the consequence of disproportionately taxing women for doing wage work. The beneficiaries of secondary earner tax reform would be working wives and mothers, with varying effects by income. The strong negative effects of current tax policies are especially severe, McCaffery argues, at the low and high income levels, and also strongly discourage middle-income women. At the lowest income levels, a woman may lose significant benefits by leaving welfare for wage work; at the highest income levels, tax rates are the highest when the economic incentive for a second income is the lowest.

How does this work for fathers? McCaffery points out that women have significantly changed their work-family roles, while men have not. Women do more wage work but men generally do not do more family work. Although women's wage work patterns look more and more like traditional male wage work patterns, women's feelings about, and commitment to, wage work are quite different from men's. McCaffery characterizes women as generally more ambivalent. Taxing women more heavily thus adds to an existing range of reasons not to engage in wage work. Women have high tax elasticity, meaning they are quite responsive to changes in tax burdens. Taxing them less would result in fewer negative consequences for women who do wage work, and therefore, presumably, would encourage more women to do wage work. To the extent that women's work patterns increase men's fathering at least in some circumstances, this would indirectly impact fathers.

In addition, McCaffery sees men as implacably tied to their work and argues that the current tax system reinforces those trends. Men are reinforced in their work role by their wives' tax burdens, and by the comparative ease of increasing their income versus adding another earner. Men have strong tax inelasticity: they are largely unresponsive to tax changes, they simply keep on working. McCaffery argues that men would tolerate a significantly higher tax burden before changing their behavior. If changing their behavior is desirable, then a higher tax burden is justified as a means of reallocating family responsibilities.

Public policy has done little to change the structure of work, despite much rhetoric about family values. The major piece of expressed workplace support for families, the Family and Medical Leave Act of 1991, is extremely time limited, unpaid, and fails to cover the full workforce (Dowd 1993). Usage of the statute discloses that very few fathers have taken leave (Selmi 1999), which is not surprising considering the strong economic disincentives to do so, and the ongoing workplace culture disincentives. Welfare "reform," the other piece of family legislation in the 1990s, requires wage work as a norm, but fails to guarantee adequate child care (and limits available care to two years). It also fails to help single parents cope with the other adjustments they would have to make in deal-ing with the more difficult work-family conflicts faced by low-in-come workers. At the same time, wage work to replace welfare ben-efits often fails to provide adequate resources to support a family.

SUMMARY

Despite a purportedly neutral legal structure, family law rules gov-erning postmarital and nonmarital families, and indirectly marital families as well, remain strongly gendered by history and context. The lived-out reality of fatherhood is clearly gendered. Marital fatherhood operates within a strictly gendered system. Marriage provides a clear line of demarcation, and as a result also buys privacy for conduct within marriage. This permits fatherhood to be hidden, presumed. Legal support is provided under the economic breadwinner definition of fatherhood. That legal support parallels the common law concern about legitimacy and primogeniture, which arose out of concerns re-lated to the distribution of real property. The labor-connected supports for economic fatherhood are thus linked to the land-connected sup-ports for fatherhood tied to family inheritance.

The postdivorce structure is equally gendered. Custody of children is overwhelmingly given to mothers. While fathers' custody roles have increased significantly, they have increased from such a small base that they are still dwarfed by the typical mother custody family. Fathers' roles most often are not as joint or near-joint physical custo-dians, but rather "visitors" or secondary parents. Over time they be-come incidental parents who see less and less of their children. The patterns are even more stark in nonmarital families. Mother custody is even more common, father custody more rare, and visitation more attenuated or absent.

Child support, on the other hand, is overwhelmingly a father's obligation. Although a tiny proportion of mothers pay support, it is understood to be a male obligation. Not automatically sought, and historically far from universally paid, it is nevertheless viewed as the primary parental obligation of fathers. Lack of payment makes one a deadbeat dad, morally and criminally reprehensible. Many fa-thers can pay, and fathers in general experience a rise in their stan-dard of living upon divorce, while the economic circumstances of women and their children drop precipitously, triggering consequences in housing, education, and other economically related factors. Again, nonmarital fathers seldom have this obligation and seldom pay it.

In sum, even as the legal system puts its greatest emphasis on fathers' economic obligations, many fathers back away from the breadwinner role after divorce or if they never marry. At the same time, fathers claim that the system not only requires an excessive economic contribution, but also that it robs them of time with their children by failing to enforce their visitation rights and failing to neutrally consider them as primary or joint custodians. Fathers see any decline in payment of child support as justified by the decline in contact with their children, regardless of the reason for that declining contact. They feel especially justified if they perceive that there is obstruction by the mother or that the support is being used for the expenses of the mother rather than for the children. At the same time, mothers see the system as failing to provide for their economic needs and those of their children as well as failing to enforce the economic obligations it does impose, while allowing fathers not present in their children's lives to control and manipulate their lives and those of their children.

Why do we have these patterns? Many fathers would argue that it is due to overwhelming judicial bias against fathers. This is a stunning complaint, the reverse of the usual feminist complaint of gender bias as a pervasive element in the legal system, grounded in the rules and concerns of the system, and the bias of an overwhelmingly male judiciary and lawmakers. In family law, male litigants are arguing that male judges (and sometimes female judges) are biased against them. Either the claim is that the feminists have captured the judiciary in this area of the law, persuading men to discriminate against men by championing the views of women, or that judges continue to be sympathetic to their socialization, which teaches that women are natural nurturers and superior caretakers of children and that men cannot fit into a caretaker role. Some see a generational difference, in that litigants are arguing before judges who have neither the socialization, nor the experience, nor the self-awareness to understand their conscious and unconscious stereotypes about men and parenting. In other words, men are fathers' worst barriers to recognition as parents. Judicial bias has to be considered against the key fact that an overwhelming majority of custody, visitation, and child support matters are resolved by agreement, not by judicial decision.

When men's intimate partnerships fail, our structure has allowed them to walk away or limit their relationships with their children to economic ones, while failing to support men's nurture within a truly egalitarian work or family environment. The patterns are even more stark in nonmarital families. The continuing cultural link of economic fatherhood to marriage, or some other form of shared household with the mother of the children, means that fathers resist even this limited conception of fatherhood outside a shared household, particularly when they move on to parent other children in a new shared household. Economic fatherhood is thus both price and privilege. It is the privilege of limited fatherhood at the price of unsupported nurture.

PART III · REDEFINING FATHERHOOD

CHAPTER 9

A New Model

> We, with love, shall force our brothers to see themselves as
> they are, to cease fleeing from reality and begin to change it.
> —James Baldwin, *The Fire Next Time*, 1962

Baldwin's eloquent assertion on behalf of civil rights is no less fitting
to the task of redefining fatherhood. Redefining fatherhood, like imag-
ining racial equality and civil rights, is not inherently difficult. The
challenge is to face the context from which we begin, decide on the
goal, and figure out the means to get there.

*My core thesis is that the redefinition of fatherhood must center
around the nurture of children.* By nurture I mean the psychological,
physical, intellectual, and spiritual support of children. This seems
simple. In fact, there is significant consensus that nurture is at the core
of parenthood for men and women. It rests on children's needs, and is
beneficial to adults and society as a whole. What is more difficult is the
task of fleshing out the definition, determining what we mean or envision when we talk about men nurturing children, and fashioning the
tools to that end.

157

What is the role of law? Because of the frequency of divorce and the number of children born to unmarried couples, the law is an active presence in the lives of many parents and children, defining their rights and responsibilities. Because it plays this critical role, it has a major impact on the construction of fatherhood. It is not, of course, exclusive; individual and social change make as much, if not more, of a difference. Indeed, many family relationships function outside legal constructs or sanctions. Yet even in those instances, families operate in the shadow of the law, either by agreement or in an effort to avoid the default model of the legal system or to avoid its biases and restrictions.

What are the questions or problems posed by the context from which we operate? That context includes the patterns and practices of fatherhood outlined in Part 1, and the existing legal structures that define and support fatherhood, described in Part 2. The interaction of these two does little to support nurture and arguably much to undermine it. If nurture is the core of fatherhood, our definition of nurture and our means to accomplish it must be clearly envisioned.

First, do we work with the patterns that we have or try to change them? Men, as they currently nurture, are strongly connected to households and their relationships with women. Many are serial fathers rather than nurturers solely of their biological children. Some are multiple fathers, caring simultaneously for children within and outside their household to whom they have biological or other connections. Many do very little nurturing of their biological children, whether in their household or not. Furthermore, men parent less than mothers, and often nurture in a secondary role. If we mean to redefine fathering as nurture, we can support nurture where it happens or strengthen relationships that are currently faltering or abandoned. For example, we could support better, and ongoing, nurture by biological and marital fathers, or support serial fathers in successive social fathering irrespective of marital status. We can support conduct, or privilege status, or do some of both. In addition, we must envision a new relationship between men (and women) as multiple parents, and determine whether that vision should include an array of relationships that vary according to conduct rather than legal status or sheer time.

Should fatherhood be supported exclusively or preferentially within marriage? Strong support of marriage may reinforce the most successful fatherhood model, or merely recognize status over substance. It might include disincentives, even deterrents, to divorce by parents. But a strong privileging of marital fathers continues to stigmatize children born outside marriage. If carried to an extreme, it would leave significant numbers of children without legal fathers, and treat fathers outside marriage like sperm donors, unconnected to their children. Regardless of how we deal with adults and marriage, we may not want to continue to draw lines and attach names to children on this basis.

How do we empower fathers without subjugating mothers? Or must we empower mothers as a means of achieving more nurture in relationships that are more economically equal? A major impetus to coequal parenting has been women's wage work position, opportunity structure, relative income, and the time demands of their work. If our goal is greater paternal nurture, perhaps women's wage work should be our primary focus. Workplace reforms might bring about structural change but utilization may be gender disproportionate. Redressing the gender imbalance might be achieved by expanding the opportunity structure for women. Dangers (or benefits) to women may lurk in such a strategy, if our goal is the reorientation of work and family for all. In addition, for mothers to be valued all forms of families must be taken into account as we redefine fatherhood.

We also need to ask whether we envision fatherhood as a single-parent or dual-parent role, and whether that should vary depending upon whether the father shares a household with the mother. We currently tend to view parenthood as a single- or primary-parent role, even though we also talk in terms of the importance of having two parents and the importance of shared, coequal, gender-neutral parenting. Despite our talk, and despite increasing similarity in the work and family roles of a significant number of men and women, we continue to have a skewed pattern of parenting where women do significantly more than men. Increasingly, all parents in two-parent and single-parent households are in wage work, and have increased work hours, which translates into less parental time with children. The pattern we currently have, in both two-parent and single-parent families, is that of a "core" parent who, to a greater or lesser degree, is supported by secondary caretakers. Fathers are usually one of those secondary caretakers when they share a household with the mother. They may also take on this role as a former spouse, or other friends or family, with paid caregivers providing the backup to the core parent. It is uncommon, however, for fathers to share the core parent role fifty-fifty or themselves be the core parent.

The question is, do we want fathers' nurture to mean that men are core parents as frequently as women, by changing the existing gendered allocation of parenting tasks, or do we want to create a truly co-equal parenting model, a new pattern? It seems clear that we have not thought through what true equality means: whether it means equally dividing a *parent* role, or whether it means doubling the amount of parenting, if both men and women are doing the *same* or *equal* parenting (and assuming only two parents of different sexes). Traditional assumptions were that mothers parented, in the nurturing sense, while fathers hardly nurtured at all or only in a limited sense. Men's parenting was conceived of primarily as breadwinning. Even if we do not expect to substantially increase the amount of parenting a child gets, achieving parity in work-family roles will be difficult. Furthermore, if we look at all families, accomplishing sufficient economic and nurturing parenting is equally difficult.

Can we support nurture while insisting on financial responsibility, and will we continue to see financial responsibility in individual, and unequal, terms? Under existing workplace structures, requiring or encouraging greater paternal nurture would likely have economic consequences that would be counterproductive and therefore counterintuitive. Because family income is dependent on the superior earnings of most men as compared to most women, economic incentives would undermine increased nurturing opportunities. They would be least effective for those men unable to obtain work that insures a subsistence income.

The economic issues surrounding fatherhood are critical to insuring the well-being of all children. They also have a significant impact on the ability of fathers (and mothers) to nurture. We must determine whether we are prepared to initiate significant structural change in the workplace or provide backup economic support. *Without an economic strategy, any redefinition of fatherhood will be confounded by the economic necessities of families and the gendered structure of the workplace.* Even if the workplace were reoriented to permit greater nurture, without economic support of caregiving work families' ability to take advantage of more flexible options would be limited to the middle class. Failure to deal with economic issues, then, will result in class-limited fatherhood and the class-limited nurture of children.

We function in a race- and class-stratified and differentiated world of fatherhood. We must define and envision fatherhood so that the consequences for children do not reinforce race and class hierarchies. Economic strategies are significantly more important for communities of color where unemployment rates remain high, unlike middle-class white communities where economics can be ignored but time is perceived as the greatest need. Marriage strategies are racial strategies as well if we fail to deal with the underlying lack of economic opportunity for men of color.

Finally, children and families function in flexible, changing structures and relationships. Family fluidity is characteristic of our current context; how do we incorporate fluidity instead of privileging specific forms of family? Children change developmentally and otherwise in a very short space of time; we have to be careful not to think of nurture as static, but rather as a constantly evolving relationship. Relational changes and differences are far more complicated than economic monitoring. Diversity is a critical value as we rethink fatherhood.

So far, the legal system has either ignored nurture or assumed it by relying on definitions or assumptions linked to biological or economic fatherhood within marriage. One of the questions raised by a focus on nurture is whether we should presume or foster nurture based on biological connection, marriage, or adoption, or simply support social fatherhood irrespective of status. Second, the legal system has been satisfied with economic parenthood, although paradoxically it has failed to ensure that economic obligations are honored. Biological models have failed because we continue to fail to establish paternity for a significant number of children. Economic models have failed because we fail to insure payment of obligations where support is capable of being paid, fail to provide adequate backup economic support when all or part of the obligation cannot be paid, and fail to insure adequate, universal support (private or public) for all children. Marriage models are insufficient because so many children are born outside marriage and so many marriages fail. The failure to support fathers outside marriage does more to harm than help children. Indeed, it is striking how little legal fatherhood, as we know it, is about nurturing and supporting children.

How, then, should fatherhood be redefined? There are no easy answers, and keeping the answers multiple and flexible may be better than a simple unitary standard or definition. The data on which we act are provisional and tentative, which may argue for caution. In the balance of this chapter I explore a range of suggestions on conceptualizing fatherhood. The perspectives are often grounded in whether one sees the current context as alarming, a "crisis" for children and men; whether the focus is on men's greater involvement and therefore on efforts to support involved fathers and determine what factors encourage father involvement; or whether the focus is on fathers' pervasive disengagement or lack of connection, and the goal is to stem the tide of disintegration. Much of the controversy among scholars and policy advocates centers around support for "traditional" fatherhood versus some "new" definition of fatherhood. In the last part of this chapter I articulate a redefinition of fatherhood grounded in nurture and social fatherhood.

In the chapter that follows I describe the challenges facing a redefinition of fatherhood as nurturing social fatherhood. These are the challenges raised by masculinity, especially the presence of homophobia and violence in masculine culture. In addition, the relationship of motherhood and fatherhood, and of work and family, poses significant challenges to a redefined fatherhood. I suggest that the answers to these issues lie in cultural and economic policies.

Finally, in the last chapter in this section I sketch the policy implications of my proposed redefinition and the questions it raises. Because of the complexity and interrelatedness of the issues surrounding fatherhood, and because political realities may limit the nature of reform, I explore a range of options.

DEFINITIONS: SOME SUGGESTIONS

Probably the strongest core definition of fatherhood is being a good provider or breadwinner for one's children. Nevertheless, this definition describes the actual conduct of fatherhood less accurately today than at any previous time. The abandonment of the breadwinner definition of fatherhood has been noted by many, but perhaps is best captured by Barbara Ehrenreich (Ehrenreich 1983; see also Kimmel 1995a:115–50). Drawing on history, sociology, anthropology and psychology, Ehrenreich looks at the transformation of fatherhood from the breadwinner ideal toward a notion of manhood without responsibility, due in part to the diminished position of fathers but also to the rise in women's wage work and the feminist rethinking of mother-hood. She describes this not just as the collapse of the breadwinner ethic, but as the revolt of men against familial responsibility. She contrasts the attitudes toward marriage and family of the 1980s with the expectations of the 1950s and earlier, exposing in the process the anti-female rhetoric of the 1950s: men's view of marriage as a trap, and of women as parasites feeding on men's work. She emphasizes a strongly differentiated male and female culture of marriage and parenthood.

Ehrenreich sees the traditional marital ideal of the breadwinner husband and homemaker wife as a system of economic dependency for women and responsibility for men, made possible by the family wage and adherence to gender hierarchy and segregation. She demonstrates how psychiatry supported this structure by declaring marriage and breadwinning as the only "normal" state for an adult male. Erik Erikson also promoted the idea of life cycle stages, with maturity tied to marriage and parenthood (Erikson 1967).

Ehrenreich documents various strands of rebellion against this ideal, from critiques of the corporate culture, to *Playboy* magazine and the sexual revolution, the Beats and the hippies, and men's liberation. This has been a movement *from* responsibility, self-discipline, commitment to women and children, *toward* a celebration of individualism seen as self-growth. The result, she argues, has been the feminization of poverty, caused by eliminating the support of women through men's wages, while not insuring either women's equal access to wages nor support for their family roles. Ehrenreich does not suggest redefining fatherhood per se, but she argues that a new vision must incorporate women's equality. Thus she would redefine fatherhood by supporting women in their work and family roles, and leave men's redefinition to themselves, as long as it was predicated on equality with women.

Redefining fatherhood to achieve gender equity is also proposed by Louise Silverstein's feminist analysis of fatherhood (Silverstein 1996). Her argument is that women are limited by their family role, and that while women have entered the wage work world of men, there has not been a corresponding emergence of men doing family work. Women are expected to be providers and nurturers, although social institutions do not support them in either role. Fatherhood, Silverstein argues, continues to emphasize the bond with the mother. "In contrast, if fathers were perceived as primary caretakers, as well as primary providers, then their relationship with, and responsibility to, their children would be defined independently of their relationships to the mothers" (Silverstein 1996:6). She also suggests that the barriers to nurturing fathering are not limited to unwillingness to give up patriarchal power, but are combined with powerful deterrents, particularly in workplace culture. She sees women's economic equality leading to more mother-headed families in the short run, although that economic equality is crucial to women's equality at home. She believes that nurturing needs to be seen independent of marriage, leaving open the issue of what the mother-father relationship should be. Her insistence that the redefinition of fatherhood should not be at the mother's expense, and her attention to issues of domestic violence as well as economic inequality, suggests that she would envision constructing that relationship in a way that does not merely reconstruct a different patriarchy.

The intractability of the gender dynamic around parenting and work-family relationships is clear:

> As a movement, feminism has long had a dilemma on its hands. If women are to be free of the undue coercion and domination of males, they must establish their own independent sphere of activities and the necessary social and legal rights to protect that sphere. Women cannot and should not leave their fate in the hands of males, much less their reproductive fates. Meanwhile, feminists have also deplored feckless, irresponsible males who leave women in the lurch. Yet if males are to be encouraged to act more responsibly, to take seriously their duties to women and children, then they must be allowed to share the right to make decisions in those domains that bear on their activities and responsibilities. Males, moreover, have rights corresponding to their duties; they should be empowered to do that which their moral duties require of them. (Callahan 1992:240)

Consistent with this equity focus, greater nurture by fathers may also be critical to reorienting men's thinking about women and women's public status. According to Scott Coltrane,

> female status and father-child relationships are significantly correlated under a variety of conditions assumed to account for the sexual division of labor in both child rearing and public decision making. . . . If we hope to understand the strength and resilience of male dominance, we cannot rely only on biological or structural explanations but must also consider the influence of child-rearing patterns and public status on each other. (Coltrane 1988:1062)

Coltrane's research was designed to test the hypothesis that male participation in raising children enhances the public status of women. The converse is that women-only child care result in less public esteem for women and the creation of male-only activities for men. Although this analysis is based on data from nonindustrial societies, Coltrane argues that the work supports the thesis that "societies with father-present patterns of child socialization produce men who are less inclined to exclude women from public activities" (Coltrane 1988:1088).

Rather than redefining fatherhood by focusing on mothers, a second perspective focuses on increasing men's nurture. One group of fatherhood scholars has argued for a model of social fatherhood, paternal involvement, and "responsible" fatherhood (Marsiglio, Day, and Lamb 2000). They define involvement as men's positive and active participation in their children's lives and connect responsible fatherhood to the notion of "generative" fathering. Responsibility is defined as "paternal responsibilities for economic support, emotional support of mothers, and direct interaction with children . . . (engagement, accessibility, and responsibility)" (Marsiglio, Day, and Lamb 2000). They also note that the concept of paternal involvement is becoming more specifically defined. For some, that definition includes involvement measured not only in terms of human capital but also in terms of financial capital, a possible backdoor reintroduction of the breadwinner ideal. The persistence of the breadwinner model seems especially connected to the position of divorced and nonmarital fathers, and perhaps also some primary breadwinner fathers in intact marital families who want to claim that breadwinning is "good enough fathering."

Marsiglio, Day, and Lamb note that there is disagreement and discomfort among some with redefining fatherhood using a "mother template." "Nurturance" seems either to be viewed as synonymous with mother care, or as requiring expansion of the term to include economic support and/or to include or emphasize activities more characteristic of fathers' involvement with children. The nurturing ideal incorporates a tension between androgyny and some claim of difference, or at least an infusion of the concept of nurture with male-identified conduct or roles. Finally, these researchers note the general absence of information in the fatherhood literature about fathers from different family structures, class, and racial and ethnic backgrounds.

Constructing a definition of nurturing fatherhood grounded in men's development as adults, in personal development and social contribution, rather than gender or race equity or fairness, is the argument made by some advocates of generative fathering (Hawkins and Dollahite 1997; Marsiglio 1995b; Snarey 1993). Those who advocate the generative model see it as an alternative to the "deficit" model of fatherhood. Generative fathering is rooted in ethics and care. "By generative fathering we mean fathering that meets the needs of children by working to create and maintain a developing ethical relationship with them. . . . [W]e believe ethics precedes and grounds all scholarly understanding of fathering and professional practice with fathers" (Dollahite, Hawkins, and Brotherson 1997:18; see also Ritner 1992). Generative fathering is also rooted in concepts of work, as epitomized by the use of the term "fatherwork" to describe a combination of love and work (Dollahite, Hawkins, and Brotherson 1997:21). These scholars hope to tap into men's work orientation in a positive way while distinguishing this from wage work. They subdivide fatherwork into stewardship work, development work, and relationship work. "This work involves the call and the capability to commit to, choose on behalf of, consecrate oneself to, care for, change for, connect with, and communicate with the next generation" (Dollahite, Hawkins, and Brotherson 1997:32).

Gerson suggests that generative parenting includes equal parental sharing, defined as equal participation in routine work, equal participation in child care, and equal sacrifices on behalf of children (Gerson 1997). Parental sharing is extremely difficult for divorced fathers and is further complicated for stepfathers (Pasley and Minton 1997). At least one scholar argues that this is connected to the breakdown of male-female relations (Doherty 1997). "Unless we deal with male-female relations, and with marriage, we will be avoiding what I believe is the heart of the problem with fathering today" (Doherty 1997:226). Others argue that the barriers are tied to workplace culture (Dienhart and Daly 1997). William Allen and Michael Connor emphasize the ethnic differences in the notion of generative fatherhood, and suggest that African-American concepts of masculinity would include economic support, racial survival, bicultural socialization, and the challenges of the workplace (Allen and Connor 1997).

The legal theorist most identified with the generist perspective and a child-centered definition of parenting is Barbara Bennett Woodhouse. Woodhouse defines this perspective as recognizing "nurture as paramount," and sees parents as trustees rather than as rights-bearers. "The generist perspective . . . would value most highly concrete service to the needs of the next generation, in public and in private spheres, and encourage adult partnership and mutuality in the work of family, as well as collective responsibility for the well-being of our children" (Woodhouse 1993:1755). In their role as trustees, parents interact with other individuals and communities, and therefore are inclusive rather than exclusive (Woodhouse 1993). Woodhouse would include this conduct-centered definition even during gestation, challenging the acceptance of gender difference rooted in biology instead of in care (Woodhouse 1993). For example, in the context of adoption, she argues for shared trusteeship between biological and adoptive parents, communities of color, and political communities, and the balancing of cultural and social identity with the need for security and nurture (Woodhouse 1995). Her concept of fatherhood is grounded in the experience of children. "Young children know their families only through concrete experience. As children mature, their needs may change. Law should empower them to act as subjects in shaping their identities according to their emerging capacity, rather than treating them as objects" (Woodhouse 1994).

Virtually all fatherhood researchers note the inattention to, but importance of, race in rethinking fatherhood. Race influences our perception of fatherhood, although rarely in a positive way. The process of redefinition demands race equity as well as gender equity. "In the discourse about fatherlessness, Black men serve only in negative roles. . . . The last thing most White Americans want is to amplify Black males' masculinity. Black men represent all of the negative aspects of fatherlessness but none of the positive potential of fatherhood" (Roberts 1998). This racial blindness and exclusion hides a different model and experience of fatherhood that particularly challenges the connection between marriage and fatherhood, and the insistence on retaining a breadwinner model. The actual involvement of Black fathers with their children, the patterns of male mentoring in the Black community, and the means of providing support even in the absence of the ability to provide significant economic support are all important, but often ignored, fatherhood practices. As Dorothy Roberts suggests, "If we want to imagine nurturing fatherhood, decoupled from the patriarchal economic model, we might begin by looking to Black Fathers" (Roberts 1998:153). That reexamination must also deal with the economic disincentives to Black fatherhood.

Black fatherhood also cautions us to be careful about our historical perspective. While the cultural construction of Black masculinity is very different, Black fathers have been affected by their inability to meet the dominant culture's patriarchal model. It makes it far more difficult to construct an oppositional role for Black men than for Black women, who in some respects have been left alone to create a strong identity (Blount and Cunningham 1996). Robert Park, an advisor to Booker T. Washington, put it this way: the African-American "is, so to speak, the lady among the races" (Gibson 1996:95). The dilemma for Black men and other disempowered men in redefining fatherhood is how to gain power without adopting the patriarchal model.

Research on Latino fatherhood indicates that some of the same issues arise for Latino men, with the focus particularly on the concept of *macho*. *Macho* is a constructed masculinity which sees its most important task as taking care of *la familia*. "Critics often look at the negative behavior of the macho and forget the positive" (Anaya 1996:66). We also forget that the definition is in process of creation, not fixed, although misunderstood as static by the dominant culture (Gonzalez 1996).

Although nurture is at the core of a redefinition of fatherhood, nurture itself is a contested term. Whether it is a universal neutral concept, and whether motherhood is at the core of nurturing fatherhood are matters of considerable debate. Sara Ruddick argues for defining fatherhood as mothering, not as parenthood, to name the reality of who has been doing the nurturing, what men need to do to care for children, and confront the injustices of current child care:

> If we see or remember child-tending accurately, we will be rid of distinctions, or more optimistically reimagine connections, between so-called physical, intellectual and emotional activities. . . . The *work* of child-tending can be, and is being, undertaken by women and men, gay and straight, single, coupled, or in many kinds of social arrangements. I speak of "mothering" rather than "parenting" as the work in which child-tending men and women engage. This terminology acknowledges the "fact" that mothering has been—and still is—primarily the responsibility of women and that history has consequences.
> . . . By contrast, the abstract notion of "parent" obscures the pervasive injustices suffered by women-mothers and, more generally, the myriad father problems that vex and divide feminists. In making the case for "mothering" as a gender inclusive and therefore genderless activity, I have been struck by the resistance even of those men who fully engage in child tending. . . . A man or women is a *mother*, in my sense

of the term, only if he or she acts upon a social commitment to nurture, protect, and train children. (Ruddick 1990:229–30)

On the other hand, those who favor a neotraditional model of fatherhood and even some generative theorists would argue that men parent differently, and that the difference should be recognized and valued. Certainly the claim of uniqueness is powerful and attractive. The child development literature seems to support it in some respects, by noting the differences in men's parenting style and activities. Overall, however, what children need and how parents practice caretaking is not gender defined (Dowd 1997a). As one scholar described it in relation to her own son, he "needs as many fully developed people in his life as possible, people who will show him ways of being that bring him, and the people in his life, joy and compassion. These people might be men, and they might be women, but the fact that they are male or female is the least important fact of all" (Burke 1996:xviii).

In terms of practical strategies and policies, Sweden leads the way in rethinking fatherhood. It exemplifies a gender-neutral, gender-equal fatherhood model. Sweden's commitment to gender equality, premised on the elimination of gender-specific roles, began in the late 1960s. The incentive to change was the need for women's labor in the wage labor market, rather than a demand from women for equality at home (Dowd 1989b). Much of Swedish policy has been directed at removing structural barriers for women, especially by providing supports in the wage labor market for parents, including child care, parental leave, part-time work, and ongoing leave time to attend to sick children or remain involved in children's lives. Policy specific to men was initially limited to "daddy days," ten days of paid leave that could be taken at birth or adoption.

Since the 1970s, Sweden has actively monitored gender differentials in the usage rates of these policies, and responded to sharp gender differentials by campaigns to educate men and the business community; by requiring companies to devise plans to support fathers in their nurturing role; and by dedicating one month of the twelve-month parental leave entitlement exclusively to fathers (Haas 1995). The structural arrangement that appears to work best for mothers who are primary or sole caretakers is a thirty-hour workweek, accomplished by working part time and using income supports. The alternative would be to reduce the workweek to thirty hours for everyone.

That alternative has been resisted, at the same time that tax changes have made additional work less heavily taxed, which may disproportionately affect men's work by encouraging longer hours.

Linda Haas has exposed the structural and cultural disincentives of the Swedish workplace that result in the low usage rates of these policies by fathers (Haas 1995). As she notes, the occupational structure remains highly sex segregated. But the other barriers, as she explains, are social-psychological, and they are more influential (Haas 1993: 257). The pattern is of sharply differentiated gender use in the context of policy designed to assist women and never thought of in terms of how to implement it and encourage its use by men (Hojgaard 1997). "The conceptualization of policies in gender-neutral terms simply conceals the differences in social conditions and cultural practices of women and men" (Hojgaard 1997:252). One of the most persistent problems across cultures is work culture and the association of men with work: "The choice of being an active father with respect to the work place culture challenges a very basic symbolic meaning of masculinity as it involves work performance" (Hojgaard 1997:258). Changing the work culture requires radical restructuring to reach the equality goals of Sweden's progressive structure (Haas 1995). "[M]ost companies' formal policies and informal practices still reinforce gender-based expectations for men's and women's roles and make it difficult for men to become more active in child care" (Haas 1995:34). Several possibilities recently explored in the Swedish context include consideration of ways to encourage or mandate that men and women equally divide the twelve-month parental leave entitlement, and programs specifically targeted at men to educate and support them in becoming and continuing to be nurturers (Frean 1998).

American political and nonprofit organizations that have sprung up around fatherhood issues are split between advocates of traditional or modified traditional models of fatherhood, and those who support a nurturing model of fatherhood. The traditionalists see fathers as distinctive and support the breadwinner role, versus a more androgenous model, the nurturing father, whom they sometimes sarcastically refer to as substitute moms. Conservatives fear the down playing of economic responsibility and discarding fathers' claims of distinctiveness; liberals fear a perceived conservative agenda of ongoing male dominance cloaked in the rhetoric of difference (Schoenfeld 1996; Seibold 1995).

Critics on the left tend to be more sanguine about the emergence of
new family structures. . . . Almost all on the left argue that single
women, given adequate resources, are perfectly capable of rearing
happy, healthy children and that families without fathers are simply
one variant among many in the continuing evolution of family forms.
Conservatives reject such optimism. To them, many of America's
most intractable problems . . . can be traced to fatherlessness . . . conservatives call for a return of fatherly authority, extol the virtues of
traditional masculinity, and see in marriage and fatherhood a way to
stem men's proclivity for sexual promiscuity and social disorder. . . .
Those on the right celebrate traditional fatherhood and see within it a
deep source of social stability and morality. (Daniels 1998:12)

The Fatherhood Project is the organization most strongly associated with the "new" nurturing father model. Its director, James
Levine, argues for a gender-specific approach rather than a "parenthood" approach. He sees the need for radical change, and emphasizes the importance of personal as well as structural and cultural
changes to reorient fathering (Carroad 1994). The Project particularly encourages community-based strategies (Levine and Pitt
1995). The National Fatherhood Institute, on the other hand, cham-
pions the unique and traditional role of fatherhood (Schoenfeld
1996; Seibold 1995). The National Fatherhood Initiative, led by
Wade Horn, is grounded in the position that fathers are unique and
irreplaceable, and that America's policy goal should be to insure the
presence of a a "responsible, committed and loving father" in every
home (Eberly 1997:218). Another more negative conservative view,
often associated with Blankenhorn, sees men as irresponsible or
blocked nurturers, and mothers as inadequate or irresponsible parents. Fathers' importance in this view is based on their uniqueness.
The policy orientation is toward forcing responsibility on the irresponsible, while unblocking the blocked nurturers by empowering
fathers (Davidson 1990).

One of the most expressly patriarchal models of fatherhood is that
of the Promise Keepers, a national men's Christian political group organized in 1990 by Bill McCartney, a former University of Colorado
football coach. Its call is for men to be more responsible husbands, fathers, and friends based on a biblical model. The strong message of
commitment mirrored in the name is tied to an understanding of the
importance of gender difference and the need for men to be leaders
and heads of their families. Promise Keepers express their concern for

the "feminization of men," and the need to reassert men's traditional role as moral and familial leaders:

> I am convinced that the primary cause of this national crisis [of moral breakdown in our society] is the feminization of the American male. When I say feminization, I am not talking about sexual preference. I'm trying to describe a misunderstanding of manhood that has produced a nation of sissified men who abdicate their role as spiritually pure leaders, thus forcing women to fill the vacuum. (Beal 1997:278, quoting Tony Evans)

Leaders of the movement claim male leadership is not characterized by domination but by service, and that it is therefore traditional not patriarchal. Promise Keepers commit themselves to building strong marriages and families through love, protection, and biblical values. The talk of family in the movement is more oriented toward the husband-wife relationship and family as a whole, rather than to a specific focus on fatherhood.

Promise Keepers are also strongly committed to racial brotherhood, although their membership is predominantly white. Their position on the issues is strikingly paralleled by the goals of the Million Man March, a march and movement directed at African-American men. In October 1995, somewhere between half a million to almost 2 million men (depending on the estimates) marched in Washington. The march, led by Louis Farrakhan, was characterized as one of "atonement, reconciliation, and responsibility" for men. It was experienced by many as a day of empowerment for Black men, and one that challenged stereotypes. One of the marchers' covenants was the promise to "serve our wives and children." The message is embedded in a strongly political, community-oriented context, rather than a familial one.

In sum, the definition of fatherhood is a matter of considerable debate among academics, policy makers, and advocacy groups. A redefinition of fatherhood can be centered around a benefit to children, parents, gender equity, and/or society. The apparent strategies include a focus on women as a means to encourage male nurture and/or a focus on male-female relationships as critical to increased male nurture. This approach sees men's fathering as inextricably relational, tied to mothering and women's equality. A second strategy focuses on the quality of nurture and the conditions to facilitate it, by exposing and describing male patterns of nurture. Traditionalists would argue that traditional fatherhood, with its focus on the breadwinner role, is a nurturing role, and that economic fatherhood is at the core of nurturing, or that it remains critical, perhaps modified by more social nurture. Advocates for social fatherhood reject that view and identify the workplace and breadwinner models as the greatest barriers to nurture, whether modeled on mothering or a distinctive male pattern.

The term "nurture" can be appropriated by any position in the fatherhood debate. The range and degree of nurture stretches across a considerable continuum. That the question of the uniqueness of male nurture versus its essential similarity to mothering is such a delicate one speaks volumes for the raw nerve of gender. Thus the definition of what constitutes nurture is critical. Traditional definitions of fatherhood ground their arguments in gender difference, and often hide gender hierarchy, as well as race and class divisiveness. "New" fatherhood is sometimes equally grounded in difference. Many commentators ignore the intersections with mothers and view fatherhood in isolation. In the next section, I offer a model that is responsive to the context and practice of fathering, and is informed by this debate among advocates.

A NEW MODEL: NURTURE AND SOCIAL FATHERING

The most important question for the redefinition of fatherhood is whether the goal of nurture would be best achieved by reinforcing or reorienting traditional definitions centered around marriage, biology, and economic responsibility, alone or in combination. The support of marital fatherhood is appealing because it suggests a commitment to a long-term relationship that accords with the developmental benefits to children from consistency of care and stability in their familial relationships. If fatherhood is understood as a permanent relationship, then marriage might arguably best support that understanding. However, the breakdown of marital patterns, as evidenced in high divorce rates, nonmarital birth rates, cohabitation rates, and men's nonmarital and postdivorce parenting, argues against a definition tethered to marriage. This is a social and cultural pandora's box that cannot be closed.

A biological definition is an appealing alternative in light of these social realities. Such a definition might be justified on the grounds that adults ought to be responsible in their reproductive behavior, and that that responsibility should be reflected in an obligation to care for the children they bring into this world. This argument is particularly appealing when minimum care is defined as sufficient economic support to insure that the child will have reasonable opportunities to develop to his or her full capacity. An economic requirement might include a similar obligation of support by the mother, pro rata reduced to reflect the value of the mother's caretaking should the father not provide any care.

The difficulty of the biological approach, however, arises when one goes beyond economic support. If nurture is the goal of redefined fatherhood, then despite the value and necessity of economic support, it is not nurture. Nurture requires a relationship, and the biological approach suggests that the father is entitled to a relationship with the child irrespective of his relationship with the mother. In the absence of marriage, cohabitation, or a prior established relationship with the child, even if there is no sharing of a household with the mother, should a biological connection entitle the father to a relationship? Any answer in the negative gives power to the mother; any answer in the positive gives power to the father.

Is there a solution that shares power, or avoids this seemingly inevitable gender conundrum? Given existing gender power relations, the widespread persistence of domestic violence and child abuse, and most significantly, the patterns of disconnection between fathers and children based on biology alone, the right to a relationship with one's child based solely on biological connection should be rejected. But biological connection rarely occurs in isolation, save for anonymous sperm donors. Rather, it is embedded within a context of relationship, conduct, and intent, and those factors can be evaluated to determine the opportunity to create, maintain, or modify a parent-child relationship. Relationship would include relationship with the mother and, if in being, the child. Intent would focus on the father's expressed feeling and actual conduct to prepare or be a father, as expressed toward the mother, the child, or other children in being. The capacity to nurture would include the father's intentions, expressed or by conduct, to establish, maintain, or improve a nurturing relationship. Conduct would include not only these relational factors, but also the father's acquisition or demonstration of nurturing skills, knowledge, and commitment, including his relationships with other children or other mothers to whom he is connected and may have, or could have, established a nurturing relationship.

Both marital and biological fatherhood also have the appeal of a status designation based on a relatively easy fact-finding of marital status or genetic relationship. Economic definitions of fatherhood are more conduct oriented, but similarly have the appeal of simplicity. Usually in conjunction with marriage, biology or adoption, economic support would be "good enough" fatherhood. Certainly the support of children is essential, although support ought not be confused with nurture. It is tempting to do so because economics has such powerful effects on children's opportunities and outcomes. In that sense, money is nurture and care. But the nurture that we seek to place at the center of fatherhood is personal and relational, not financial. Furthermore, prioritizing breadwinning for fathers gets in the way of nurture, and it is that very conflict that we must address, most significantly for fathers but also for mothers. The more difficult question about economics is whether we would impose economic responsibilities as a consequence of conceiving or adopting a child, but not guarantee an opportunity to establish and maintain a social relationship. The arguments for separating economic and social relationships are very strong. There is nothing in the provision of economic support, moreover, that should entitle one to a social relationship. *We should stop supporting the notion that money buys rights to children.*

In contrast to other alternatives, social fathering directly promotes nurture as the core definition of fatherhood. Social fatherhood is grounded foremost in the needs of children, second on the needs of society, and third on its benefits to individuals. Social fathering means focusing on the conduct of fathers, with nurture as the most critical conduct. This most strongly supports fathering as we know it without foreclosing support of any of the more traditional definitions of fatherhood, at least in some respects. Marital fatherhood, if it actually works as it is presumed to work, would satisfy a social fathering definition. Biological fathers who establish actual relationships with mothers and children would also be covered, although they would lose some automatic rights that they might have had under a status-based definition. Economic fathers would know that their financial support was not sufficient nor enabling of a relationship with their child.

Valuing nurture by examining conduct makes it incumbent on us to define nurture. Defining nurture requires us to articulate both a quantitative and qualitative standard. If fatherhood is defined as social fatherhood, as conduct instead of status, then we must define what we mean by nurture. Nurture means care—physical, emotional, intellectual, spiritual—gauged by one's conduct and the consequences for children's positive development. It is responsive to the different needs of children at different ages. Thus nurture is not a static conception. It means more than simply doing; it also means the manner in which things are done, and their results for children.

Translating this into policy requires us to attend to economic, cultural, and racial issues. The economic issues include the reorientation of work and family interconnections to support nurture for all children, which inevitably requires some form of family support to make nurturing fathering possible. Another challenge is the need for cultural policies that affirmatively educate and reeducate men about nurturing children, and about cooperating with other caretakers of their children. Economic and cultural policies must also take race into account, both in identifying positive models among men of all races and in remaining grounded in the realities of fatherhood as practiced in different communities. The means to achieve a redefined fatherhood must be gender relevant, gender conscious, and gender specific.

Adopting nurture as the core concept of fatherhood is more difficult conceptually, and involves a more balanced understanding, than does a biological or economic model. In that respect, it is less clear-cut than those models or definitions, which can rely on genetic testing or some level of economic contribution as a standard, measures which seem clearer and more easy to apply. The more nuanced standard of nurture opens the door to a variety of definitions and understandings, and to differences over when a standard of nurture has been met. The critique of the "best interests" standard in family law should make us cautious about adopting a standard that seems equally capable of being ambiguous and discretionary. But it should not dissuade us. The task is to articulate an inclusive, diverse standard that focuses on the needs of children and emphasizes men's presumed ability to nurture. Moreover, another benefit of describing and defining nurture is that we make the work of taking care of children more visible and more valued.

By using "nurture" instead of "father," we incorporate what we know of men's ability to care for children. A nongendered word is appropriate here, to counter the cultural and historic tendency to essentialize and naturalize fatherhood, and to associate it with genetic and economic factors. Yet the content of nurture is unavoidably woman-connected. It is disproportionately women who have engaged in the care of children. Much of the definition and image of nurture therefore can therefore be filled in by looking to mothers, and to our expectations of their nurturing. I do not mean to ignore the critique of our expectations of mothers and simply accept prevailing standards. But I want to suggest that the challenge of defining "nurture" can be resolved by critical analysis of mothers and mothering, both in the interest of fathers and of mothers.

There are dangers and challenges to making explicit the feminine, feminist source of the definition of nurture. If we specify and acknowledge that mothering is our model, men may respond with a sense of distance and rejection rather than inclusion. I would not cling to the necessity of identifying nurture as a mothering, mother-oriented model, if that would distance men and turn them off. But I am unconvinced that we cannot acknowledge the value and contour of what mothers do without alienating fathers. Furthermore, acknowledging mothering and valuing it as a model also rejects devaluing women or their work with children because of who historically has done, and currently does more, of the work.

The qualitative component of nurture can be defined, then, by the work of caring for children, based particularly on what we know of women's affirmative mothering. That definition must include not only the physical incidents of care and the manner in which it is rendered, but also the intellectual and psychological commitment, management, planning, and judgment involved in such care. Our qualitative description must also include a range of care defined according to cultural, ethnic, and racial diversity. Nurture must be seen in connection to the other work of the household, and in relation to wage work. Household work should not be separated from child care, and should include the care given to other adults as well as children. The connection of family work and wage work is essential, both in the short-term daily sense and in terms of its impact on long-term opportunities and economic security.

Nurture must also be defined and understood quantitatively, in relationship to the child and to other caregivers. Just as important as what it is we define nurture to be, is the context in which we imagine it will occur, both the immediate context of the household, and the broader context of individual support networks and extended family, community supports, and overall social and cultural values. We operate in a context strongly modeled on a primary caretaker. Other than the small number of fathers who are themselves sole or primary parents, most fathers who nurture do so in circumstances characterized by distinctly unequal direct parenting, in addition to indirect parenting. Do we want to support this quantitative and relational model of nurture? If we understand such fathering to be a legitimate model of nurture, then we must degenderize the model so that both mothers and fathers can perform as the primary or secondary parent. If, on the other hand, our model is one of coequal parenting, including both direct and indirect parenting, then we are aiming for a radical change both in the way fatherhood is defined and in teh way it relates to motherhood or other caretakers.

In addition, there is the purely relational issue of whether we want to promote a definition of fatherhood that is independent of or connected to motherhood. Our existing model of fatherhood seems essentially at war with itself on this issue. The marital emphasis of the traditional, and to some extent still current, definition of fatherhood would reject a concept of fatherhood that is independent of mothers. On the other hand, the deemphasis of differences between marital and nonmarital fathers, and the imposition of economic obligations tied to biological fatherhood suggest that we value a model of lifelong father-child relationships irrespective of the relationships between fathers and mothers, and perhaps even overriding them.

If society has a definition of fatherhood that is dependent on the relationship of the father to the other parent, is it insuring the best interests of the child or simply handing a powerful weapon, capable of being abused, to the other parent? If we assume that we are operating on a primary-parent model where fathers and mothers can both be the primary parent, we are assuming that the primary parent will appropriately exercise his or her power. Martha Fineman would argue for this approach, by elevating the Mother-Child dyad (and requiring men to be mother equivalents if they want to occupy the preferred position of the Mother) (Fineman 1995; see also Trost 1996).

Much can be said for this approach, since the data indicate that some of the difficulty that men, especially postdivorce men, have with their fathering role stems from their difficulty with the increased power position of their former wives. If that power position fosters equality, then one can argue that it is a good thing. On the other hand, if it fosters vengeful inequality, even if it might seem to balance former inequality in the other direction, it would not be good to do. Calling the power person Mother is also consistent with the argument that doing so values the work that mothers have traditionally disproportionately done, trusts their likelihood of acting in their children's best interests, and requires fathers to act more like mothers or negotiate with mothers rather than being given automatic equal rights regardless of their conduct, past or present, or promised in the future.

Fineman would also argue that this promotes fathers' best interests and gender dynamics by making it more likely that fathers would be included, based on the positive quality of the relationship they had or maintain with the mother. The more casual the relationship, the less likely nurturing fatherhood might be, but that would depend on the relationship with the mother. This scenario seems to maximize choice (in the sense of including men who quantitatively and qualitatively nurture very little) and gender equity. In a coequal parenting situation, both parents are primary, and neither parent would have a controlling role. This would require both parents to work cooperatively or to choose a mechanism to resolve differences.

Related to this issue are three further questions: how this works in the absence of a relationship; how this works in the absence of a shared household; and how this works at birth, when conduct by which a relationship can be measured may be limited. The first two questions require a focus on the relationship between the social father and the mother. That relationship can develop in the absence of intimacy and shared living, but requires cooperation, respect, and nonviolence. In such a model, mutuality is valued and no particular structure is privileged. It also has an inclusive concept of parenthood, supporting cooperation among multiple parenting figures who function in the best interests of the child. At birth, relational conduct may be minimal in terms of the child, but would certainly exist in relation to the other parent and intention could be expressed in planning. The intent to nurture should be strongly supported within a relationship of mutual cooperation and respect.

Redefining fatherhood around nurture and a model of social fatherhood, means that I would answer the initial questions raised in this chapter by arguing that we should work with existing patterns of fatherhood rather than resisting them. The strongest of these patterns are social, connected to relationships and households. Parenting relationships that are not socially connected would not be disadvantaged by this definition, but those that are currently ignored would be better supported. In addition, we would more strongly recognize other sources of stability and care, including extended family and networks of friends.

Second, this definition would not privilege marriage, as it is flexible enought to recognize the value of actual conduct within marriage or other relationships. Third, social fatherhood resolves the question of supporting fatherhood without undermining motherhood. The focus is on relationships, between father and child, and between father and other caretakers. Fourth, the economic parameters of this definition are essential. If we continue to operate within current ways of supporting children and their parents, inevitably this definition will require coordination with private obligations of support. In addition, the choice of a two-parent versus single-parent model of parenting would largely be resolved in favor of perpetuating the single-parent, or primary-parent model.

The consequence, then, of remaining within the existing economic framework would be to limit options and put enormous pressure on the need to reorient work and family policy and encourage a transformation in primary parenting away from its currently gendered practice of mother care. In addition, remaining within existing economic parameters would severely limit the impact of any redefinition toward social fathering to middle-class and upper-class fathers, and whites over families of color. On the other hand, social fatherhood would value the nonmarital patterns more dominant in nonwhite communities, and perhaps make alternative cultural conceptions of fatherhood more visible. Finally, social fatherhood best responds to the need for flexibility, given the context of significant family fluidity and change.

It is important to recognize the challenges posed by reorienting fatherhood around nurture, instead of around economics, biology, or marriage. The most difficult challenges are two gender intersections: the relationship of fatherhood to masculinity, and that of fatherhood to motherhood. Those barriers must be recognized and addressed if we are to practice a redefined fatherhood. It is to those challenges that I now turn, before I return to a more detailed examination of redefined fatherhood.

CHAPTER 10

Gender Challenges: Masculinities and Mothers

> To develop a new kind of father, we must encourage a new
> kind of man
> —Garbarino, 1993

Fatherhood is connected to two gender intersections: the concept of masculinity and the relationship between fatherhood and motherhood. Men's identities as fathers do not exist in isolation from their identities as men. Indeed, that broader masculine identity arguably poses the most difficult challenge to a redefined and differently lived fatherhood. As long as masculinity identifies nurture and care as feminine and unmanly, men's socialization will work against them rather than for them. As long as masculinity is defined in opposition to femininity, and requires devaluing and stigmatizing things labeled feminine, men will be blocked from or conflicted by learning from female role models. The learning and valuing of nurture is blocked by misogyny and homophobia, even for (and perhaps more so for) those men who do not feel privileged by male position and privilege. It is also challenged by the embrace of violence as a part of masculinity, a value or trait antithetical to nurture and care.

The second gender circle is relational rather than individual: the relationship between fatherhood and motherhood. Fatherhood does not exist in isolation. The redefinition of fatherhood should not be at the expense of motherhood. The strong role of mothers as gatekeepers and mediators of men's relationships with their children suggests that they are central to any new redefinition. It also points to the importance in thinking from a relational perspective. While a gender-specific strategy may be essential, it must be done with both mothers and fathers in mind. Connected to this is the relation between family and work, as constructed for men and women and between men and women.

MASCULINITIES

"Masculinity is not only constructed, it is performative, that is, we don't merely play out a constructed role, we also play with, perform within that role, which means the role is fluid and temporal, not fixed" (Berger, Wallis, and Watson 1995). Seeing masculinity as a cultural construction rather than a biologically essentialist characteristic is one of the core insights of the study of masculinities (Clatterbauth 1990; Connell 1995; Kimmel and Messner 1992; McLearn, Carey, and White 1996; Messner 1997). A second core understanding is that masculinity is not singular, although a single ideology may dominate (Carrigan, Connell, and Lee 1992; Messner 1997). Because multiple masculinities exist, the dominant masculinity is subverted and there is potential for change from within (Carrigan, Connell, and Lee 1992). Nevertheless, the power of the dominant masculinity must not be ignored, since it constrains men to act within its boundaries. Finally, sex and race intersect powerfully in the construction of masculinity (hooks 1995).

Robert Brannon reduces the dominant masculinity role into four basic rules: "No Sissy Stuff," "Be a Big Wheel," "Be a Sturdy Oak," and "Give 'em Hell" (Kimmel 1996:282). Michael Kimmel describes the core dilemma of masculinity as the need to constantly prove oneself to be a man (Kimmel 1996). What is fascinating in the dominant account is the absence of a focus on fathering. In contrast, when feminists and others talk about women, they do not get very far without discussing motherhood. Masculinity seems to focus on the way men live their lives, which makes family subservient to everything else. Fathering is tied to manliness only as a demonstration of virility—the ability to produce a child—not as the conduct of caretaking and nurturing.

The power of masculinity is perhaps nowhere more apparent than in its medical, scientific operation. Anne Fausto-Sterling explores how the norms of biological, medical maleness have been constructed by social and cultural expectations in the context of medical opinion of sex assignment at birth. Genetic females should always be raised as females, preserving reproductive potential regardless of how severely the patients are virilized. In the genetic male, however, the assignment of gender is based on the infant's anatomy, predominantly the size of the phallus (Fausto-Sterling 1995:130, quoting Donahue, Powell, and Lee 1991). Fausto-Sterling goes on to explain that the average phallus at birth is 3.5 cm. If a baby has a penis less than .9 cm that is considered normal, but if the penis is less than .6 cm, many physicians will recommend that the child not remain a male. Surgery will remove a penis that could give an orgasm and replace it with a clitoris that may not. So the construction of masculinity at birth is social: as an adult, the person must be able to pee standing up and have heterosexual intercourse, with heterosexuality taking precedence over sexual pleasure (Fausto-Sterling 1995).

Psychologists have dominated the study of masculinity. Lynne Segal critiques traditional psychological theory as tending to ignore gender power relations in its articulation of the way masculinity and gender role are acquired (Segal 1990). She argues that masculinity should be viewed as a combination of individual identity and social and cultural practice. That is, masculinity is part of the individual's construction of his individual identity, but it is also connected with institutional structures, especially family, workplace, state, and the rituals of public places. Segal argues that a major theme of masculinity is hierarchy and dominance. Dominance is combined with threat: "Masculinity is surrounded by its enemies . . . within, femininity and male homosexual desire . . . without, women and the feminine must be subordinated and held in place" (Segal 1990:103). Subordination is increasingly more difficult:

The point is that it is insufficient for the *men* to be distinguished from the *boys*; the *men* must be distinguished from the *women*. Without the return of full-blooded patriarchy, many men are today condemned to live with ever increasing levels of insecurity over the distinctiveness of their *manliness*. For it is no longer so easy to imagine that there are many significant activities or areas of life which, by definition, forever exclude women. Just as it is not so easy to imagine that there are many activities or areas of life which, by definition, can never include men. And this becomes ever more apparent, however much the reality of men's dominance continues to reproduce significant areas of actual exclusion for women, and opting out by men. (Segal 1990:132)

David Gilmore, who has studied manhood cross-culturally, sees masculinity as a critical social organizing tool, a way for the community to encourage people to act in certain ways. Gender roles are therefore a communal problem-solving mechanism. He describes the role as imposing a triad of requirements for men: to be a man, you must impregnate women, protect your dependents from danger, and provide for your family. If the basic needs of society are production and reproduction, he sees women as taking care of the latter. The male role is then a response to women's role and society's needs. However, he sees an emphasis on nurture within the provider role:

[M]anhood ideologies always include a criterion of selfless generosity, even to the point of sacrifice. . . . Manhood therefore is also a nurturing concept, if we define that term as giving, subverting or other-directed. It is true that this male giving is different from, and less demonstrative and more obscure than, the female. It is less direct, less immediate, more involved with externals. (Gilmore 1990:229)

The harmful and limiting aspects of masculinity have been well chronicled. Privilege comes with a price. Andrew Kimbrell blames much of the declining significance of fathers on the impact of industrialization, creating the structural separation of men from their children:

The separation of men, and men's work, from the family may well be the most significant personal and social disruption men have ever had to face. For generations industrial society has been conducting an unparalleled anthropological experiment: What is the effect of virtual father absence on the family, children and the redefinition of men's role in society. After several generations the tragic results of this experiment are being seen in the growing crisis for men and masculinity. (Kimbrell 1995:39)

The most ominous consequences, he thinks, are those confronting boys, whose masculine models are no longer in their homes, but must come from the culture. He also argues that industrialization has destroyed men's friendship with each other and replaced it with competition, and destroyed gender complementarity (Kimbrell 1995:41). Kimbrell blames the legal system for distancing fathers from their children in divorce and custody decisions. He sees a reduction of the hours of work as the major workplace reform necessary for involved fathering. He argues for a vision centered around a core ethic of *husband*, not as a noun but as a verb, meaning a caretaking, caregiving ethic tied to a dominant, head of household role.

At the center of this postindustrial toxic masculinity Kimbrell sees the ideal of the machine: "the cult of efficiency, the premier mechanical trait, remains at the heart of the masculine mystique's emotional impoverishment of men" (Kimbrell 1995:65). Symbolized by the "machine man" and the "profit man," this economic focus is not only hard on men, he argues, but also has become more and more difficult if not impossible to attain under current economic conditions (Kimbrell 1995:109). "If white men who are becoming increasingly irrelevant to the family and to the high-technology global economy want to know about their future, they need only speak with their African-American brothers, who for so long have been virtually invisible, but waiting to be seen and heard" (Kimbrell 1995:277).

Toxic masculinity is also the target of Frank Pittman, especially the ways in which traditional masculinity literally hurts men (Pittman 1993). Men live seven years less than women, have higher death rates by homicide, suicide, and accidents, and suffer more from lung cancer, cirrhosis of the liver, and other ailments. He emphasizes that masculinity norms require that masculinity be fought for all life long. Indeed, he notes one description of being a real man as *The Big Impossible*. He connects the passion for masculinity to this lifelong quest, tied to the masculine mystique:

> Why do men love their masculinity so much? Because men have been trained to sacrifice their lives for their masculinity, and men always know they are far less masculine than they think they should be. Women, though, have the power to give a man his masculinity or take it away, so women become both terrifyingly important and terrifyingly dangerous to men. It's all quite crazy. (Pittman 1993:17)

He links toxic masculinity to men being raised by women without male role models. In his view, if men raised children they would save their lives, and save the world. On the other hand, John Stoltenberg views toxic masculinity from a strongly antimasculinist, radical feminist perspective, arguing that masculinity can be serious, pervasive, and hateful (Stoltenberg 1989).

One of the strongest themes of masculinity is gender difference (Connell 1995; Segal 1990). Yet one of the more interesting discoveries by psychologists is that there are few significant psychological differences exist between men and women (Connell 1995). Connell also explains the low interest of men in changing their masculinity as tied to self-interest, and the difficulty of organizing a powerful group who nevertheless do not feel their power or want to reclaim it (Connell 1995).

One of the most significant attempts at reworking the conceptualization of masculinity is Joseph Pleck's work on men's sex roles (Levant and Pollack 1995; Pleck 1992). Pleck argues that the gender role identity paradigm that previously dominated psychological thought was not well supported by empirical data, and reified gender dichotomy and essentialism. Under traditional theory, men and women must acquire their identity, manifested by the appropriate traits, attitudes, and interests, which would give them the stamp of an appropriate identity. This helped pinpoint what constituted too little masculinity or too much, with too little being the primary concern (Pleck 1992). Pleck's alternative paradigm is a gender role strain paradigm with the following principles:

> gender roles are contradictory and inconsistent; the proportion of persons who violate gender roles is high; violation of gender roles leads to condemnation and negative psychological consequences; actual or imagined violation of gender roles leads people to over conform to them; violating gender roles has more severe consequences for males than for females; and certain prescribed gender role traits . . . are too often dysfunctional. . . . [G]ender roles are defined by gender role stereotypes and norms and are imposed on the developing child by parents, teachers, and peers. (Pleck 1995:3)

According to this model, the "problem" with masculinity is its definition, not men's inability to live up to it (Pleck 1995:23).

But that inability imposes severe limits on men. Shame plays a significant role in male culture, as the mechanism which insures the metaphor of life as a contest (Auerbach 1997). Shame is a powerful agent in self-regulation and social integration (Krugman 1995:94). "Male difficulties with intimacy and with parenting—especially following divorce—can be usefully understood in terms of how hard it is to handle vulnerable and exposed states that generate shameful feelings" (Krugman 1995:94). Shame is a tool to control one's feelings and their expression, together with the valuing of aggression (Krugman 1995:122).

The emotional consequences of traditional masculinity are particularly troublesome in terms of nurturing children and coparenting with other caretakers. Early in life, boys are more emotional than girls. "Through the ordeal of emotional socialization, males learn to tune out, stifle, and channel their emotions" (Levant 1995a:236–37). We have an extraordinarily negative view of boys that ironically reflects this socialization (Mariani 1995). Male children are seen as "belligerent, willful creatures naturally avaricious and aggressive, in need of constant punishment if he is to learn the avoidance of transgression" (Mariani 1995:136). A critical event in all boys' lives, according to one theorist, is their felt need to disconnect from their mothers, which he describes as not so much a disconnection from a person as from relationship itself (Bergman 1995:74). Relationship is thereby experienced as comparison, and leads to competition, aggression, and even violence. "The fantasy is that by achieving, a man will win love. For example, the *Hi Mom!* syndrome: pro football players on the sidelines after making a great play, when caught by the TV camera, invariably turn, raise an index finger to indicate they are Number One, and shout, *Hi, Mom!*" (Bergman 1995:75). In contrast, fathers are often described as distant or absent. Friends can be as much a source of fear as of connection. "[T]he charm of buddies does not last long: ask any man about his boyhood and you will hear hair-raising stories filled with incredible cruelty, violence, and daily terror. . . . No discussion of men's development can ignore male violence or male power" (Bergman 1995:78). The consequences for men are *action empathy*, the inability to know their own emotional lives; channeling vulnerable emotions through anger; and channeling caring emotions through sexuality (Levant 1995a:237). According to Levant, a high number of men suffer from at least mild alexithymia—"the inability to identify and describe one's feelings in words" (Levant 1995a:238). Levant sees men's lack of involvement in child care as tied to skill deficits, as well as seeing child care as women's work and therefore not something men should have to do, which he links to separation from mothers (Levant 1995a:246).

The psychological tasks are immensely more complicated for men of color:

> African-American males have adopted distinctive actions and atti-
> tudes known as "cool pose." . . . Emphasizing honor, virility, and phys-
> ical strength, the Latino male adheres to a code of machismo. . . . The
> American-Indian male struggles to maintain contact with a way of
> life and the traditions of elders while faced with economic castration
> and political trauma. . . . Asian-American men resolve their uncer-
> tainty privately, in order to save face, and surrender personal auton-
> omy to family obligations and needs. (Lazur and Majors 1995:338)

The dominant model and the community culture are both factors in the masculinity norms of minority men.

The pop culture men's movement has evolved apart from these academic debates about masculinity and most strongly reflects the ongoing need to ground masculinity in difference. The major strands of the movement include the mythopoetic men's move-ment, the profeminist men's movement, fathers' rights groups, men's rights groups, the Christian men's movement, men's thera-peutic groups, and the fatherhood movement. Some are traditional-ists whose arguments are often biologically or theologically based. Others advocate for men's rights using equality arguments to claim both that women have achieved equality and that men have an equal need for liberation and equality (Kimmel 1995a:301; see also Bertoia and Drakich 1993). Most significantly, and ironically, these groups reflect a sense of lack of power (Kimmel 1995a). Men feel *dis*empowered even as they have power: "Ironically, as [middle-class, white, middle-aged heterosexuals] men are everywhere in power, that aggregate power of that group does not translate into an individual sense of feeling empowered" (Kimmel 1995a:18). The focus of the mythopoetic movement, inspired by Robert Bly's *Iron John*, is on gender distinctions, the feminization of manhood, the search for lost fathers, and the retrieval of heroic archetypes. Inter-estingly, fathers are present only in the concept of the *father wound*, the anguish over not being parented. Grief for their fathers does not seem to lead men to rethink their own fatherhood.

Most significant for this book is the fathers' rights movement, because of what it says about the law. Most vocal and organized are non-custodial fathers, mostly divorced, who see the legal system as strongly biased in favor of women, and mothers as disproportionately powerful in custody (see, for example, Conine 1989; Dudley 1996). An emerging newer theme is an equality-based argument that critiques paternity law, arguing that men should have equal rights to choose whether to become parents or not, just as women can choose to have or not to have an abortion (Marsiglio 1997). The prime goal of these groups is the elimination of economic obligations based solely on genetic fatherhood. These movements entwine arguments of gender neutrality (to attack gender bias in the system) and gender uniqueness (to argue for fathers as essential).

Summary

In sum, the intersection of fatherhood with masculinity teaches us that reconceptualizing and redefining fatherhood is connected to redefining what it means to be a man. Fatherhood cannot be looked at in isolation, since it is not experienced that way. Whether men become fathers or not, the possibility of that role and life experience affects them as men, just as being men affects the ways in which they father.

Thinking of fatherhood within the broader picture of masculinity emphasizes the cultural perspective of redefining fatherhood. Masculinity is a cultural construct, socially and personally taught and reworked. Cultural change seems least likely a subject, or object, of law. In this sense, rethinking fatherhood exposes the limits of law. If the change needed is cultural, then law cannot mandate it. It must come from below, from an individual and communal desire to reorient fatherhood, implemented by lived changes in men's lives. Arguably much that has shifted in the past few decades concerning fatherhood is traceable to cultural and social shift, rather than to legal change.

At the same time, law can have an impact on culture in several powerful ways. First, because the law reflects cultural constructions, a reoriented sense of fatherhood could be more clearly reflected in the law. The broader masculinity perspective suggests that law reflects an understanding of fatherhood not limited to the usual places; rather, wherever the law constructs a definition of manhood, it may construct an understanding of fatherhood. In addition, the law not only reflects but also determines culture. Particularly when the law takes on the task of not only defining but also educating, it is explicitly used to create or mold culture. If redefining fatherhood is understood as intimately connected to defining masculinity, then law is being used in this way. If the project of redefinition inescapably requires connecting that new image with a holistic, pluralistic concept of manhood, law is one among many mechanisms that could contribute to cultural change, if that cultural change is deemed necessary. Whether justified as civic education, public health education, sex education, or the promotion of family values, law's mandate will be critical to reorienting culture.

The intersection of fatherhood with the broader concept of masculinity brings in sharp relief the role of the state in responding to barriers and limitations to achieving social and communal goals. The connection between fatherhood and masculinity exposes the way current constructions of fatherhood are connected to aspects of masculinity deemed essential to separating men from women, giving men power only by thinking in terms of hierarchy, and defining power as violence. Masculinity is a significant barrier to fathering, at least certain aspects of masculinity as currently constructed. Men are defined by limitation, by fear of being seen as gay or as acting like a girl. Ways of behaving, feeling, and communicating are proscribed by these powerful deterrents. Resistance to nurturing, defined and associated as a womanly trait, prevents the reorientation of fatherhood by raising the flags of homophobia and misogyny. A nurturing model of parenting is a womanly, motherly one. Gender-neutral language of parenting cannot hide that. As long as that is so, the resistance to woman-identified labels and conduct will create the need to claim a distinct father model, biologically based, to prevent the feared taint of female models. The critique of masculinity exposes the need to honor and value a feminine-inspired model, while expanding it with positive aspects of male-identified culture. Reorienting fatherhood is an example of empowerment without hierarchy, by valuing and validating of women-identified roles, conduct, and experience.

Two aspects of traditional masculinity are particularly problematic for fatherhood: homophobia and violence. In the next two sections I examine both in greater detail.

Homophobia

Would nurturing fatherhood be problematic or even precluded because of homophobia? Probably not, if redefining fatherhood recasts fatherhood and manhood in ways that expand the definition of masculinity while maintaining homophobia. The more challenging way, however, is to redefine fatherhood and manhood so that it also destabilizes discrimination against gays and lesbians. Because of the link between sexual orientation discrimination and sex discrimination, this would destabilize discrimination against women as well. It might be said, then, that the cultural barriers include both homophobia and sexism.

Homophobia is fear or hatred of homosexuality and gay and lesbian persons, while heterosexism is denial, denigration, or stigmatization of any nonheterosexual form of behavior, identity, relationship or community (Stein 1996:39; see generally De Cecco and Shively 1985). The term was first coined in the early 1970s. It is a defining characteristic of being a man, that is, it is normative for men (Herek 1993). Kimmel notes the key role of homophobia in controlling men:

> Masculinity defined through homosocial interaction contains many parts, including the camaraderie, fellowship, and intimacy often celebrated in male culture. It also includes homophobia. Homophobia is the fear of other men—that other men will unmask us, emasculate us, reveal to us and the world that we do not measure up, are not real men. . . . The word "faggot" has nothing to do with homosexual experience or even with fears of homosexuals. . . . [I]t comes out of the depths of manhood: a label of ultimate contempt for anyone who seems sissy, untough, uncool. (Kimmel 1996:8, quoting David Leverenz)

Some leading researchers prefer the term heterosexism for the reason that the phenomenon is not a true phobia, and that it deflects attention from systemic, institutional, and cultural beliefs by focusing on individual feelings, reactions, and beliefs (Herek 1996).

The very term homosexuality is a nineteenth-century invention, pathologizing behavior and making it an illness. This has been a powerful mechanism for controlling the rest of society, by devaluing and despising things feminine and denying their legitimacy for men, as well as denying sexual expression to men. It simultaneously limits men and devalues women (Law 1988). Only since the early 1970s has homosexuality been viewed as a "normal" sexual orientation rather than as a psychological disease (Stein 1996).

Violence against gays and lesbians, but especially gay men, is pervasive and serious. This violence shapes the identity and life experience of all gays and lesbians, as well as heterosexuals. It is the visible sign of widespread homophobia, ranging from verbal abuse to serious physical injury or death, and may be done by individuals, groups, and by state authorities, including the police (Berrill 1992; Brenner 1992; Stein 1996). The consequences for homosexuals are depression, vulnerability, denial, and self-blame (Stein 1996), beyond the extensive physical consequences (Berrill 1992) and the experience of threat and stigma (Herek 1991).

The connections between homophobia/heterosexism and misogyny are close: as one study of this phenomenon in secondary schools notes, "[t]he dual Others to normative heterosexual masculinities in schools are girls/women and non-macho boys/men. It is *against* these that many, perhaps most, boys seek to define their identities" (Epstein 1997:113). Homophobia is linked to social pressure to avoid being like a girl, which makes the socialization and culture of boys hostile to fathering. For example, cultural messages and stereotypes cast young men in a role that emphasizes power, assertiveness, and sex for its own sake and without responsibility (Cusick 1989). Girls are trained to be mothers; boys are socialized to "score" (Cusick 1989). One of the most important messages about not acting like a girl, reinforced by homophobia, is that "boys don't cry," which translates into adult male emotional inexpressiveness and/or dangerous fearlessness (Goodey 1997). One researcher refers to this as boys' "emotional illiteracy" (Brody 1985; Goodey 1997:401). But it is felt and experienced quite differently, not as loss but as gain. The "value" of homophobia, if one can call it that, lies in self-righteousness and fear (Goleman 1990). It may be a source of self-esteem, a means to categorize, and may resolve individual conflicts (Davies 1996; Herek 1991 and 1993).

The impact of homophobia on straight men is particularly clear with respect to intimacy with other men. In general, it means a lack of intimacy in male friendships (Devlin and Cowan 1985). The limits of what is acceptable in being a man, grounded in homophobia, have an impact on the sharing of affection and nurture in friendships. Safe relationships with other men reinforce competition, distance, and the stigmatizing of women. While it might have less strong an impact on children, the same consequence is also likely. In addition, the labeling or reinforcement of certain professions as female blocks those employment opportunities for men who fear being labeled as gay. For example, teaching in preschool or elementary school, which demands a caring, nurturing teacher, is seen as incompatible with masculinity (King 1998).

Homophobia constrains fatherhood in several ways. It imposes significant limitations on men through fear of identification or disclosure as homosexual. Particularly constrained is the development of emotional and psychological skills that are strongly connected to nurturing parenting. This affects both parent and child. It also limits or contorts any redefinition of fatherhood as nurture. Nurture may have to be defined in "masculine," read "heterosexual," terms to be permissible. The demonstration of care by engaging in traditional masculine pursuits might be one example of this. Alternatively, the nurturer could balance emotional and psychological nurture with "manly" conduct, such as a sports figure being a tender and loving father while being indisputably strong, aggressive, and conducting himself in a manly way, doing manly things. The development of these skills, then, must be masked or paired with conduct or attitudes that reassure and define the self as heterosexual. Far more radical, of course, would be a challenge to homophobia and heterosexism itself, opening up the limits and boundaries of masculinity. That is, instead of redrawing the boundary, we might eliminate it; we might define masculinity affirmatively, rather than in terms of difference and denigration to others.

Gay and lesbian culture and individual lives have enormous liberation potential, and therefore gay culture is subversive of majority culture (Pronger 1990). "Gay men [offer] a creative alternative to traditional heterosexual lives, and [seek] to find new ways to [be] men, emphasizing community instead of alienation, comradeship instead of isolation, love instead of competition, the struggle against sexism and ageism instead of enslavement to commercialism and the latest fashion" (Segal 1990:148).

The solutions here, as with masculinity in general, are cultural. In addition, vigorous defense of rights, antidiscrimination laws, and legal recognition of gay and lesbian families, including fair treatment of gay and lesbian parents, are essential.

Domestic Violence

Another aspect of masculinity that stands in the way of redefining fatherhood is male violence. Both the conduct and the culture of violence are associated with masculinity, as a definition of manhood. The conduct of violence is directed toward partners and children. The culture of violence is pervasive, societal, but especially male-identified. This sanctioning, even glorifying, of violence is contrary to parenting both in the sense of the way adults relate to, teach, and act toward children, and the way in which they model behavior for their children. Current concepts of masculinity support violence as a symbol or sign of manliness. Ironically, masculinity even arguably makes violence consistent with care. Defense of one's family is deemed one of the highest modes of caring. The most heroic but also the most violent acts are justified by this principle. Discipline of one's children, including verbal abuse and physical punishment, is also viewed by some as consistent with, and even necessary to, nurturing parenting. Both discipline and defense are modes of parenting more strongly associated with fathers than mothers. Where homophobia and misogyny impose limits on men's behavior, the tolerance or even veneration of violence permits and encourages behavior inconsistent with nurture and care.

Although child abuse is notoriously difficult to estimate, the data suggest that between 1 and 10 percent of American children may be victims of physical abuse (Sternberg 1997:291). In 1997, more than 3 million children were identified as abused or neglected; physical abuse was present in 22 percent of the confirmed cases; sexual abuse in 8 percent; neglect in 54 percent; emotional maltreatment in 4 percent, and other maltreatment in 12 percent (National Committee to Prevent Child Abuse 1998:1). The rate of reported victims is 47 children per 1,000 in the population. Eighty percent of the abusers are parents. Biological mothers and fathers are about equally prevalent as abusers (fathers 54 percent, mothers 65 percent), but given the caretaking patterns, the rate of abuse of children by their fathers is sharply higher than that for mothers. In addition, children abused by other parents, parent substitutes, or nonparental persons were far more likely to be hurt by males (80 to 90 percent) than by females (14 to 15 percent) (Sedlak and Broadhurst 1996:17).

Child abuse is inconsistent with the concept of nurture. The ultimate sanction for child abuse is termination of parental rights, alone or in combination with criminal prosecution. Short of that, removal of children to foster care under civil protection proceedings, with the potential for reunification of the family, has been a solution. This solution has varied over time from a policy that maximized the potential for family reunification to the current preference for providing children with quicker placement in a permanent, stable family to prevent long-term foster care (Adoption and Safe Families Act of 1997, 42 U.S.C. § 671). Short of removal, other options are denial of custody and supervised or no visitation so that children can be separated from their abusers, when the parents separate and only one parent is identified as an abuser. The difficulty with such identification is that even the parent who did not participate in the abuse may be deemed guilty of abuse under failure to protect laws (Jacobs 1998). Because the standard for termination of parental rights is high, and because the custody and visitation structure considers abuse as a factor or presumption but rarely as a *per se* basis for denial of custody, and even more rarely for complete denial of visitation, this structure permits, even orders, ongoing relationships between abusers and their children when the circumstances or evidence fall short of the termination standard.

Equally inconsistent with nurture is violence directed at intimate partners. This form of violence is far less addressed, however, in the legal regulation of the parent-child relationship. Domestic violence against partners impacts on fatherhood in two ways. Fathers' abuse of their intimate partners affects both the father-child relationship and children's development. In addition, fathers' domestic violence affects their relationships with the mothers of their children, or those who act as mothers to their children or to other children that they parent. Because fatherhood as practiced is so strongly connected to fathers' relationships with mothers, the presence of domestic violence cannot be segregated from men's parental role. *The practice of nurture at the core of a redefined fatherhood requires not only particular conduct toward children, but also a healthy, violence-free relationship with other caretakers.*

Domestic violence is a serious and pervasive problem (ABA Commission on Domestic Violence 1998). Even if defined only as serious physical violence, the most conservative estimates place the number of incidents per year at 1 million; other estimates are as high as 4 million incidents per year. According to one estimate, 39,000 Americans were killed fighting in Vietnam between 1967 and 1973; during the same six years, 17,500 American women and children were killed by family members (Quirion et al. 1997:505). One in three adult women experience at least one physical assault from a partner during adulthood.

The incidence of domestic violence crosses ethnic, racial, age, national origin, sexual orientation, religious, and socioeconomic lines. Nevertheless, a disproportionate number of separated or divorced women have been both victims of domestic violence and welfare recipients (ABA Commission on Domestic Violence 1998; Quirion et al. 1997). Similarly, a disproportionate number of those on welfare have been victims of domestic violence: studies show that more than half of women receiving benefits are or have been battered (J. Meier 1997: 205). Younger women are more likely to report domestic violence, which means the likelihood of children being present is greater. While domestic violence is not limited to men, it is overwhelmingly a male behavior: 95 percent of the perpetrators of domestic violence are male (ABA Commission on Domestic Violence 1998:2). Furthermore, the behavior tends to reflect a pattern rather than one-time behavior. One of the more common behaviors is that the seriousness of the violence escalates when women leave, so that a significant amount of domestic violence occurs when the batterer and the victim no longer share the same household. The ongoing connection between batterers and their victims is often through their children.

> Children are strongly affected by domestic violence in their homes. Repeated trauma in adult life erodes the structure of the personality already formed, but repeated trauma in childhoodforms and deforms the personality. The child trapped in an abusive environment is faced with formidable tasks of adaptation. She must find a way to preserve a sense of trust in people who are untrustworthy, safety in a situation that is unsafe, control in a situation that is terrifyingly unpredictable, power in a situation of helplessness. (Quirion et al. 1997:508)

More than 3 million children are exposed to domestic violence annually (ABA Commission on Domestic Violence 1998:5). The likelihood that the children will be abused as well increases astronomically in these situations: their risk of abuse is fifteen hundred times greater than that of the average population. Between 40 and 60 percent of men who abuse women also abuse children.

Little or no research has been conducted on the fathering of men who batter their partners (Sternberg 1997). Considerable research, however, has been conducted on the impact of domestic violence on children who witness it or who are aware of it. The consensus of researchers who have studied such children is that it has a significant detrimental impact on them (Cahn 1991; Quirion et al. 1997). Children witness abuse 87 percent of the time, and nearly all are aware of domestic violence that occurs in their home (Quirion et al. 1997: 508). Children suffer emotional and behavioral problems including withdrawal, low self-esteem, nightmares, self-blame, and aggression against others. Witnessing violence, according to the available research, has implications for children in the behavioral, emotional, social, cognitive, and physical realms (Kolbo, Blakely, and Engleman 1996). The reaction of children varies by age, stage of development, and gender. Witnessing domestic violence triggers both short-term and long-term effects (Jaffe and Geffner 1998). Delinquent children frequently have family violence or abuse in their family history.

Children also suffer from the impact of violence on their mother's parenting, especially when it occurs when the children are young. This is the same developmental period when trust, reciprocity, consistency, and child-centered nurture have the strongest and most lifelong effect on their development (Quirion et al. 1997:513). And tragically, sons learn domestic violence from their fathers: boys who witness domestic violence are three times more likely to abuse their own partners, and the sons of the most violent fathers are a thousand times more likely to beat their own partners (Cook 1997). Ongoing contact with batterers perpetuates the cycle of violence, passing it on to the next generation.

Despite this clear evidence of the harmful and ongoing consequences of domestic violence on children, many fathers have ongoing relationships with their children even after the mothers or caretakers have left the household of the batterer. In addition, abuse of partners is generally not considered relevant evidence nor an independent ground for terminating parental rights (Haddix 1996). One researcher has found that children's relationships with their fathers was the single most problematic and difficult aspect of their adjustment in the aftermath of violence (Edleson 1996). Nevertheless, little has been written on the relationship between children and the fathers whom the children have witnessed abusing their mothers (Edleson 1996).

Ironically these children are far more likely to be in the custody of their fathers. Fathers who batter mothers are twice as likely to seek sole physical custody of their children (ABA Commission on Domestic Violence 1998). Custody litigation is frequently threatened or used as a power play by batterers (Quirion et al. 1997:514). And the presence of domestic violence does not bar them from custody or visitation. The realities of fatherhood and domestic violence only become more and more paradoxical in the treatment of this issue under custody and visitation laws, and in conjunction with the treatment of mothers under failure to protect laws. Although children are often the reason that battered women leave their batterers, courts frequently treat claims of domestic violence as manufactured for leverage at divorce (Jaffe and Geffner 1998). Neither custody nor visitation is prohibited; to the contrary, courts routinely support ongoing relationships between fathers and their children under the expressed policy of custody statutes that support the ongoing relationship of the child with both parents (Cahn 1991). Furthermore, courts seem to take the view that the violence directed against the mother in the past (and even in the present) does not affect the father-child relationship. With the physical separation of the batterer and the victim, courts are even less inclined to view violence between adults as impacting the relationship between adults and children (Cahn 1991).

States have taken three basic approaches to the issue of domestic violence and custody. First, some states require that domestic violence must be considered before joint custody can be awarded; second, some state statutes include domestic violence as a factor to be considered in applying the "best interest" standard when determining the primary or sole custodian; and third, some states direct that domestic violence should be taken into account in making certain legal determinations, such as whether a mother has abandoned her children if she can show that her "abandonment" was a "flight from violence" instead. Although most states have an explicit consideration of domestic violence in their custody statutes, virtually all could consider it under the "best interests" standard as there is considerable range in the weight given to domestic violence in custody statutes (Cahn 1991; Kurtz 1997; Stark 1995). Some states permit denial of custody or visitation, but very few mandate denial of visitation, even in the worst instances of abuse. The 1994 Model Code on Domestic and Family Violence of the National Council of Juvenile and Family Court Judges provides for a presumption against custody, but not a bar (Quirion et al. 1997). The presumption is rebuttable but requires fact-finding and evidence of sufficient weight to rebut it. In the vast majority of cases, domestic violence is either deemed irrelevant or is not taken seriously in custody decisions, and it is uncommon to deny visitation or to require supervised visitation (Cahn 1991; Stark 1995).

> A lack of information about family violence and the danger it poses to adult and child victims has led the courts to consider the abuse of wives or mothers by male partners as largely irrelevant to custody deliberations and awards, concluding either that men who are violent toward their partners may, nonetheless, be very good fathers or that domestic violence has little effect on the children or that even if the father was violent during cohabitation, he will cease beating and terrorizing the mother upon separation. (Quirion et al. 1997:502)

At the same time, states frequently treat mothers quite differently in the domestic violence scenario. If domestic violence is reported by a mother, her children may be removed from the home; if children are directly abused, the mother's inability to protect the children may be criminally prosecuted as "failure to protect" them (Miccio 1995; Rabin 1995; Stark 1995). As Michelle Jacobs points out, the standard of parenting to which mothers are held and the rate of prosecution in failure to protect and abuse proceedings are dramatically different for mothers and fathers (Jacobs 1998). Furthermore, child abuse is treated separately from domestic violence, both conceptually and legally (Sternberg 1997). The ultimate sanction for abuse is termination of parental rights. The relation between termination and removal into foster care has varied over the years but currently favors quicker dispositions over family reunification, although foster care "drift" remains a significant issue. Short of termination, where evidence of abuse exists custody and visitation are limited or denied.

Masculinity norms and socialization are linked to domestic violence, although they are by no means the sole cause of domestic violence (O'Toole and Schiffman 1997). The current thinking on causes is that no one single theory or cause can explain domestic violence, but that the combination and interaction of theories is the most useful approach. Thus, researchers combine biological, psychological, and sociological approaches into a "biopsychosocial" model, while other researchers combine complex causative factors including class, income, age, and unemployment with the feminist theories that point to the critical role of patriarchy, male dominance, and gender roles (McKenry, Julian, and Gavazzi 1995). All these theories and models, however, recognize that the honoring of violence within masculinity norms, along with the connection of masculinity to dominance over women, links two aspects of masculinity to the strongly gendered pattern of domestic violence. Furthermore, some researchers also report that the presence of domestic violence is connected to departures from traditional gender roles: that is, when men are unable to be economic providers, or perceive themselves as less powerful when their partner takes on a nontraditional economic or social role, they may respond by asserting their power by means of emotional, psychological, or physical violence (Anderson 1997).

The legal response to domestic violence has focused primarily on the victims, not on the batterers. It separates the relationship of adult partners from the children they share, separates child abuse from partner abuse, and distinguishes the witnessing of abuse from direct victimization. The treatment of batterers has been largely inadequate (Tolman 1996).

What impact does this have on redefining fatherhood? First and foremost, the presence of domestic violence (both partner abuse and child abuse) as part of the context of fatherhood means that any empowering of fathers can be dangerous for children and for women. Thus, we must reject any construction of fatherhood as an independent relationship unconnected to men's relationships with children's mothers, or children's reactions or consequences as a result of those relationships. Redefining fatherhood must rest on the premise and protection of a violence-free relationship between fathers and mothers, and fathers and their children. Unless and until domestic violence becomes a rarity, we should not construct fatherhood as an independent relationship of men with their children; rather, we must recognize fathers' relationships with other caretakers and the importance of those relations being healthy ones for the benefit of their children.

Second, given the impact of domestic violence on children, existing law should move in the direction of barring custody, and limiting or barring visitation. Partner abuse should also be relevant evidence and an independent basis for termination of parental rights. The evidence is consistent and powerful that witnessing domestic violence is harmful to children, and that the harm is long lasting. The evidence is also clear that courts ignore the consequences of domestic violence when making custody and visitation decisions. This is an area that cries out for nondiscretionary rules to correct this judicial bias, and to insure that parenting is understood to exclude violence against both one's children and the caretakers of one's children. Of all the ambiguous and difficult decisions to make regarding the redefinition of fatherhood, this one stands out as a clear limitation. Either custody and visitation should per se or presumptively be barred, or termination should be more vigorously used and include all forms of domestic violence that adversely impact children.

Some further considerations ought to be taken into account. First, domestic violence must be carefully defined to include all forms of violence that are harmful to children. The focus must be on the significant harm to children rather than conviction on a criminal charge. Second, there must be provision in the law to insure that a rule barring custody and allowing only supervised visitation or even barring visitation is not misused. Finally, there must be provision for modification in the event that a treatment program is successfully completed and there is no recidivism, and if there is evidence that reestablishment of a parent-child relationship, or an expanded relationship, would best serve the child.

Beyond a reform of custody and visitation law, a proactive strategy requires the recognition of violence as a cultural issue which in turn requires an affirmative approach to teach and adopt principles of nonviolence, especially within the context of masculinity. The larger connection between fatherhood and masculinity, as well as the specific issue of domestic violence, requires a cultural strategy to reorient and reeducate fathers. The strategy must be gender specific, gender conscious, and gender relevant. The state should act as a moral agent and as a public health agent in addressing these issues. This reorientation in culture should be as pluralistic in conception and method as possible, but its clear goal should be the reduction of gender violence.

How would this be done? I will address this issue in more detail in the chapter that follows, but AIDs education, sexual harassment training, and gender-equity programs developed at all levels of education and in sports, all suggest means of reorienting culture and social practices. Reducing gender violence includes thinking this comprehensively, reaching boys as early as preschool as well as fathers at divorce, teaching the skills of nurture and peaceful problem solving while directing their energy and aggression into positive outlets. The approach must be sensitive to existing gender differences, akin to the gender-specific, even gender-segregated, approach taken under Title IX. One author calls this a "gender-relevant" approach:

> Gender-relevant programs involve both boys and girls, and attempt to thematize, that is, bring to light for examination and discussion, the gender dimension in social life and education. . . . The gender-relevant logic is not the same as gender-neutrality, that is simply attempting to avoid gender distinction. Quite the contrary: Gender-relevant programs name and address gender. A much more interesting, gender-inclusive, pedagogy becomes possible, as pupils have the opportunity to see the world from standpoints they normally regard as Other. . . . [T]his process is critical in sex education, and [is called] "learning to be the opposite sex." (Connell 1996)

We do not leave women out of the equation, or assume they have no role in either the problems or the solutions. To the contrary, thinking in interconnected terms is essential both here and with respect to other aspects of the reformulation of fatherhood. It is to the intersections and necessary connections between fatherhood and motherhood that I now turn.

FATHERHOOD AND MOTHERHOOD

The second gender intersection that challenges the redefinition of fatherhood is the relationship between fatherhood and motherhood. It is essential that fatherhood not be viewed in isolation. Much of what we know about fatherhood indicates that it is strongly mediated by motherhood. Men's relationships with children are strongly affected by the nature of their relationship with their children's mother. Fathering happens in connection with relationships to other caregivers; fatherhood must be reworked by looking at that larger picture.

A movement away from status (biological or marital) and an emphasis on social fathering means that fatherhood must be practiced in a shared power model with other parents, including other men. This would also address some of the power issues raised by domestic violence. The relational requirement means that we do not envision fatherhood as a status apart, but one that exists in relation to children and other caretakers, and so puts the burden of creating and maintaining that relationship on the caretakers (not solely on the mothers).

Men's involvement as fathers is also strongly connected to women's employment. Thus, on both the family and work sides, fathers are connected to mothers and the work-family patterns of each are strongly interrelated. The larger patterns of men and women's work-family relationships are tied to structural constraints that strongly affect parents on the basis of gender, race, and class. Integral to fatherhood, then, is a redefinition that does not denigrate motherhood or women, but rather supports mothers and women's equality. That cannot be done without men addressing patriarchy, or it will yet again be reconstituted, but only with a new emphasis on fatherhood as nurture.

Relational Issues: Coparenting

Fatherhood is currently strongly connected to, and practiced in relation to, motherhood. The ideology of masculinity and in particular the oppositional use of women and homosexuals to define manhood reflects the negative cast to the mother-father relationship. Fatherhood has been strongly gendered, defined as different and separate, unique and essential. Fatherhood has also been seen as complementary to motherhood, making them a connected whole. In its most negative sense the connection between the two is seen in domestic violence, with children used as a means of control to prevent women from leaving their batterers. In its most positive sense the connection was traditionally one between the complementary housewife and breadwinner roles. Contemporary notions of gender equality and gender neutrality suggest a vision of fatherhood and motherhood that is sharply different from this older expressly gendered norm. The new vision is one of degendered "parenthood" that men and women are equally capable of performing and sharing coequally. However, competing visions suggest that gender difference remains alive and well in notions of the uniqueness of fathers to families. Yet, fathers are seen as connected to mothers, rather than as separate, independent actors in relation to children.

Within the context of fatherhood as *practiced*, however, fatherhood and motherhood connections are very dissimilar. While fathers and mothers are strongly connected to each other, the nature of the connection is not grounded in the same experience. Looking at the connection from the mother's perspective, it is most often a connection of backup support for her primary parenting. Whether economic or nurturing support (directly to her or to the children), or both, the connection provides critical support for caretaking and nurture to take place. This is what Martha Fineman has called women's derivative dependency, derived from the dependency of children and the caretaker's need to be cared for in order to provide that care (Fineman 1995).

Looking at the connection from the father's perspective, however, mothers are the gatekeepers or facilitators to men's relationships with their children. The extent of men's nurture is strongly connected to mothers and households. Those who father serially show this most clearly: they successively parent the children present in the households they share with the women with whom they have intimate relationships. The connections and disconnections between nonmarital and divorced fathers and their children also demonstrate the nature of the father-mother connection. It is perhaps most evident, however, in the patterns of dual wage earners who share a household but often do not share the care of children or housework.

A break in the connection between father and mother due to separation or divorce typically has different consequences for women and men. When fathers maintain a connection with their children, they are far more likely to do so either when they share their household with a female intimate partner or when they have established a cooperative relationship with their former partner. Many fathers, however, lose their connections with their children when they are unable to maintain or establish a good relationship with their former spouse or the partner they never married. Men reconnect with children through another woman. On the other hand, mothers may lose economic resources but can fill the backup nurturing role with a support network without requiring a connection with another man.

The critical mediating function of women for fathers can also act as a block to men's nurture. Several studies have noted that men learned to nurture their children more quickly and competently when they were forced into situations where they had to parent alone (Dowd 1997a; Gerson 1993). Where men and women physically coparented, fathers were more likely to cede control to mothers, and mothers were more likely to assert a dominant role. That this happens is not surprising both in terms of socialization differences regarding parenting, and general differences in masculinity and femininity that more strongly support nurturing skills for women than men. In addition, the devaluing of women elsewhere may make them reluctant to cede their power in the family (Cahn 1999).

The connections between fathers and mothers are important. Parenting is rarely done in isolation. But given the dominant-subordinate pattern of existing fatherhood-motherhood connections, that pattern must be kept in mind not only in order to value and support these connections, but also to change and improve them. Clearly any change or improvement is related to whether we mean to adopt a single-parent or dual-parent model for fatherhood. A single-parent model might leave the nature of the connections the same, but simply seek to change the person who holds each role long enough to remove the gender association of the dominant position with mothers, and the backup position with fathers. On the other hand, if the model is dual equal parenthood, then the connection to be supported is one of mutuality and similarity. The relational connections also extend beyond mothers in those instances where there are multiple parents.

It is essential that the connections between fathers and mothers, and other caretakers, be nonviolent; that the nature of the connection not be skewed because of sex; and that issues of power and dominance be addressed, since they were presumed by traditional models and continue to exist in much of our practice. Much of the discourse that has raised this issue has been adversarial rather than connecting. Fathers' rights groups have pushed relational issues not to repair their relationships with mothers, but to ignore them and override mothers' relationships by protecting their "right" to connect with their children. Some fathers have pushed for the right to prevent mothers from perceived prevention of visitation or alleged brainwashing of children to turn them against their fathers, or to control financial support. But as Karen Czapanskiy has shown, there has been no corresponding mandate to maintain fathers' relationship with their children by enforcing visitation (Czapanskiy 1991).

Embedded in the relational issue is the question of how we conceive parents: whether we want to do so in terms of rights or in a different way. Elizabeth Scott has argued that rights are still a useful way of conceptualizing parents, the main goal being to encourage adults to make sacrifices for the well-being of their children (Scott 1994; Scott and Scott 1995). Barbara Woodhouse, on the other hand, focuses on social, experiential parenting in support of "generist" parenting, which sees parenthood in terms of fiduciary obligations to provide nurture (Woodhouse 1994). But the relational question of the interaction between fathers and mothers is perhaps most clearly brought into view by the work of Martha Fineman (Fineman 1995). Fineman is concerned not only with the question of nurture that Scott and Woodhouse focus on, but also with the relationship of the nurturer to other caretakers. Fineman largely presumes the existing pattern of primary and secondary caretaking (although she does not preclude coequal caretaking), and would center family law around primary caretaking. She challenges the conceptualization of family in terms that focus on the adult sexual pair, which she calls the concept of the sexual family, and which privileges the intimate bond between husband and wife, and historically, the power of the head of the household, presumed to be the father (Fineman 1995). She argues for recasting family law to focus on and support the nurturing parent-child relationship, which she calls the Mother-Child dyad. Relationships between the dyad and others would be negotiated and contracted rather than existing as a matter of status or rights. Her conceptualization is not gender-specific; rather, it seeks to value and name caretaking work for those who have done that work most often, namely, mothers:

> I have deliberately (even defiantly) chosen not to make my alternative vision gender neutral. . . . Historically, and in terms of its cultural cachet, mothering is a gendered concept and, partly for that reason, is qualitatively different from terms currently (incorrectly) substituted for it such as caretaker. . . . Motherhood has unrealized power—the power to redefine our concept of the family, which may be why men have tried for so long to control its meaning. . . . I believe men can and should be Mothers. In fact, if men are interested in acquiring legal rights of access to children (or other dependents), I argue they *must* be Mothers in the stereotypical nurturing sense of that term—that is, engaged in caretaking. (Fineman 1995:234–35)

Bottom line, what is critical is that fatherhood must not be defined in isolation from motherhood; the connections between fathers and mothers, and/or fathers and other caretakers, must be attended to as they are critical to the successful practice of any redefined fatherhood, and integral to the very notion of parenthood. The relational aspect of fatherhood also raises the question of whether we perpetuate the very different experience of this connection for most women and most men, and the implicit difference between women's linear and primary parenting role, and men's serial and secondary parenting role.

Structural Issues: Work and Family

The second level at which fatherhood and motherhood intersect is the connection between work and family, and the skewed patterns of fatherhood and motherhood. The subordinate position of fathers and the prevention of fathers' nurture by virtue of existing work and family structures poses a serious challenge to the redefinition of fatherhood. If relational issues operate at an individual level (although affected by dominant gender-role socialization and culture), work and family issues operate on an institutional, structural level that severely limits the reorientation of fatherhood and its relation to motherhood. Because existing work and family structures privilege men with respect to work and because wage work is more highly valued than parenting, the harm to fathering has been hidden. The assumption is often made that men could make different choices and father more. To some extent that may be true. But fathers are significantly constrained in their choices by the economic realities produced by this skewed structure. Those economic realities perfectly fit the cultural message that above all fatherhood means being a good provider.

The structure of the workplace is very hostile to parenting of any sort. The conflicts between wage work and family operate on multiple levels. First, conflicts of time constrain any wage earner from parenting. Due to the number of hours committed to work and the scheduling of work, there is not enough time for both family and full-time wage work. Mothers disproportionately carry the stress of the time conflict, since they continue to do a disproportionate share of family work. Fathers' increased share of family work, however, increases their conflict, and a truly equitable allocation of family work would merely distribute the conflict equally rather than resolve the problem (Dowd 1989a).

A second time problem is inflexibility, which causes conflicts between school schedules and work schedules, makes it difficult to respond to emergencies, and magnifies problems when attending non-emergency, but no less important, events. School vacations, summer breaks, and after-school time also create significant challenges for full-time working parents, as do unexpected, unscheduled school closings.

A more fundamental, long-term time problem is the clash between family life cycles and occupational opportunity structures. Work demands are greatest and the stakes highest at the earlier stages of one's work life, although the opportunity structure plateaus earlier in blue-collar than in white-collar occupations. During the same period, family demands are also at their peak due to marriage, childbearing, and for some, due to partnering transitions. Again, the consequences are disproportionately borne by women. Although women's work patterns are converging with male work patterns, women still spend more time away from work, do more part-time work, and make more occupational choices that accommodate family responsibilities. Fathers continue to have a higher work-force participation rate, more frequently work full-time and more frequently work longer hours and overtime. Fathers also do significantly different work than mothers do. Job segregation between and within occupations continues to be extremely pronounced, and the gender maldistribution coupled with the asymmetrical parenting patterns of fathers and mothers reinforce work and family presumptions in male-identified work that severely undermine the worker's ability to nurture children (Dowd 1989a and 1997a). If men have children, their linear, uninterrupted, upward progression at work and the kinds of work they do requires a family worker who does a disproportionate share of the family work, and allows for fathers' separation from the family in order to be what Joan Williams calls the "ideal worker" (Williams 1999).

The choices presented by the wage work structure, then, are the devalued, underpaid patterns of women's work, identified as the paths consistent with nurture, or the valued, demanding, higher paid patterns of men's work, modeled on a breadwinner supported by a flow of family work, but disconnected from the nurture of his children. Joan Williams argues that since women do not benefit from a similar flow of family work, they are significantly disadvantaged by the existing structure (Williams 1999). Both fathers and mothers are faced with the conflict between nurture and work; fathers, disproportionately, resolve that conflict against nurture.

That fathers resolve work and family conflict differently than mothers is partly tied to relative burdens, but also reflects different ideal roles and gendered paradigms of the work-family relationship. It is also connected to conflicts between the role of parent and ideal worker, the values associated with each role, and the assumption by the workplace that the roles are in conflict. For men, work is definitional, family support is expected, and becoming a parent reinforces those assumptions with the perpetuation of the breadwinner paradigm. Work requires the sacrifice of family, by clearly communicating in workplace culture that work comes first, family second. Men's assumption of greater family responsibilities is not valued or supported; rather, it is often viewed as demeaning or, at the least, a barrier to ultimate workplace success. The pervasive stereotyping of women as mothers or potential mothers and therefore as less than ideal workers since they presumably will put family first, has its mirror in the assumption that fathers will rededicate themselves to work in order to be good providers, and that families will support their sacrifice of family time and presence for economic gain. In addition, the value structures of worker and parent are presumed to be in opposition: family and parenting are associated with love, connection, and caregiving, in contrast to the competitive, hierarchical workplace role of employees where the assumed motivators are fear and greed. The presumed difference in characteristics is also reflected in the low valuing of caring work in the wage workplace.

Fathers' experiences of work-family conflict push strongly against nurture. The sources of the conflict are structural and cultural. The strongest factor in maintaining this pattern is economic. Men's incomes, although falling, remain primary in most families; at the same time, dual incomes are more essential to family success. The differential in opportunity structures for men and women plus the income factors thus perpetuate men's secondary, nonnurturing parenting. Because a single salary is insufficient for many families, and because part-time work is underpaid and normally without benefits, the option of taking reduced work hours with no significant loss of opportunity is less available for fathers than for mothers. Where a single salary is sufficient to support a family allowing one parent to be at home, that single salary is far more likely to be the man's salary. Thus family triggers a stronger male tie to work and fewer options. Full-time work by both parents provides the least family time. Differential gender opportunity throughout the economic structure significantly constrains fathers.

It should be noted, however, that the constraints are cultural as well. Many women work full-time, many do so in "men's" work, and many do not significantly reduce their family responsibilities. They do less housework, but do not significantly reduce child care. In many households with two full-time, dual wage earners, family responsibilities have not been equally shared. When men take on an equal share of family work, it is not normally because of equal time demands, but rather because mothers have equal or greater incomes and equal or greater career opportunities. This suggests that although the skewed occupational patterns are a major constraint, they are exacerbated by cultural and social issues that undermine shared family work. One of those issues is the undervaluing of nurture and family because it is female identified; another is that achieving equality for fathers requires not only taking on woman-identified roles and work, but also giving up masculine privilege.

The ongoing valuing and support of work, and the defining of manhood and fatherhood by work, severely undermines equality goals. Family is socially defined as secondary, in opposition to the worker role. From the moment parenthood begins, nurture is either discouraged or unsupported by the structure of the workplace. This happens in a variety of ways. The ideal employee is the economic parent and the ideal relationship between work and family is seen as separation (Dowd 1989a). Work hours and schedules best reflect this. Occupational opportunity structures also reflect this, and then construct the family-driven conduct of employees as *choice*. The benefit and tax structures also support the primary worker, not the primary or co-equal parent.

Public policy has done little to change the structure of work, despite much rhetoric about "family values" (Dowd 1993). The major piece of workplace legislation supporting families, the Family and Medical Leave Act of 1991, is extremely time limited, provides unpaid leave, and fails to cover the full workforce (Dowd 1989a and Dowd 1993). Very few fathers have taken leave (Selmi 1999). This is not surprising, considering the strong economic disincentives to do so and the ongoing workplace cultural disincentives. Welfare "reform," the other recent piece of family legislation, requires wage work as a norm and fails to guarantee even adequate child care, much less any other adjustments that would support mostly single parents in dealing with the more difficult work-family conflicts faced by low-income workers. Finally, child care support, while increasing, continues to be far less than universally available, much less available at some guaranteed level of quality.

Every policy measure that limits the opportunities of women to do wage work limits the fathering opportunities of men. Every effort to increase men's involvment in nurturing children will flounder on the economic realities of wage work unless we consider both a serious restructuring of the workplace and support for greater nurturing roles at home. The intersection of fatherhood and motherhood thus requires serious attention to economic policies, but also to cultural and social policies supportive of nurturing fatherhood instead of economic fatherhood.

In reorienting policy, it is also critical that the class and race implications for all fathers be taken into account. Class influences the ability to achieve or change roles, and to deal with the conflicts work and family currently create. At the most fundamental level, class means sheer survival. A significant proportion of poor households are the working poor (Dowd 1990). The rising poverty rate of children is linked to the inability to make a living wage and the disproportionate growth of low-wage jobs. Mothers are disproportionately linked to poverty issues due to the gender patterns of income. Any reorientation of policy to permit more nurturing fatherhood must insure economic sufficiency for all children; nurturing parenting should not be limited to those above the poverty line. Furthermore, any restructuring must include the structural difference between low- and high-income jobs, and value the families and communities of low-income people. One of the ironies of the class configuration of work-family patterns is that blue-collar men do more child care than higher-income men (Cohen 1998). Split care is an economic strategy that works above poverty-level income, but drops off at higher incomes levels. This bespeaks the powerful impact of the provider role, masculine norms, and the role of economic policy in redefining fatherhood.

Class issues are issues of race as well, because of the skewed racial distribution of income. Economic issues are clearly a priority for Black fathers and other fathers of color. Arguably Black fathers ought to be at the center of the redefinition of family, in order to deal with the core economic challenges to redefining fatherhood as nurture, as well as to learn from models of nurture in the Black community. Extended family structure, broad kinship networks, and community support provide a positive model for fathers and families, even as the difficulty of raising children in a racist society calls upon other fathers to understand the race and gender teachings of their parenting. By focusing on Black fathers, in addition to supporting and appreciating the diversity of fathers, we confront the existing reality that patriarchy weakens only for a racial price, and we are challenged to achieve fatherhood neither grounded in patriarchy nor privileging any group of fathers (Dowd 1990).

CHAPTER 11

Redefined Fatherhood

My redefinition of fatherhood centers around nurture. It moves away from the marital model of traditional fatherhood and the bioeconomic model of recent legal reforms toward affirmative means to support men's nurture of children and their connections with mothers and other caretakers. The means to achieve this are closely tied to the definition of nurture and how we imagine fatherhood in relation to motherhood. The change will be radical if we implement it wholly. If men are to significantly nurture children during their lives in a way that does not diminish or devalue mothers and motherhood, then we are contemplating serious change. It is serious and radical because it cannot be achieved without confronting two critical issues. First, we have to insure the economic support of children and those who care for them. Second, we must implement true egalitarian, cooperative, mutual support models of parenting. Accomplishing these two goals for *all* children, not just privileged children, is an enormous task. Furthermore, what must be given up is difficult to surrender. What must be given up is patriarchal and racial power by those who have benefited from it, even if unconsciously.

In this chapter, I suggest some policy implications of redefining fatherhood as social fatherhood in view of the challenges to men's nurture of children. First I focus on eliminating aspects of the existing system that support patriarchal fatherhood, epitomized by the system of distinguishing between legitimate and illegitimate children, and linking the payment of money to entitlement to a social relationship. I then propose an affirmative restructuring that would support nurturing, social fatherhood. Policy efforts are needed in the economic, cultural, and educational arenas. I explore both an expansive and a more limited set of policy goals. Either we can envision radical change that opens the door to male nurture of children as a societal norm, or we can imagine something more limited that might support only those already committed to, or open to, this concept of fatherhood.

The policy recommendations presume the definition of nurture outlined in chapter 9. Nurture encompasses both quantitative and qualitative characteristics, practiced cooperatively with other caretakers. Social fatherhood is defined as the practice of nurture, either alone or in combination with other caretakers, as the sole or primary parent, or contributing as closely as possible to an equal amount of caregiving in partnership with the other primary parent or parents. It is nonexclusive, cooperative parenting.

Economic policy is foremost and will drive much of what we do, because it releases the time and room for nurture. Without significant economic support of families and the reorientation of workplace structures, nurture is difficult if not impossible for most men. Economic pressure and ongoing sex discrimination against women contribute to the perpetuation of breadwinner fatherhood. Limited or no economic support means class-limited fatherhood. Just as important as economic policy, however, is cultural policy. Cultural policy designed to support a reoriented fatherhood role, or roles, is essential and arguably more difficult to implement. It is difficult not because we may fear the state's advocacy of a particular definition of fatherhood—the state does that already by supporting "responsible" fatherhood (Knitzer et al. 1997). Rather, the difficulty lies in the ability to challenge entrenched concepts of masculinity.

An important caveat is that although the policy recommendations that I propose are frequently gender specific, in ends or means, they do not reflect an essentialist view of men or ignore the needs of women. In some instances, the policies recommended here would equally apply to women. For example, a commitment to the economic support of children would address women's impoverishment as mothers. In other instances, however, the needs of women and men are different. Indeed one might argue that women's needs should be addressed first, that by meeting their needs we would best open the space for men to nurture. For example, eliminating employment discrimination and increasing benefits for part-time work would support women's wage work, which is demonstrably tied to more nurture of children by men. For the moment, however, I speak solely to fathers, in order to more clearly expose their needs, but not to claim priority for their needs. We ought not to create a hierarchy, but rather should constantly and persistently keep the needs of both women and men in view, since they are connected in the goal of nurturing children. We must constantly keep asking the woman question as we focus on men. If we focus on the benefits to children, perhaps we will stop becoming entangled in false dichotomies between adults.

DISMANTLING PATRIARCHAL FATHERHOOD

Under a model focused on nurture, the support of older models must be eliminated. One critical step is the elimination of the distinction between marital and nonmarital children, completing the journey away from common law conceptions of fatherhood. Second, in conjunction with that step, we should eliminate the status of illegitimacy and view all children as legitimate and valued. We should seek the universal establishment of paternity, for purposes of identity and medical information. Third, to the extent that we retain adults "private economic obligations to children, those support obligations should not trigger social entitlement. This does not require dismantling a legal coupling of the two, but should reinforce the policy judgment that money is not a determinant of social relationship with any child. Fourth, we must make a concerted effort to track down and eliminate bias in the family law system, being careful to examine the bias claims of both fathers and mothers, and to determine whether there are intersections between them. Finally, we should vigorously enforce and affirmatively support women's equality in the workplace under existing antidiscrimination laws, as a critical indirect means to promote more nurture by men.

Eliminating distinctions between marital and nonmarital children, eliminating the concept of legitimacy and illegitimacy as we know it, and universally establishing paternity are all instrumental in dismantling the concept of fatherhood as defined by marriage. By so doing we follow the principle of the constitutional cases on illegitimacy to their logical conclusion, that is, no sufficient policy reason exists to stigmatize and punish children for the conduct of adults.

Legitimacy is a patriarchal concept that has no place in a legal system devoted to equality. Children should not have to live with labels imposed on them by the conduct of the adults who brought them into the world, nor be controlled solely by the decision of their fathers to acknowledge them or not. Such status discrimination has no rational basis. If we want to retain the concept of legitimacy, we should reform it to be the status all children acquire at birth. All children should be viewed as "legitimate." Moreover, fathers do not benefit from this distinction, other than to avoid responsibility for the support of their children and protection against claims by mothers. The expansion of obligations for child support by unmarried fathers has largely erased the distinction, along with changes in social attitudes that no longer condemn cohabitation. Eliminating the privileged position of marriage with respect to fatherhood eliminates children as the victims or targets for promoting marriage. If parenting within marriage is good because it promotes commitment and nurturing, then married fathers should easily satisfy a social fathering standard. The strong connection of fathers to households suggests that marital commitment and sharing a household are concurrent with nurturing, and that such fathers would satisfy the social fathering standard.

A logical progression from eliminating the concept of legitimacy is eliminating any special significance of marriage to determining fatherhood. Thus, any form of marital presumption like the one at issue in *Michael H. v. Gerald D.* (1989) would be inappropriate as a basis for blocking the establishment of biological identity and/or the existence of a social father. The status of a biological father, then, would be evaluated in terms of the social fathering standard and the best interests of the child. The best interests standard would not presume to favor the exclusivity of a relationship to the marital father.

If marriage no longer triggers fatherhood status, neither would biology. The purpose of establishing paternity would be to establish biological identity and insure access to essential medical information for the benefit of the child. It would not give the adult a right to establish a social relationship with the child. That determination, consistent with the definition of social fathering, would depend on the intent and conduct of the biological father, including his relationship with the mother. In the context of adoption, this would place the father in much the same position as he is in today under the "biology plus" requirement of the unwed father cases that have reached the Supreme Court. Under a social fathering standard, the "plus" would be elevated to a standard of nurture that demands more than the Court's current doctrine, which currently permits a relatively minimal showing to satisfy its requirement. On the other hand, paternity may trigger economic responsibility, depending on the structure of public economic support available to children.

The separation of economic responsibility and social connection should not be limited to unwed fathers, or to fathers no longer sharing the same household with children. Rather, it should be recognized for all fathers. Economic support is critically important to children, but it does not constitute nurture as I have defined it here. Economic support, whether private, public, or some combination of the two, is an obligation owed to children. Nurture, on the other hand, is social care and a relationship that cannot be bought. It must be practiced, and when practiced, strongly supported. This principle is recognized in theory in many custody statutes, by virtue of the proposition that visitation may not be denied on the basis of nonpayment of child support. The countervailing proposition, that payment of child support entitles one to visitation or that the denial of visitation entitles one to cease payment of support, is, however, a widespread assumption shared by fathers. Some use this assumption as the basis for policy proposals in light of studies that show that there is a connection between the two (that is, that fathers who maintain a relationship with their children pay their child support more consistently than those who diminish or lose contact with them) (Pearson and Thoennes 1988). The connection of nurture with payment of child support should not be encouraged or supported. Like the concept of legitimacy, it is grounded in patriarchal concepts of fatherhood that limit fathers primarily to a breadwinner role, and see an economic role as sufficient fathering. It perpetuates a view of children as property "owned" by virtue of economic support. It is also tied to control of mothers, frequently expressed in the literature on divorced fathers as a desire to control the economic decisions or resources of custodial mothers when fathers contribute economic support. Linking nurturing relationships to economics perpetuates a view of children as property, and gives men dominance over children and women.

The claim of mother preference and father bias in family law determinations requires careful exploration under a social fathering standard. Custody and visitation awards, as well as actual conduct, should be examined to determine the validity of suh claims. This examination should include mothers' claims of bias in the system, which point to different problems. Mothers especially focus on the economic consequences of the system and the lack of realistic acknowledgment of the costs of primary nurturing, as well as issues of control and cooperation. Fathers, on the other hand, focus on skewed custody patterns, lack of enforcement of visitation, and controlling child support resources for the direct use of their children. We also need more information from and about children and their nurturers, as we continue to function with information skewed by class and race exclusion.

The structuring of postdivorce and nonmarital, noncohabiting parental relationships should be grounded on the record of nurture and the ability to create a holistic context that will benefit the children at issue. This should include consideration of the father's record of nurturing other children (or lack thereof). This requires fact-intensive, case-by-case determinations that look to the father-child relationship and the father's relationship with other caregivers. Where a record of nurture is unavailable due to a father's inability to establish a relationship, his efforts to establish a relationship as well as his intent and planning for a future relationship must be balanced against the best interests of the child. While joint custodial arrangements are appropriate as an option, they should not be presumed and should be limited to joint physical custody, which presumably would be based on a coequal parenting history. Equal parenting would mean fifty–fifty, or no more than forty-five–fifty-five, distribution of nurture. Joint legal custody, if not premised on coequal nurture, would be eliminated. Such custody values status over conduct, and replicates the patriarchal model of power without responsibility or social conduct. Thus, joint custody would mean equally nurturing parenting.

Nurturing relationships should be maintained and/or increased, and mothers and fathers should carefully plan and be counseled as to how that can occur, and be supported in their efforts. Social fatherhood is not a status once achieved. It is earned every day, by *doing* parenting. One of our problems is that we do not have a strong concept of cooperative parenting. We also need to have a mechanism for adjustment if nurture does not continue over time to incorporate other caretakers. That includes better support for formal and informal stepfathers, and better support for mothers who have become sole or primary custodial parents in a legally structured joint custodial model.

Custody norms must include multiple adults who can nurture children, rather than seeing the parental role as limited to no more than two people at any given time. The social fathering by informal or formal stepparents should be supported and recognized by the legal system. Third-party visitation statutes can be used to accomplish nonexclusive parenthood, or new legislation specifically targeted at stepparents, to support ongoing relationships when households are no longer shared.

The changes suggested here also incorporate the recommendations on dealing with domestic violence included in chapter 10. Most fundamentally, those recommendations would strengthen existing custody and visitation statutes to prohibit custody and unsupervised visitation in situations of child abuse or a child's witness of domestic violence against a partner. It would also establish a rebuttable presumption against supervised visitation, with the burden on the parent who has engaged in child abuse or abuse of a partner to defeat the presumption that ongoing contact with an adult who has been abusive to a child or a partner is not in the best interests of the child. That presumption would have to be defeated on the basis of clear and convincing evidence.

Finally, greater support of social fatherhood rests on women's equality in the workplace. The data clearly indicate the connection between greater nurture by men and greater labor force participation and opportunity for women. Antidiscrimination laws and equal pay legislation, if vigorously enforced, would have an enormous indirect impact on fathers. Although there are significant limitations on the ability to achieve significant structural or cultural change in the workplace through existing law, nevertheless it is a tool that should not be ignored. In addition, the affirmative support of parenting provided by the Family and Medical Leave Act and parallel state acts, if complemented by expansion to the full labor force, inclusion of wage replacement, and coverage of nonemergency, nonserious absences to attend to children's illnesses, could significantly increase paternal use of this time benefit. Finally, vigorous enforcement of affirmative efforts to achieve gender equity in education would contribute to the education of young women for all segments of the workplace and young men for nurturing parenthood.

AFFIRMATIVE POLICY
Economic Support for All Children

If we dismantle parts of the existing legal structure that support marital, biological, or economic definitions of fatherhood we will have only limited success in attaining the goal of better support for nurturing fatherhood. To accomplish the restructuring necessary to support that ideal we require policies aimed at the economic support of children as well as policies aimed at changing the cultural norms of fatherhood. Two components are thus necessary to support fatherhood redefined around nurture. First, we must construct a system of economic support of families that values and supports the nurture of children. Second, we must eliminate work-family conflicts by restructuring the workplace and by supporting the care of children. Both changes must be implemented in a way that supports men's nurture of children and assures equity and support to women as well.

Economic policy is critical to redefining fatherhood. It dictates the shape of other policies and reflects the inclusiveness and equity of our ultimate vision. From a race and gender perspective, economic issues are the most critical. Patterns of fatherhood—unlike those for mothers—are significantly differentiated along racial lines. We have essentially three choices in designing a system of economic support. First, we can use the existing system, composed of child support (presumed to occur within marriage and by legal order outside marriage) and the welfare system. As not all children receive the support they are entitled to under this system, our efforts could be directed at maximizing the establishment of support orders and payment, and insuring max-imized benefits under the limited welfare system we now have. This approach essentially represents current policy regarding fathers.

Second, we could modify the existing system by guaranteeing backup child support payment if support is not paid, and supplement-ing the support amount if it is insufficient to meet the needs of the child and the primary caretaker. Under such a system the obligation to pay support would not cease, but rather sufficient support would be guaranteed. The state, rather than private individuals, would pursue nonpayment. In addition, we could increase the benefit levels under the welfare system to replicate those available under the social secu-rity system for children of widows or widowers, and either eliminate welfare time limits or transfer families to the social security system to insure basic economic support. This modified private system would include more government backup designed to insure sufficient re-sources for children to eliminate the negative outcomes for children of poverty. Under this scheme, we would enable the primary parent to nurture while working no more than part-time.

Third, we could adopt a system of family supports with the goal of supporting the nurture of all caretakers. Such a system would not only insure a minimum level of economic support for children and their caretakers, but would also value the nurturing work of parents both in the short and long term. Family supports might take the form of uni-versal, non–needs-based subsidies, tax benefits to individuals and businesses, paying salaries and benefits to nurturers, or supporting credits in the employment and pension structures for nurturing work, akin to the valuing of military service through the range of veteran's benefits and preferences. Family support might also include a reexam-ination of the relative benefits attached to part-time work, as well as the wages for such work. Economic support would also include paid time benefits, such as more extended leave, entitlement to part-time work until children are in elementary or middle school, universal health insurance, and universal high-quality child care as well as pre-school and after-school care. The economic support models must ad-dress the question of whether we imagine nurture to take place within a primary parent or coparenting model, or whether we wish to support both visions of parenting.

If we were committed to providing guaranteed resources to chil-dren, that would open a far more creative space for thinking about children, nurture, and patterns of fathering. On the other hand, if we refuse to move from our private-oriented model of inadequate support, we are limited to maximizing support out of the existing structure, by maximum enforcement of child support obligations, universal establishment of paternity, and maximizing the economic returns from the reformed welfare structure. However, maintaining the private model, even with full enforcement, means that we ignore the economic circumstances of a significant proportion of children. Strong evidence demonstrates that even if the system were fully implemented and all support were paid, the support would be inadequate to meet the needs of children. Most scholars have concluded that we will neither economically rescue children nor socially involve fathers by taking this route (Dowd 1997a). An additional backup system is vital. Welfare as we now know it was not intended to provide this kind of support. The time limitation on entitlement is especially insidious for the long-range welfare of children, not to mention the lack of child care and inadequate income from workfare or many "real" jobs.

One of the most difficult aspects of redefining fatherhood is determining the place of economic obligations in light of the strong traditional position of breadwinning in the definition of good fatherhood and good manhood, and contemporary concerns regarding poverty and individual responsibility. If we do not impose economic responsibility, do we foster irresponsibility and disconnection? Will we make things worse? Given children's poverty statistics and the racial and class implications of economic disparity in male breadwinning opportunities, family support is necessary. We must equalize children's opportunities, support caretaking by all fathers, and dismantle the patriarchal structure that limits fathers' nurture as well as mothers' economic empowerment. The danger of providing economic support to families is not that it would promote irresponsibility, but rather that we might avoid dealing with the more difficult structural problems faced by men disadvantaged by race, class, or sexual orientation, especially the lack of economic opportunity tied to educational, housing, and employment problems.

If we take the most radical route, that of ensuring sufficient economic resources to children, then we must follow the children to the nurturers, and support those who nurture. A commitment to the welfare of all children would mean devoting resources based on children and their caretakers, rather than by virtue of biological or marital connections. It would mean committing ourselves to egalitarianism and communal support of all children. We continue to presume that economic resources will come through individual contribution, through a network of employment equally available to all. That individualistic approach has severe racial consequences due to ongoing discrimination. If we continue to use that approach, we must address the bias in the economic opportunity structure so that fatherhood is not racially defined. Maximizing the use of existing race discrimination statutes would be a significant part of this strategy. Some would argue that at best this would result in limited change, while others would argue that vigorous enforcement and affirmative action could generate significant differences. However, in the absence of structural workplace change, even the most wildly successful use of existing structures would leave us far short of the goal of greater nurture for children.

To the extent that we impose private economic responsibility, it should be tied to biology or intent, but should not trigger any parental rights in the absence of social fatherhood. Economic responsibility ought to be separated from the right to presence and access in order to disconnect the notion that children are property and that access can be bought. Economic responsibilities should be independent of nurturing, which should not be seen as a mandated responsibility, but rather as a social good and privilege that should be strongly supported. Economic responsibility ought to be grounded in a responsibility to life created and brought into this world, whereas rights of connection and relationship are grounded in care and nurture. Ideally, economic responsibility should be imposed with recognition of the limits of our economic system and sensitivity to the impact of responsibility in a system skewed by race and class bias. In addition, those biases should not disadvantage fathers or, more importantly, children. A system of commitment to a basic level of economic resources is the most preferable, which would require a combination of public and private resources.

Work-Family Restructuring

Second, we must restructure the workplace. Father researchers agree that workplace conditions and demands are a major barrier to involved, nurturing fatherhood. Programs like parental leave are useful but limited, because they provide episodic rather than ongoing opportunities to combine work and family. The restructuring needed includes addressing the varieties of conflict between work and family responsibilities that currently plague the workplace. Time demands must be more flexible on a daily basis, and the sheer length of time worked by the "ideal" worker must be reduced.

This would also involve thinking more creatively and using part-time workers to their full worth. Periodic time to deal with family emergencies or family demands should also be liberally available. Occupational structures must be recast to permit commitment to family without sacrifice of opportunity. Opportunity must be broadened throughout the workplace by achieving gender equality and race desegregation of the workplace.

The culture of work must accept and support family responsibilities, and value family work. This means addressing pervasive gender stereotyping of jobs and employees. It also means a reorientation, top-down, of workplace values and culture, similar to the efforts to reorient workplace culture to deal with sexual harassment. Formal policies accomplish little. The informal adoption of new mores has a far greater effect.

We have to visualize parenting and working being combined in a variety of ways and in ways that are not gender defined or likely to play out according to gender. How we conceptualize parenting (a primary-secondary parent model, or a coequal parent model, and variations for other family configurations) will have a major impact. If we expect all parents to nurture along some range of conduct, then our planning and structure must reflect all parents. If we visualize this as a singular role, then the range of possibilities includes sharing roles, or taking the entire role and trading off with the other parent, or dividing it other than in equal shares, to be maintained or changed over time. In addition, variables by age and number of children must be considered, such as the differences between preschool care and after-school care for high school students. In addition to daily time and schedule issues, school breaks and summers must be factored in as well.

How much of this is for fathers only? By looking at men's work barriers, the hope would be to widen the opportunity structure for women as well. In the workplace, it is important to communicate that doing nurturing work is a positive, not a negative. Most of what is needed would be neutral in structure, but the corporate culture's implementation and support of such policies must be very gender specific. Workplace restructuring requires neutral goals but must acknowledge the structural, cultural, and occupational differences in the average situations of mothers and fathers. Women are still fighting for an equal opportunity to do the full range of wage work, while also taking care of their children. A small proportion of men fight to nurture, but wage work and economic demands due to men's better opportunities get in the way.

We must be aware of the limitations of existing attempts to expand men's role in the nurture of their children. The Swedish example gives us powerful insights into the differences and interconnections in work-family roles. While Swedish men's role in family care has increased, the progress has been slow, disproportionate in certain areas, and women remain distinctly second-class in the wage workforce (Dowd 1989b; Haas 1995). Attempts to revision work and family have so far focused almost exclusively on women, on the assumption that women will primarily care for children. But women have rarely been in control of policy, and, as the Swedish example shows us, it is possible to construct strong family supportive policies without making any impact on women's wage work positions or public equality positions, or on men's nurture of children. If we are to focus on fathers, our efforts to encourage a reorientation of work and family cannot be limited to men, and cannot occur at the expense of women. The two must occur in tandem, with recognizing that the needs of fathers and mothers are significantly different, even if intertwined.

Cultural Change: Fatherhood Education

What we know from the context of fatherhood is that more than economic factors and workplace structures limit the ability of men to nurture. Cultural barriers prevent them from parenting as well. Policies can be stymied by the clear communication in the workplace that those who devote time to their families sacrifice economic opportunity, particularly when such opportunity guarantees the very economic base viewed as essential to one's family. Sexual harassment policies, proactive diversity policies, and a vast array of human resource knowledge on managing and supporting employees, all provide us with models for implementing and supporting changes in workplace culture *if* a commitment is made to the value of nurturing children.

The context of fatherhood and its practice also reveals, however, that the need for this kind of cultural change goes deeper. Men's socialization and education give them few models of nurturing fatherhood, and core concepts of masculinity, including homophobia and violence, pose serious challenges to a vision of manhood that includes fatherhood. The practice of fatherhood, particularly by men who are single custodial parents or who coparent at a significant level, indicates that men can parent as successfully as women, and engage in parenting in essentially the same way that women do. Although some follow the example set by their own fathers, and others create a new model that rejects the practice of their own fathers, it is nonetheless revealing that many have been thrust into fatherhood by the course of events and did not see caring for children as part, or even as the core, of manhood.

All this suggests that we need to focus on ways to support men's capacity and skills to nurture. This requires education efforts and other bottom-up strategies to provide a network of support. However, the education needed should not stop at fathers themselves. It is also necessary to reorient those institutions and people who most directly deal with fathers—such as courts and hospitals—so that they do not perpetuate assumptions that undermine social fathering.

From what we know about fathers, this kind of education and support could be especially effective at childbirth or adoption, and at divorce. At childbirth or adoption, everything we know about fathers—whether biological, social, married, or unmarried—suggests many have a strong motivation and desire to remain connected to the children to whom they have already been attached emotionally and intellectually as they anticipated their birth or arrival. At the same time, the message of difference between mothers and fathers seems strongest at this stage, without a corresponding message to fathers of their importance. We must support both parents, as well as a cooperative and shared parenting relationship between them. Education at this stage can focus on skills as well as modeling the relationship between parents. The relatively recent change from men's total absence from childbirth to their accepted, even expected presence, suggests that a cultural shift in expectations can have enormous implications. Extending the vision from the limited demands of men's presence and support at childbirth to a coequal nurturing role in parenting is a more complex task, but building on the commitments and interest of fathers at this stage is essential.

More recent efforts at increased paternity establishment are beginning to work with this pattern of men's fathering and encourage their connection with their children. This work should be extended to social fathers as well. We must not only provide supportive mechanisms at the hospital, but also reorient hospital staff to welcome and encourage those men who can become fathers, rather than treat them disparagingly, or simply ignoring them. The time frame of hospital-based programs is short, given the short stays of mothers in hospitals after normal deliveries. It is essential that fathers and mothers be supported for long enough time to develop the patterns and skills needed for cooperative parenting. This might be accomplished in stages, with intensive support for the first six months after birth or adoption, and less intensive assistance for up to two years. Given the importance of the preschool period for children's development, a third stage might extend until kindergarten. The different socialization of women and men and the different contexts from which they operate may well require gender-specific training and support. Primary-care physicians are an important resource, as are the health care delivery system in general as well as the daycare and preschool educational systems. Early medical and educational intervention and support for children intersects with the support of familial nurture. We must also be attentive to class- and race-differentiated delivery of services under the existing health care and educational systems, with the goal of universal, high-quality support.

Education and support for nurturing fathering are also essential at divorce. Many fathers face their lack of skills only when they must parent their children alone, either as a custodial parent or during visitation with their children. This challenge comes at the same time as they are working through their feelings in relation to their former spouse. They need to be supported not only in their nurture of their children, but also in building their confidence that they can manage this and do it well alone. In addition, both parents, now former partners, need to help to develop an ongoing postdivorce relationship to construct cooperative parenting. This is especially challenging if they did parent cooperatively during the marriage.

All these tasks will be complicated by the presence, either immediate or long-term, of new relationships and eventual stepparents and blended families, a strong likelihood given the high remarriage rates and the higher propensity of divorced fathers than divorced mothers to share their household with a partner. Some of the help needed by such families is already present in existing parenting and conflict-resolution courses, and post-divorce family planning done by some courts. But this effort needs to be more strongly supported by realistically confronting the patterns of postdivorce fathering and devising better ways to support social fathering. Stepparents, informal and formal, should also be supported as part of this process. If we accept serial fatherhood, we need to focus on men learning to nurture the children they live with, and if they practice serial fatherhood as multiple fathers, men must learn to nurture cooperatively with their former wives or partners and the other social fathers or mothers with whom their former partners currently share a household. This view of the cultural and educational task would accept current patterns of fatherhood, rather than focus exclusively on reinforcing, supporting, or mandating ongoing relationships between biological or marital fathers and their children when they are no longer part of the children's household.

The focus on childbirth and divorce should not mean that we ignore fatherhood at other times. Institutional and legal structures are simply more readily available to fathers at those stages. Birth programs can be attached to public health programs and preschool educational programs. Divorce programs can be attached to the family court process. In addition, we need to go beyond these institutional frameworks in order to reach other fathers. Models can be found in the grassroots, community-based initiatives to support poor fathers and teenage fathers (Levine and Pitt 1995; Knitzer et al. 1997). In addition, some men's groups and fathers' rights groups have provided support to fathers (Levine and Pitt 1995:170–193). Just as we favor public health initiatives like AIDs education or universal inoculation, we can find ways to provide resources to insure that men are supported in becoming nurturing fathers. We need community-based strategies rather than top-down ones.

If we are to challenge the concepts of self and lack of skills that block men's nurture, we need to think about educational efforts for young boys as well. New research is beginning to reveal that the socialization of boys imposes significant limits on the very skills and developmental resources needed for good parenting. The shutdown begins early. An effort to combat this tendency, literally to challenge the very construction of boyhood, would need to be part of a comprehensive plan to deal with issues of gender equity, included in, for instance, the goals of Title IX, the federal statute that mandates gender equity in education (Title IX of the Education Amendments of 1972, 21 U.S.C. § 1681 [1972]). Educating men for nurturing fatherhood must also be seen as a race-equity goal, so that all fathers are suppported and diversity of ways in which nurturing fatherhood is practiced is respected. In addition to educating boys and men, we must teach their teachers, who reinforce dominant masculinity norms in both direct and subtle ways.

The goal of encouraging men's nurture and of seeing it as a pervasive norm, not just as fringe behavior, is a radical one. The tricky challenge in this is not to become wedded to a single norm. Much of the fatherhood debate has been entangled by arguments about traditional versus nontraditional models. There is an opportunity here for us to coalesce around what we can agree on, without committing ourselves to a singular ideal. To some extent, more nurture in the lives of children is a place of agreement without regard to whether we see that limited to a particular model. On the other hand, we have not traditionally supported unmarried fathers, poor fathers, and men of color. We must keep the most disadvantaged fathers at the forefront to insure that our efforts to support fatherhood are not race- and class-limited.

GENDER-SPECIFIC AND GENDER-RELEVANT STRATEGIES

To achieve a redefined fatherhood model, we must be prepared to use gender-specific strategies. It is tempting to use gender-neutral terminology when thinking about fathering, since it affirms the evidence that men fundamentally parent like women, and that fathering as nurturing is the same as mothering. Yet at the same time, fathers and mothers are differently situated both socially and legally. Even as the goal may be gender equity and neutrality, the means to get there must be gender specific. The downfall of a gender-neutral approach can be seen in the structure, implementation, and experience of usage of the leave guaranteed by the Family and Medical Leave Act. Another example of failed gender neutrality is family law's treatment of custody, visitation, and child support.

The most important reason why the means need to be gender specific is because men practice fatherhood and conduct themselves as fathers in such different ways from women. Furthermore, the essence of gender role and gender identity moves in the direction of seeing gender as significant with respect to parenting. I propose that we use a gender-specific, gender-conscious means to accomplish a gender-neutral, but gender-diverse end. Such an approach takes account of the actual conduct of fathering and therefore of the ways in which men's conduct should change, or that we hope it will change. It provides fathers the opportunities and support to do so, reflecting a conscious social, communal choice that sees men's nurture and involvement in the lives of children as a positive good and one that should not be gender-limited.

The challenge is how to be gender specific without reinforcing social constructions of difference. It is tempting to argue that men and women are different, that those differences are critical to children, and that a gender-specific approach is therefore needed to allow men to make the unique contribution that they can make *as men* to children's development. Much of the men's movement and fathers' rights movement make precisely this sort of argument, either openly or implication. It is not to be doubted that men can contribute much to children's development; but this is not due to their uniqueness, or to some hard-wired gender essentialism. The very socialization that may act as a barrier to nurture can also contribute to nurture, and as some have suggested, there are admirable aspects of masculinity that children should be encouraged to learn. But the differences do not overwhelm the sameness of parental nurture.

A gender-specific approach can be modeled upon Title IX, which has authorized and mandated gender-specific approaches to achieve gender equity in sports. What has been accomplished in twenty years under Title IX is phenomenal. It has transformed women's sports and women's educational opportunities. Average physical differences and other factors have been used to justify gender segregation as part of the gender-specific approach, that is, that equity could not be achieved with gender integration. Title IX has also been the basis for the development of curricular changes at all levels of education, which more closely parallels the socially constructed differences, hierarchy, and need for gender-specific approaches with respect to parenting.

A second area where gender-specific approaches have been used in order to take socially constructed difference into account is sexual harassment. The pressure of potential legal liability and the affirmative defense of a strong proactive antiharassment, policy has generated significant change in workplace culture. Creative strategies to vigorously implement employment discrimination law to eliminate cultural and structural elements of gender discrimination may provide a similar legal "stick" to press for proactive changes to support a gender-conscious resolution of work-family conflict.

Finally, race- and gender-conscious educational and employment policies under affirmative action doctrine provide another model. What is different here is that the beneficiaries of affirmative legal action—men—are a group historically priviledged in many respects who would be offered support and encouragement and opportunity to frame their relationships with their children in a different way. Rather than overcoming the prejudices and biases of others, this would be overcoming men's own socialization and privilege. At the same time, we must remember that some men are heavily disadvantaged because of race, a factor which must be taken into account in designing any model for change.

In sum, the policies that flow from fatherhood redefined as nurture must begin with economic support. The direction and comprehensiveness of economic policy will determine in large degree the success of our attempts to redesign wage work and family nurture. Our model of parenthood also affects workplace policies and family law expectations. Finally, education efforts focused on challenging the dominant masculinity and offering another model, as well as teaching the skills of nurture, are critical companions to economic support. Cultural change, after all, has gotten us where we are, both positively and negatively.

Epilogue

The redefinition, and lived difference, of fatherhood centered around nurture would be a tremendous change. Achieving it is a significant challenge. It is easy to mistake what is involved, and to see this as a simple test of will and mere presence. At a fatherhood conference I attended in late 1998, one speaker relayed comments from a Washington conference on the importance of "responsible" fatherhood. The gist was that we have a solution to significant problems with children and families that can be implemented with "no new taxes"—namely, fathers. Appealing to men as unique and essential, the message suggests that presence alone is significant to children. Simplistic arguments can rarely capture the complexity of an issue, but this kind of position far underrates what is needed to afford men an opportunity to engage in nurturing their children, and underrates what children need as nurture. It also suggests that the problem can be solved without economic investment in the importance of nurture for our children and for men, which is an unrealistic prospect for most men and children.

How soon will it be before Father's Day changes from a rest for dad from his breadwinner role to a celebration of his caretaking role? In the meantime, perhaps we can focus on care and nurture, and begin to educate our sons. We can begin with "Take Our Sons Home Day," which would be a national day of gender-conscious mentoring. Because so many children do not have fathers actively in their lives, we would have to rely on the father figures, other male family members, and men of the community to take on the task of teaching the next generation. In order to teach, we must know this for ourselves. We could teach our sons by the conduct of nurture. We could also educate employers about the nurturing activities of their employees, how businesses could better facilitate men's nurture of their children, as well as how businesses benefit from employees' nurture of their families. We could honor those who nurture, as well as recognizing curricula, workplaces, and other programs that support social fathering.

Our ultimate progress will be measured not in small symbolic steps, but rather in our ability to envision and implement a different construction of fatherhood for this generation. Our success will be measured not in the statistics and reports of the government, but in the common perception of preschoolers about daddies, who they are and what they do. When my son grows up, I hope he will be as much a nurturer as he is now, and that he will teach other boys and men, and maybe his own son, that what it means to be a real man is embraced in the love and care one gives to another. And in that, I hope, he will not be an unusual man at all.

References and Bibliography

BOOKS AND ARTICLES

ABA Commission on Domestic Violence. 1998. Http://www.abanet.org/domviol/ stats.html.

Adams, Michelle, and Scott Coltrane. 1997. "Children and Gender." In *Contemporary Parenting: Challenges and Issues*, edited by Terry Arendell. Thousand Oaks, Calif.: Sage.

Adler, Jerry. 1996. "Building a Better Dad." *Newsweek* 127:58.

Allen, Katherine R. 1997. "Lesbian and Gay Families." In *Contemporary Parenting: Challenges and Issues*, edited by Terry Arendell. Thousand Oaks, Calif.: Sage.

Allen, Mike, and Nancy Burrell. 1996. "Comparing the Impact of Homosexual and Heterosexual Parents on Children: Meta-Analysis of Existing Research." *Journal of Homosexuality* 32:19.

Allen, William D., and Michael Connor. 1997. "An African-American Perspective on Generative Fathering." In *Generative Fathering: Beyond Deficit Perspectives*, edited by Alan J. Hawkins and David C. Dollahite. Thousand Oaks, Calif.: Sage.

235

Allen, William D., and William J. Doherty. 1996. "The Responsibilities of Father-hood as Perceived by African American Teenage Fathers." *Families in Society: The Journal of Contemporary Human Services* 77:142.

Almeida, David M. 1993. "Continuity and Change in Father- Adolescent Relations." *New Directions for Child Development* 62:27.

Altimari, Daniela, and Matthew Daly. 1999. "Same-Sex Family Adoption Derailed." *Hartford Courant* (June 4).

Amato, Paul R. 1994. "Father-Child Relations, Mother-Child Relations, and Offspring Psychological Well-Being in Early Adulthood." *Journal of Marriage and the Family* 56:1031.

American Bar Association. 1998. "Family Law in the Fifty States 1996–1997: Case Digests." *Family Law Quarterly* 31:667.

"The American Freshman: National Norms for Fall 1996." 1998. Los Angeles: Higher Education Research Institute, UCLA.

Anaya, Rudolfo. 1996. "I'm the King: The Macho Image." In *Muy Macho: Latino Men Confront Their Manhood,* edited by Ray Gonzalez. New York: Anchor Books.

Anderson, Elijah. 1989. "Sex Codes and Family Life among Poor Inner-City Youths." In *The Ghetto Underclass: Social Science Perspectives,* edited by William Julius Wilson. Newbury Park, Calif.: Sage.

Anderson, Kristin L. 1997. "Gender, Status, and Domestic Violence: An Integration of Feminist and Family Violence Approaches." *Journal of Marriage and the Family* 59:655.

Andrews, Amy, and Lotte Bailyn. 1993. "Segmentation and Synergy: Two Models of Linking Work and Family." In *Men, Work, and Family,* edited by Jane C. Hood. Newbury Park, Calif.: Sage.

Arendell, Terry. 1995. *Fathers and Divorce.* Thousand Oaks, Calif.: Sage.

Aschenbrenner, Joyce. 1983. "Extended Families among Black Americans." *Journal of Comparative Family Studies* 14:257.

Ashe, Marie, and Naomi Cahn. 1994. "Child Abuse: A Problem for Feminist Theory." In *ThePublic Nature of Private Violence: The Discovery of Domestic Abuse,* edited by Martha Albertson Fineman and Roxanne Mykitiuk. New York: Routledge.

Atkinson, Maxine P., and Stephen P. Blackwelder. 1993. "Fathering in the Twentieth Century." *Journal of Marriage and the Family* 55:975.

Auerbach, Carl 1997. "Transforming Patriarchal Fathering: The Role of Shame and Organizing Metaphors." *Society for the Psychological Study of Men and Masculinity Home Page.* Http://web.indstate.edu/spsmm/posstat.html.

Bahr, Stephen J., Jerry D. Howe, Meggin Morrill Mann, and Matthew S. Bahr. 1994. "Trends in Child Custody Awards: Has the Removal of Maternal Preference Made a Difference?" *Family Law Quarterly* 28:247.

Bainham, Andrew. 1997. "Sex, Gender, and Fatherhood: Does Biology Really Matter?" *Cambridge Law Journal* 56:3.

Baldwin, James. 1962. *The Fire Next Time*. New York: Dell Publishing.

Ball, Richard E. 1983. "Family and Friends: A Supportive Network for Low-Income American Black Families." *Journal of Comparative Family Studies* 14:51.

Barnett, Rosalind C., and Grace K. Baruch. 1988. "Correlates of Father's Participation in Family Work." In *Fatherhood Today: Men's Changing Role in the Family*, edited by Phyllis Bronstein and Carolyn Pape Cowan. New York: John Wiley.

Barret, Robert L. 1990. *Gay Fathers*. Lexington, Mass.: Lexington Books.

Barry, Margaret Martin. 1997. "The District of Colombia's Joint Custody Presumption: Misplaced Blame and Simplistic Solutions." *Catholic University Law Review* 46:767.

Barta, Carolyn. 1997. "Masculinity Is Fast Becoming a Scholarly Endeavor in Schools." *Dallas Morning News* (May 25).

Bartlett, Katharine T. 1984. "Rethinking Parenthood as an Exclusive Status: The Need for Legal Alternatives When the Premise of the Nuclear Family Has Failed." *Virginia Law Review* 70:879.

Beail, Nigel, and Jacqueline McGuire. 1982. *Fathers: Psychological Perspectives*. London: Junction.

Beal, Becky. 1997. "The Promise Keepers' Use of Sport in Defining Christlike Masculinity." *Journal of Sport and Social Issues* 21:274.

Becker, Mary E. 1989. "The Rights of Unwed Parents: Feminist Approaches." *Social Service Review* 63:496.

Bederman, Gail. 1995. *Manliness and Civilization: A Cultural History of Gender and Race in the United States, 1880–1917*. Chicago: University of Chicago Press.

Behrman, Richard E., ed. 1997. *The Future of Children*. Los Altos, Calif.: Center for the Future of Children and the David and Lucile Packard Foundation.

Bell, Derrick. 1995. "The Race-Charged Relationship of Black Men and Black-Women." In *Constructing Masculinity*, edited by Maurice Berger, Brian Wallis, and Simon Watson. New York: Routledge.

Berger, Maurice, Brian Wallis, and Simon Watson, eds. 1995. *Constructing Masculinity*. New York: Routledge.

Bergman, Stephen. 1995. "Men's Psychological Development: A Relational Perspective." In *A New Psychology of Men*, edited by Ronald F. Levant and William S. Pollack. New York: Basic Books.

Berman, Phyllis W., and Frank A. Petersen, eds. 1987. *Men's Transitions to Parenthood: Longitudinal Studies of Early Family Experience*. Hillsdale, N.J.: Lawrence Erlbaum.

Bernard, Jessie. 1992. "The Good-Provider Role: Its Rise and Fall." In *Family in Transition: Rethinking Marriage, Sexuality, Child Rearing, and Family Organization*, edited by Arlene S. Skolnick and Jerome H. Skolnick. New York: HarperCollins.

Bernstein, Fred A. 1996. "This Child Does Have Two Mothers . . . and a Sperm Donor with Visitation." *New York University Review of Law and Social Change* 22:1.

Berrill, Kevin T. 1992. "Anti-Gay Violence and Victimization in the United States: An Overview." In *Hate Crimes: Confronting Violence against Lesians and Gay Men*, edited by Gregory M. Herek and Kevin T. Berrill. Newbury Park, Calif.: Sage.

Berry, Judy O., and Julie Meyer Rao. 1997. "Balancing Employment and Fatherhood: A Systems Perspective." *Journal of Family Issues* 18:386.

Bertoia, Carl, and Janice Drakich. 1993. "The Fathers' Rights Movement: Contradictions in Rhetoric and Practice." *Journal of Family Issues* 14:592.

Best, Stephen Michael. 1996. "Stand by Your Man Richard Wright, Lynch Pedagogy, and Rethinking Black Male Agency." In *Representing Black Men*, edited by Marcellus Bount and George P. Cunningham. New York: Routledge.

Bianchi, Suzanne M. 1995. "The Changing Dynamic and Socioeconomic Characteristics of Single Parent Families." *Marriage and Family Review* 20:71.

Bianchi, Suzanne M., and Daphne Spain. 1997. *Women, Work, and Family in America*. New York: Russell Sage Foundation.

Bigner, Jerry J., and Frederick W. Bozett. 1989. "Parenting by Gay Fathers." *Marriage and Family Review* 14:155.

Bigner, Jerry J., and Brooke R. Jacobsen. 1989. "Parenting Behaviors of Homosexual and Heterosexual Fathers." *Journal of Homosexuality* 18:173.

Biller, Henry. 1993. *Fathers and Families: Paternal Factors in Child Development*. Westport, Conn.: Auburn House/Greenwood.

Blankenhorn, David. 1995. *Fatherless America: Confronting Our Most Urgent Social Problem*. New York: Basic Books.

Bloom, David E., Cecilia Conrad, and Cynthia Miller. 1996. *Child Support and Fathers' Remarriage and Fertility*. Cambridge, Mass.: National Bureau of Economic Research.

Blount, Marcellus, and George P. Cunningham, eds. 1996. *Representing Black Men*. New York: Routledge.

Bly, Robert. 1990. *Iron John*. Reading, Mass.: Addison-Wesley.

Boumil, Marcia Mobilia. 1996. *Deadbeat Dads: A National Child Support Scandal*. Westport, Conn.: Praeger.

Bowen, Gary L., and Dennis K. Orthner. 1991. "Effects of Organizational Culture on Fatherhood." In *Fatherhood and Families in Cultural Context*, edited by Frederick W. Bozett and Shirley M. H. Hanson. New York: Springer.

Bowman, Phillip J. 1992. "Coping with Provider Role Strain: Adaptive Cultural Resources among Black Husband-Fathers." In *African American Psychology: Theory, Research, and Practice*, edited by A. Kathleen Hoard Burlew, Curtis W. Banks, Harriet Pipes McAdoo, and Daudi Ajani ya Azibo. Newbury Park, Calif.: Sage.

Bowman, Phillip J., and Tyrone A. Forman. 1997. "Instrumental and Expressive Family Roles among African American Fathers." In *Family Life in Black America*, edited by Robert Joseph Taylor, James S. Jackson, and Linda M. Chatters. Thousand Oaks, Calif.: Sage.

Bozett, Frederick W. 1988. "Gay Fatherhood." In *Fatherhood Today: Men's Changing Role in the Family*, edited by Phyllis Bronstein and Carolyn Pape Cowan. New York: John Wiley.

———. 1989. "Gay Fathers: A Review of the Literature." *Journal of Homosexuality* 18:137.

———. 1993. "Gay Fathers: A Review of the Literature." In *Psychological Perspectives on Lesbian and Gay Male Experiences*, edited by Linda D. Garnets and Douglas C. Kimmel. New York: Columbia University Press.

Bozett, Frederick W., and Shirley M. H. Hanson, eds. 1991. *Fatherhood and Families in Cultural Context*. New York: Springer.

Bray, James H., and Sandra H. Berger. 1990. "Noncustodial Father and Paternal Grandparent Relationships in Stepfamilies." *Family Relations* 39:414.

Brayfield, April. 1995. "Juggling Jobs and Kids: The Impact of Employment Schedules on Fathers' Caring for Children." *Journal of Marriage and the Family* 57:321.

Brenner, Claudia. 1992. "Survivor's Story: Eight Bullets." In *Hate Crimes: Confronting Violence against Lesbians and Gay Men*, edited by Gregory M. Herek and Kevin T. Berrill. Newbury Park, Calif.: Sage.

Bright, Josephine A., and Christopher Williams. 1996. "Child Rearing and Education in Urban Environments: Black Fathers' Perspectives." *Urban Education* 31:245.

Brinig, Margaret F., and F. H. Buckley. 1998. "Joint Custody: Bonding and Monitoring Theories." *Indiana Law Review* 73:393.

Brod, Harry. 1992. "The Case for Men's Studies." In *The Making of Masculinities: The New Men's Studies*, edited by Harry Brod. New York: Routledge.

Brod, Harry, ed. 1992. *The Making of Masculinities: The New Men's Studies*. New York: Routledge.

Brody, Leslie R. 1985. "Gender Differences in Emotional Development: A Review of Theories and Research." *Journal of Personality* (June) 53:102.

Bronstein, Phyllis. 1984. "Differences in Mothers' and Fathers' Behaviors toward Children: A Cross-Cultural Comparison." *Developmental Psychology* 20:6.

———. 1988. "Father-Child Interaction, Implications for Gender Role Socialization." In *Fatherhood Today: Men's Changing Role in the Family*, edited by Phyllis Bronstein and Carolyn Pape Cowan. New York: John Wiley.

———. 1994. "Fathering after Separation or Divorce: Factors Predicting Children's Adjustment." *Family Relations* 43:469.

Bronstein, Phyllis, and Carolyn Pape Cowan, eds. 1988. *Fatherhood Today: Men's Changing Role in the Family.* New York: John Wiley.

Brooks, Gary R., and Lucia Albino Gilbert. 1995. "Men in Families: Old Constraints, New Possibilities." In *A New Psychology of Men,* edited by Ronald F. Levant and William S. Pollack. New York: Basic Books.

Brooks, Gary R., and Louise B. Silverstein. 1995. "Understanding the Dark Side of Masculinity: An Interactive Systems Model." In *A New Psychology of Men,* edited by Ronald Levant and William S. Pollack. New York: Basic Books.

Bruce, Judith, Cynthia B. Lloyd, and Ann Leonard. 1997. *Families in Focus: New Perspectives on Mothers, Fathers, and Children.* New York: Population Council.

Bureau of Census. 1991. *U.S. Department of Commerce, Family Disruption and Economic Hardship: The Short-Run Picture for Children.*

———. 1992a. *U.S. Department of Commerce, Who's Helping Out? Support Networks among American Families: 1988.*

———. 1992b. *U.S. Department of Commerce, Who's Minding the Kids? Child Care Arrangements: Fall 1988.*

———. 1992c. *U.S. Department of Commerce, Studies in Household and Family Formation, When Households Continue, Discontinue, and Form.*

———. 1992d. *U.S. Department of Commerce, Marriage, Divorce, and Remarriage in the 1990s.*

———. 1994a. *U.S. Department of Commerce, The Diverse Living Arrangements of Children: Summer 1991.*

———. 1994b. *U.S. Department of Commerce, Dynamics of Economic Well-Being, Labor Force, and Income, 1990 to 1992.*

———. 1994c. *U.S. Department of Commerce, Who's Minding the Kids? Child Care Arrangements: Fall 1991.*

———. 1995a. *U.S. Department of Commerce, Child Support for Custodial Mothers and Fathers: 1991.*

———. 1995b. *U.S. Department of Commerce, What Does It Cost to Mind Our Preschoolers?*

———. 1995c. *U.S. Department of Commerce, Who Receives Child Support?*

———. 1995d. *U.S. Department of Commerce, Current Population Reports, Marital Status, and Living Arrangements: March 1994.*

———. 1996a. *U.S. Department of Commerce, Poverty in the United States: 1995.*

———. 1996b. *U.S. Department of Commerce, Dynamics of Economic Well-Being: Poverty, 1992–1993, Who Stays Poor? Who Doesn't?*

———. 1996c. *U.S. Department of Commerce, Dynamics of Economic Well-Being: Program Participation, 1992–1993, Who Gets Assistance?*

———. 1996d. *U.S. Department of Commerce, Who's Minding Our Preschoolers?*

———. 1996e. *U.S. Department of Commerce, Marital Status, and Living Arrangements: March 1994.*

———. 1996f. *U.S. Department of Commerce, Current Population Reports, Household and Family Characteristics: March 1994.*

———. 1996g. *U.S. Department of Commerce, Current Population Reports, Fertility of American Women: June 1994.*

———. 1997a. *U.S. Department of Commerce, My Daddy Takes Care of Me! Fathers as Care Providers.*

———. 1997b. *U.S. Department of Commerce, National Population Trends, U.S. Population Estimates, by Age, Sex, Race, and Hispanic Origin: 1990 to 1994.*

———. 1998a. *U.S. Department of Commerce, Current Population Reports, Marital Status and Living Arrangements: March 1996.*

———. 1998b. *U.S. Department of Commerce, Current Population Reports, Household and Family Characteristics: March 1997.*

Bureau of National Affairs. 1989. *The 1990s Father: Balancing Work and Family Concerns.* 1989. Washington, D.C.: Bureau of National Affairs.

Burgess, Adrienne. 1997. *Fatherhood Reclaimed: The Making of the Modern Father.* London: Vermillion.

Burke, Iris. 1997. "Paternity, Fatherhood, and Illegitimacy." Unpublished paper presented at Faculty Symposium, University of Florida College of Law, October 24.

Burke, Phyllis. 1996. *Gender Shock: Exploding Myths of Male and Female.* New York: Anchor Books.

Burlew, A. Kathleen Hoard, Curtis W. Banks, Harriet Pipes McAdoo, and Daudi Ajani ya Azibo, eds. 1992. *African American Psychology: Theory, Research, and Practice.* Newbury Park, Calif.: Sage.

Butler, Judith. 1995. "Melancholy Gender/Refused Identification." In *Constructing Masculinity*, edited by Maurice Berger, Brian Wallis, and Simon Watson. New York: Routledge.

Butterworth, Dawn. 1994. "Are Fathers Really Necessary to the Family Unit in Early Childhood?" *International Journal of Early Childhood* 26:1.

Cahn, Naomi R. 1991. "Civil Images of Battered Women: The Impact of Domestic Violence on Child Custody Decisions." *Vanderbilt Law Review* 44:1041.

———. 1997. "Reframing Child Custody Decision Making." *Ohio State Law Journal* 58:1576.

Cahn, Naomi R. 1999. "Gendered Identities: Women and Household Work." *Villanova Law Review* 44:525.

Callahan, Daniel. 1992. "Bioethics and Fatherhood." *Utah Law Review* 1992:735.

Cameron, Paul, and Kirk Cameron. 1996. "Homosexual Parents." *Adolescence* 31:124.

Caplan-Cotenoff, Scott A. 1987. "Parental Leave: The Need for a National Policy to Foster Sexual Equality." *American Journal of Law and Medicine* 13:71.

Carrigan, Tim, Bob Connell, and John Lee. 1992. "Toward a New Sociology of Masculinity." In *The Making of Masculinities: The New Men's Studies*, edited by Harry Brod. New York: Routledge.

Carroad, Diane L. 1994. "Getting Men Involved with Childrearing. An Interview with Jim Levine." *Children Today* 23:24.

Cashman, Tracy. 1997. "When Is a Biological Father Really a Dad?" *Pepperdine Law Review* 24:959.

Casper, Virginia, Steven Schultz, and Elaine Wickens. 1992. "Breaking the Silences: Lesbian and Gay Parents and the Schools." *Teacher's College Record* 94:109.

Cath, Stanley H., Linda Gunsberg, and Alan Gurwitt, eds. 1989. *Fathers and Their Families*. Hillsdale, N.J.: Analytic Press.

Cazenave, Noel A. 1981. "Black Men in America: The Quest for Manhood." In *Black Families*, edited by Harriet Pipes McAdoo. Newbury Park, Calif.: Sage.

Cazenave, Noel A., and George H. Leon. 1987. "Men's Work and Family Roles and Characteristics: Race, Gender, and Class Perceptions of College Students." In *Changing Men: New Directions in Research on Men and Masculinity*, edited by Michael S. Kimmel. Newbury Park, Calif.: Sage.

Chambers, David L. 1984. "Rethinking the Substantive Rules for Custody Disputes in Divorce." *Michigan Law Review* 83:477.

———. 1995. "Fathers, the Welfare System, and the Virtues and Perils of Child Support Enforcement." *Virginia Law Review* 81:2575.

Chase-Landsdale, P. Linsday, and Jeanne Brooks-Gunn, eds. 1995. *Escape from Poverty: What Makes a Difference for Children*. Cambridge: Cambridge University Press.

Christian, Amy C. 1997. "The Joint Return Rate Structure: Identifying and Addressing the Gendered Nature of the Tax Law." *Journal of Law and Politics* 13:241.

Christmon, Kenneth. 1990. "Parental Responsibility of African-American Unwed Adolescent Fathers." *Adolescence* 25:645.

Clatterbauth, Ken. 1990. *Contemporary Perspectives on Masculinity: Men, Women, and Politics in Modern Society*. Boulder: Westview Press.

———. 1995. "Mythopoetic Foundations and New Age Patriarchy." In *The Politics of Manhood: Profeminist Men Respond to the Mythopoetic Men's*

Movement (And the Mythopoetic Leaders Answer), edited by Michael S. Kimmel. Philadelphia: Temple University Press.

Cochran, Donna L. 1997. "African American Fathers: A Decade Review of the Literature." *Families in Society* 78:340.

Cohen, David. 1998. "The Changing Role of Low-Income Fathers: Using a Public Health Model to Guide Social Policy." In *News and Issues*. New York: Columbia University School of Public Health National Center for Children in Poverty.

Cohen, Theodore F. 1993. "What Do Fathers Provide? Reconsidering the Economic and Nurturent Dimensions of Men as Parents." In *Men, Work, and Family*, edited by Jane C. Hood. Newbury Park, Calif.: Sage Publishing.

Colb, Sherry F. 1992. "Words that Deny, Devalue, and Punish: Judicial Responses to Fetus-Envy?" *Boston University Law Review* 72:101.

Coleman, John C. 1994. "The Trouble with Boys: Parenting the Men of the Future." *Journal of Adolescence* 17:309.

Collett, David. 1996. "Family Man: Fatherhood, Housework, and Gender Equality." *Law Institute Journal* 70:7.

Collier, Richard. 1995a. *Masculinity, Law, and the Family*. London: Routledge.

———. 1995b. "Waiting till Father Gets Home: The Reconstruction of Fatherhood in Family Law." *Social and Legal Studies* 4:1.

Coltrane, Scott. 1988. "Father-Child Relationships and the Status of Women: A Cross-Cultural Study." *American Journal of Sociology* 93:1060.

———. 1995. "The Future of Fatherhood: Social, Demographic, and Economic Influences on Men's Family Involvements." In *Fatherhood: Contemporary Theory, Research, and Social Policy*, edited by William Marsiglio. Thousand Oaks, Calif: Sage.

———. 1996. *Family Man: Fatherhood, Housework, and Gender Equity*. New York: Oxford University Press.

Coltrane, Scott, and Elsa O. Valdez. 1993. "Reluctant Compliance: Work-Family Role Allocation in Dual-Earner Chicano Families." In *Men, Work, and Family*, edited by Jane C. Hood. Newbury Park, Calif.: Sage.

Comer, James P. 1989. "Black Fathers." In *Fathers and Their Families*, edited by Stanley H. Cath, Linda Gunsberg, and Alan Gurwitt. Hillsdale, N.J.: Analytic Press.

Committee on Ways and Means. 1996. *Green Book*. 104th Congress, 20th Session.

Conine, Jon. 1989. *Fathers' Rights: The Sourcebook for Dealing with the Child Support System*. New York: Walker.

Connell, Bob. 1995. "Men at Bay: The Men's Movement and Its Newest Best-Sellers." In *The Politics of Manhood: Profeminist Men Respond to the Mythopoetic Men's Movement (And the Mythopoetic Leaders Answer)*, edited by Michael S. Kimmel. Philadelphia: Temple University Press.

Connell, R. W. 1995. *Masculinities*. Berkeley: University of California Press.

———. 1996. "Teaching the Boys: New Research on Masculinity, and Gender Strategies for Schools." *Teacher's College Record* 98:206.

Cook, Philip W. 1997. *Abused Men: The Hidden Side of Domestic Violence*. Westport, Conn.: Praeger.

Cooksey, Elizabeth C., and Michelle M. Fondell. 1996. "Spending Time with His Kids: Effects of Family Structure on Fathers' and Children's Lives." *Journal of Marriage and the Family* 58:693.

Cornell, Drucilla. 1998. "Fatherhood and Its Discontents: Men, Patriarchy, and Freedom." In *Lost Fathers: The Politics of Fatherlessness in America*, edited by Cynthia Daniels. New York: St. Martin's Press.

Costello, Cynthia, and Barbara Kivimae Krimgold, eds. 1996. *American Woman, 1996–97, Where We Stand: Women and Work*. Washington, D.C.: Women's Research and Education Institute.

Cowan, Philip A. 1988. "Becoming a Father, A Time of Change, An Opportunity for Development." In *Fatherhood Today: Men's Changing Role in the Family*, edited by Phyllis Bronstein and Carolyn Pape Cowan. New York: John Wiley.

Craig, Linda. 1997. "Fatherhood and the Unmarried Fertile Man." *New Law Journal* 147:6778.

Crockett, Lisa J., David J. Eggebeen, and Alan J. Hawkins. 1993. "Father's Presence and Young Children's Behavioral and Cognitive Adjustment." *Journal of Family Issues* 14:355.

"Culture and Ideas." 1997. *U.S. News and World Report* (May 12).

Cunningham, George P. 1996. "Body Politics: Race, Gender, and the Captive Body." In *Representing Black Men*, edited by Marcellus Blount and George P. Cunningham. New York: Routledge.

Curriden, Mark. 1992. "No Forced Fatherhood: State High Court Rules for Ex-Husband in Frozen Embryo Case." *American Bar Association Journal* 78:35.

Curtner-Smith, Mary Elizabeth. 1995. "Assessing Children's Visitation Needs with Divorced Noncustodial Fathers." *Families in Society* 76:341.

Cusick, Theresa. 1989. "Sexism and Early Parenting: Cause and Effect?" *Peabody Journal of Education* 64:113.

Czapanskiy, Karen. 1991. "Volunteers and Draftees: The Struggle for Parental Equality." *University of California at Los Angeles Law Review* 38:1415.

Daly, Kerry. 1993. "Reshaping Fatherhood: Finding the Models." *Journal of Family Issues* 14:510.

———. 1996. "Changing Fatherhood: An Interdisciplinary Practice." *Journal of Marriage and the Family* 58:802.

Daniels, Cynthia, ed. 1998. *Lost Fathers: The Politics of Fatherlessness in America*. New York: St. Martin's Press.

Daniels, Pamela, and Kathy Weingarten. 1988. "The Fatherhood Click, The Timing of Parenthood in Men's Lives." In *Fatherhood Today: Men's Changing Role in the Family*, edited by Phyllis Bronstein and Carolyn Pape Cowan. New York: John Wiley.

Davidson, Nicholas. 1990. "Life without Father: America's Greatest Social Catastrophe." *Policy Review* 51:40.

―――. 1996. "Changing Fatherhood: An Interdisciplinary Practice." *Journal of Marriage and the Family* 58:3.

Davies, Dominic. 1996. "Homophobia and Heterosexism." In *Pink Therapy: A Guide for Counsellors and Therapists Working with Lesbian, Gay, and Bisexual Clients*, edited by Dominic Davies and Charles Neal. Buckingham, Pa.: Open University Press.

Davis, Angela. 1989. *Women, Culture, and Politics.* New York: Random House.

Day, Randal D., and Wade C. Mackey. 1989. "An Alternate Standard for EvaluatingAmerican Fathers." *Journal of Family Issues* 10:401.

De Cecco, John P., and Michael G. Shively, eds. 1985. *Bashers, Baiters, and Bigots: Homophobia in American Society.* New York: Haworth Park Press.

Delgado, Richard, and Jean Stefanic. 1995. "Minority Men, Misery, and the Marketplace of Ideas." In *Constructing Masculinity*, edited by Maurice Berger, Brian Wallis, and Simon Watson. New York: Routledge.

De Luccie, Marie F., and Albert J. Davis. 1991. "Father-Child Relationships from the Preschool Years through Mid-Adolescence." *Journal of Genetic Psychology* 152:225.

DeMaris, Alfred, and Geoffrey L. Grief. 1997. "Single Custodial Fathers and Their Children When Things Go Well." In *Generative Fathering: Beyond Deficit Perspectives*, edited by Alan J. Hawkins and David C. Dollahite. Thousand Oaks, Calif.: Sage.

Dennehy, Katherine, and Jeylan T. Mortimer. 1993. "Work and Family Organizations of Contemporary Adolescent Boys and Girls." In *Men, Work, and Family*, edited by Jane C. Hood. Newbury Park, Calif.: Sage.

Devlin, Patty K., and Gloria A. Cowan. 1985. "Homophobia, Perceived Fathering, and Male Intimate Relationships." *Journal of Personality Assessment* 49:467.

Diamond, Michael J. 1995. "Becoming a Father: A Psychoanalytic Perspective on the Forgotten Parent." In *Becoming a Father: Contemporary, Social, Developmental, and Clinical Perspectives*, edited by Jerrold Lee Shapiro, Michael J. Diamond, and Martin Greenberg. New York: Springer.

Dienhart, Anna, and Kerry Daly, 1997. "Men and Women Cocreating Father Involvement in a Nongenerative Culture." In *Generative Fathering: Beyond Deficit Perspectives*, edited by Alan J. Hawkins and David C. Dollahite. Thousand Oaks, Calif.: Sage.

Dobrin, Adam, Brian Wiersema, Colin Loftin, and David McDowall, eds. 1996. *Statistical Handbook on Violence in America*. Phoenix, Ariz.: Oryx Press.

Dodson, Lisa. 1998. "This River Runs Deep: Father Myths and Single Mothers in Poor America." In *Lost Fathers: The Politics of Fatherlessness in America*, edited by Cynthia Daniels. New York: St. Martin's Press.

Doherty, William J. 1997. "The Best of Times and the Worst of Times." In *Generative Fathering: Beyond Deficit Perspectives*, edited by Alan J. Hawkins and David C. Dollahite. Thousand Oaks, Calif.: Sage.

Dolgin, Jane L. 1993. "Just a Gene: Judicial Assumptions about Parenthood." *University of California at Los Angeles Law Review* 40:637.

———. 1994. "The Intent of Reproduction: Reproductive Technologies and the Parent-Child Bond." *Connecticut Law Review* 26:1261.

———. 1997. *Defining the Family: Law, Technology, and Reproduction in an Uneasy Age*. New York: New York University Press.

Dollahite, David C., Alan J. Hawkins, and Sean E. Brotherson. 1996. "Narrative Accounts, Generative Fathering, and Family Life Education." *Marriage and Family Review* 24:349.

———. 1997. "Fatherwork: A Conceptual Ethic of Fathering as Generative Work." In *Generative Fathering: Beyond Deficit Perspectives*, edited by Alan J. Hawkins and David C. Dollahite. Thousand Oaks, Calif.: Sage.

Donahue, Patricia, David M. Powell, and Mary M. Lee. 1991. "Clinical Management of Intersex Abnormalities." *Current Problems in Surgery* 8:527.

Dowd, Nancy E. 1989a. "Work and Family: The Gender Paradox and the Limitations of Discrimination Analysis in Restructuring the Workplace." *Harvard Civil Rights-Civil Liberties Law Review* 24:79.

———. 1989b. "Envisioning Work and Family: A Critical Perspective on International Models." *Harvard Journal on Legislation* 26:311.

———. 1990. "Work and Family: Restructuring the Workplace." *Arizona Law Review* 32:431.

———. 1993. "Family Values and Valuing Family: A Blueprint for Family Leave." *Harvard Journal on Legislation* 30:335.

———. 1994. Book Review. "A Feminist Analysis of Adoption." *Harvard Law Review* 107:913.

———. 1995. "Stigmatizing Single Parents." *Harvard Women's Law Journal* 18:19.

———. 1996. "Rethinking Fatherhood." *Florida Law Review* 48:523.

———. 1997a. *In Defense of Single-Parent Families*. New York: New York University Press.

———. 1997b. "Women's, Men's, and Children's Equalities: Some Reflections and Uncertainties." *Southern California Review of Law and Women's Studies* 6:587.

Downey, Douglas B. 1994. "The School Performance of Children from Single-Mother and Single-Father Families: Economic or Interpersonal Deprivation?" *Journal of Family Issues* 15:142.

Dudley, James R. 1996. "Noncustodial Fathers Speak about Their Parental Role." *Family and Conciliation Courts Review* 34:410.

Duncan, Greg J., and Gretchen Caspary. 1997. "Welfare Dynamics and the 1996 Welfare Reform." *Notre Dame Journal of Law, Ethics, and Public Policy* 11:605.

Eberly, Don. 1997. Prepared statement of Don Eberly, Chairman of National Fatherhood Initiative, before the House Education and the Workplace Committee.

Edleson, Jeffrey L. 1996. "Controversy and Change in Batterers' Programs." In *Future Interventions with Battered Women and Their Families,* edited by Jeffrey L. Edleson and Zvi C. Eisikovits. Thousand Oaks, Calif.: Sage.

———. 1998. "Responsible Mothers and Invisible Men: Child Protection in the Case of Adult Domestic Violence." *Journal of Interpersonal Violence* 13:294.

Edleson, Jeffrey L., and Zvi C. Eisikovits, eds. 1996. *Future Interventions with Battered Women and Their Families.* Sage Series on Violence against Women, Volume 3. Thousand Oaks, Calif.: Sage.

Eggebeen, David J., Anastasia R. Snyder, and Wendy D. Manning. 1996. "Children in Single-Father Families in Demographic Perspective." *Journal of Family Issues* 17:441.

Ehrenreich, Barbara. 1983. *The Hearts of Men: American Dreams and the Flight from Commitment.* New York: Anchor Books.

Ehrensaft, Diane. 1987. *Parenting Together: Men and Women Sharing the Care of Their Children.* New York: Free Press.

Eichler, Margrit. 1993. "Clarifying the Legal Dimensions of Fatherhood." *Canadian Journal of Family Law* 11:2.

Eisler, Richard M. 1995. "The Relationship between Masculine Gender Role Stress and Men's Health Risk: The Validation of a Construct." In *The New Psychology of Men,* edited by Ronald Levant and William S. Pollack. New York: Basic Books.

Ellwood, David T. 1988. *Poor Support: Poverty in the American Family.* New York: Basic Books.

Elovitz, Marc E. 1995. "Adoption by Lesbian and Gay People: The Use and Mis-Use of Social Science Research." *Duke Journal of Gender Law and Policy* 2:207.

Elrod, Linda D. 1997. "Child Support Reassessed: Federalization of Enforcement Nears Completion." *University of Illinois Law Review* 1997:695.

Elrod, Linda D., and Robert G. Spector. 1998. "A Review of the Year in Family Law: A Search for Definitions and Policy." *Family Law Quarterly* 31:613.

"Employment Characteristics of Families in 1997." 1998. Bureau of Labor Statistics (news release).

Epstein, Debbie. 1997. "Boys' Own Stories: Masculinities and Sexualities in Schools." *Gender and Education* 9:105.

Erickson, Rebecca J., and Viktor Gecas. 1991. "Social Class and Fatherhood." In *Fatherhood and Families in Cultural Context*, edited by Frederick W. Bozett and Shirley M. H. Hanson. New York: Springer.

Erikson, Erik H. 1967. *Identity and the Life Cycle*. New York: International Universities Press.

Espada, Martin. 1996. "The Puerto Rican Dummy and the Merciful Son." In *Muy Macho: Latino Men Confront Their Manhood*, edited by Ray Gonzalez. New York: Anchor Books.

Everett, Joyce E. 1990. "Teen Parenting." In *Black Adolescence: Current Issues and Annotated Bibliography*. Boston: G. K. Hall.

Fagan, Jay. 1996. "A Preliminary Study of Low-Income African American Fathers' Play Interactions with Their Preschool-Age Children." *Journal of Black Psychology* 22:7.

"Family Structure and Children's Health." 1988. Washington, D.C.: National Center for Health Statistics.

Farrakhan, Louis. 1995. "In the Name of Allah, the Beneficent, the Merciful: A Holy Day of Atonement and Reconciliation." Speech presented during the Million Man March, October 16.

Fausto-Sterling, Anne. 1995. "How to Build a Man." In *Constructing Masculinity*, edited by Maurice Berger, Brian Wallis, and Simon Watson. New York: Routledge.

Fineman, Martha Albertson. 1995. *The Neutered Mother, the Sexual Family, and Other Twentieth-Century Tragedies*. London: Routledge.

Fitzgerald, Wendy A. 1994. "Maturity, Difference, and Mystery: Children's Perspectives and the Law." *Arizona Law Review* 36:11.

Fox, Greer Litton, and Priscilla White Blanton. 1995. "Noncustodial Fathers following Divorce." *Marriage and Family Review* 20:257.

Frankel, Judith, ed. 1993. *The Employed Mother and the Family Context*. New York: Springer.

Franklin, Clyde W. II. 1992. "Surviving the Institutional Decimation of Black Males: Causes, Consequences, and Intervention." In *The Making of Masculinities: The New Men's Studies*, edited by Harry Brod. New York: Routledge.

Frean, Alexandra. 1998. "Equality Time for Fathers." *New York Times* (June 6).

Freshman, Clark. 1997. "Re-Visioning the Dependency Crisis and the Negotiator's Dilemma: Reflections on the Sexual Family and the Mother-Child Dyad." *Law and Social Inquiry* 22:97.

Furstenberg, Frank F. 1990. "Divorce and the American Family. "*Annual Review of Sociology* 16:379.

———. 1992. "Good Dads—Bad Dads: Two Faces of Fatherhood." In *Family in Transition: Rethinking Marriage, Sexuality, Child Rearing, and Family Organization*, edited by Arlene S. Skolnick and Jerome H. Skolnick. New York: HarperCollins.

———. 1995. "Fathering in the Inner City: Paternal Participation and Public Policy." In *Fatherhood: Contemporary Theory, Research, and Social Policy*, edited by William Marsiglio. Thousand Oaks, Calif.: Sage.

Furstenberg, Frank F., and Andrew J. Cherlin. 1991. *Divided Families: What Happens to Children When Parents Part*. Cambridge: Harvard University Press.

Furstenburg, Frank F., and Kathleen Mullan Harris. 1993. "When Fathers Matter/Why Fathers Matter: The Impact of Paternal Involvement on the Offspring of Adolescent Mothers." In *The Politics of Pregnancy: Adolescent Sexuality and Public Policy*, edited by Deborah Rhode. New Haven, Conn.: Yale University Press.

Gadsden, Vivian L., and Ralph R. Smith. 1994. "African American Males and Fatherhood: Issues in Research and Practice." *Journal of Negro Education* 63:634.

Gallagher, Maggie. 1998. "Father Hunger." In *Lost Fathers: The Politics of Fatherlessness in America*, edited by Cynthia Daniels. New York: St. Martin's Press.

Garbarino, James. 1993. "Reinventing Fatherhood." *Families in Society: The Journal of Contemporary Human Services* 74:51.

Garfinkel, Irwin, and Sara McLanahan. 1995. "The Effects of Child Support Reform on Child Well-Being." In *Escape from Poverty: What Makes a Difference for Children?* edited by P. Lindsay Chase-Lansdale and Jeanne Brooks-Gunn. New York: Cambridge University Press.

Garfinkel, Irwin, and Patrick Wong. 1990. "Child Support and Public Policy." In *Lone Parent Families: The Economic Challenge*, edited by Elizabeth Duskin. Washington, D.C.: Organization for Economic Co-operation and Development Centre.

Garrison, Marsha. 1996. "How Do Judges Decide Divorce Cases? An Empirical Analysis of Discretionary Decision Making." *North Carolina Law Review* 74:401.

———. 1998. "Autonomy or Community? An Evaluation of Two Models of Parental Obligation." *California Law Review* 86:41.

Gatson, Sarah N. 1997. "Labor Policy and the Social Meaning of Parenthood." *Law and Social Inquiry* 22:277.

Geiger, Brenda. 1996. *Fathers as Primary Caregivers*. Westport, Conn.: Greenwood Press.

Gerson, Kathleen. 1993. *No Man's Land: Men's Changing Commitments to Family and Work*. New York: Basic Books.

Gerson, Kathleen. 1997. "An Institutional Perspective on Generative Fathering: Creating Social Supports for Parenting Equality." In *Generative Fathering: Beyond Deficit Perspectives*, edited by Alan J. Hawkins and David C. Dollahite. Thousand Oaks, Calif.: Sage.

Gibson, Donald. 1996. "Chapter One of Booker T. Washington's *Up from Slavery* and the Feminization of the African American Male." In *Representing Black Men*, edited by Marcellus Bount and George P. Cunningham. New York: Routledge.

Gilmore, David D. 1990. *Manhood in the Making*. New Haven: Yale University Press.

Goger, Thomas J. 1998. "Right of Putative Father to Custody of Illegitimate Child." *American Law Reports* 45:216.

Goldberg, Stephanie B. 1997. "Make Room for Daddy." *American Bar Association Journal* 1997:48.

Goldsmith, Scott J. 1995. "Oedipus or Orestes? Aspects of Gender Identity Development in Homosexual Men." *Psychoanalytic Inquiry* 15:112.

Goldstein, Jacob, and Abraham C. Fenster. 1994. "Anglo-American Criteria for Resolving Child Custody Disputes from the Eighteenth Century to the Present: Reflections on the Role of Socio-Cultural Change." *Journal of Family History* 19:35.

Goleman, Daniel. 1990. "Homophobia: Scientists Find Clues to Its Roots." *New York Times* (July 10).

Golombok, Susan, and Fiona Tasker. 1994. "Children in Lesbian and Gay Families: Theories and Evidence." *Annual Review of Sex Research* 1994:73.

Gonsiorek, John C. 1991. "The Definition and Scope of Sexual Orientation." In *Homosexuality: Research Implications for Public Policy*, edited by John C. Gonsiorek and James D. Winrich. Newbury Park, Calif.: Sage.

Gonzalez, Ray, ed. 1996. *Muy Macho: Latino Men Confront Their Manhood*. New York: Anchor Books.

Goodey, Jo. 1997. "Boys Don't Cry: Masculinities, Fear of Crime, and Fearlessness." *British Journal of Criminology* 37:401.

Gorenberg, Carol A. 1998. "Fathers' Rights v. Children's Best Interests: Establishing a Predictable Standard for California Adoption Disputes." *Family Law Quarterly* 31:169.

Green, Dorsey G., and Frederick W. Bozett. 1993. "Lesbian Mothers and Gay Fathers." In *Psychological Perspectives on Lesbian and Gay Male Experiences*, edited by Linda D. Garnets and Douglas C. Kimmel. New York: Columbia University Press.

Greenfeld, Lawrence A. 1996. "Child Victimizers: Violent Offenders and Their Victims." Washington, D.C.: Bureau of Justice Statistics.

Greif, Geoffrey L. 1990. *The Daddy Track and the Single Father*. Lexington, Mass.: Lexington Books.

———. 1992. "Lone Fathers in the United States: An Overview and Practical Implications." *British Journal of Social Work* 22:565.

———. 1995a. "Single Fathers with Custody following Separation and Divorce." *Marriage and Family Review* 20:213.

———. 1995b. "When Divorced Fathers Want No Contact with Their Children: A Preliminary Analysis." *Journal of Divorce and Remarriage* 23:75.

Greif, Geoffrey L., and Cynthia Bailey. 1990. "Where Are the Fathers in Social Work Literature?" *Families in Society: The Journal of Contemporary Human Services* 71:88.

Greif, Geoffrey L., and Alfred DeMaris. 1993. "Balancing Work and Single Fatherhood." In *Men, Work, and Family*, edited by Jane C. Hood. Newbury Park, Calif.: Sage.

———. 1995. "Single Fathers with Custody: Do They Change Over Time?" In *Fatherhood: Contemporary Theory, Research, and Social Policy*, edited by William Marsiglio. Thousand Oaks, Calif.: Sage.

Griswold, Robert L. 1993. *Fatherhood in America: A History*. New York: Basic Books.

———. 1998. "The History and Politics of Fatherlessness." In *Lost Fathers: The Politics of Fatherlessness in America*, edited by Cynthia Daniels. New York: St. Martin's Press.

Grogger, Jeff, and Nick Ronan. 1995. *The Intergenerational Effects of Fatherlessness on Educational Attainment and Entry-Level Wages*. Washington, D.C.: Bureau of Labor Statistics.

Groombridge, Nic. 1995. "Families without Fatherhood." *British Journal of Criminology* 35:2.

Grossman, Frances K. 1988. "Fathers and Children: Predicting the Quality and Quantity of Fathering." *Developmental Psychology* 24:82.

Gurwitt, Alan. 1997. "Fathers and Developmental Psychopathology." *Journal of American Academy of Child and Adolescent Psychiatry* 36:710.

Guttmann, Joseph. 1989. "The Divorced Father." *Journal of Comparative Family Studies* 20:247.

Haas, Linda. 1993. "Nurturing Fathers and Working Mothers: Changing Gender Roles in Sweden." In *Men, Work, and Family*, edited by Jane C. Hood. Newbury Park, Calif.: Sage.

———. 1995. "Company Culture and Men's Usage of Family Leave Benefits in Sweden." *Family Relations* 44:28.

Haddix, Amy. 1996. "Unseen Victims: Acknowledging the Effects of Domestic Violence on Children through Statutory Termination of Parental Rights." *California Law Review* 84:757.

Hamilton, John R. 1988. "The Unwed Father and the Right to Know of His Child's Existence." *Kentucky Law Journal* 76:949.

Hanson, Shirley M. H., and Frederick W. Bozett. 1985. *Dimensions of Fatherhood.* Beverly Hills, Calif.: Sage.

Harris, Kathleen Mullan. 1996. "Poverty, Paternal Involvement, and Adolescent Well-Being." *Journal of Family Issues* 17:14.

Harris, Leslie Joan. 1996. "Reconsidering the Criteria for Legal Fatherhood." *Utah Law Review* 1996:2.

Hawkins, Alan J. 1991. "Are Fathers Fungible? Patterns of Coresident Adult Men in Maritally Disrupted Families and Young Children's Well-Being." *Journal of Marriage and the Family* 53:958.

Hawkins, Alan J., Shawn L. Christiansen, Cathryn Pond Sargent, and E. Jeffrey Hill. 1993. "Rethinking Fathers' Involvement in Child Care: A Developmental Perspective." *Journal of Family Issues* 14:531.

Hawkins, Alan J., and David C. Dollahite. 1997. "Beyond the Role-Inadequacy Perspective of Fathering." In *Generative Fathering: Beyond Deficit Perspectives*, edited by Alan J. Hawkins and David C. Dollahite. Thousand Oaks, Calif.: Sage.

—— eds. 1997. *Generative Fathering: Beyond Deficit Perspectives*. Thousand Oaks, Calif.: Sage.

Heath, Terri D. 1994. "The Impact of Delayed Fatherhood on the Father-Child Relationship." *Journal of Genetic Psychology* 155:511.

Herek, Gregory M. 1991. "Stigma, Prejudice, and Violence against Lesbians and Gay Men." In *Homosexuality: Research Implications for Public Policy*, edited by John C. Gonsiorek and James D. Winrich. Newbury Park, Calif.: Sage.

——. 1993. "On Heterosexual Masculinity: Some Psychical Consequences of the Social Construction of Gender and Sexuality." In *Psychological Perspectives on Lesbian and Gay Male Experiences*, edited by Linda D. Garnets and Douglas C. Kimmel. New York: Columbia University Press.

——. 1996. "Heterosexism and Homophobia." In *Textbook of Homosexuality and Mental Health*, edited by Robert P. Cabaj and Terry S. Stein. Washington, D.C.: American Psychiatric Press.

Herek, Gregory M., and Kevin T. Berrill, eds. 1992. *Hate Crimes: Confronting Violence against Lesbians and Gay Men*. Newbury Park, Calif.: Sage.

Hetherington, E. Mavis, and Sandra H. Henderson. 1997. "Fathers in Stepfamilies." In *The Role of the Father in Child Development*, edited by Michael E. Lamb. New York: John Wiley.

Hetherington, E. Mavis, and Margaret M. Stanley-Hagan. 1997. "The Effects of Divorce on Fathers and Their Children." In *The Role of the Father in Child Development*, edited by Michael E. Lamb. New York: John Wiley.

Hewlett, Barry S. 1987. "Intimate Fathers: Patterns of Paternal Holding among Aka Pygmies." In *The Father's Role: Cross Cultural Perspectives*, edited by Michael E. Lamb. Hillsdale, N.J.: Lawrence Erlbaum.

Hewlett, Barry S. ed. 1992. *Father-Child Relations: Cultural and Biosocial Contexts*. New York: Aldine de Gruyter.

Hill, John Lawrence. 1991. "What Does it Mean to Be a Parent? The Claims of Biology as the Basis for Parental Rights." *New York University Law Review* 66:353.

Hochschild, Arlie, and Anne Machung. 1992. "The Second Shift: Working Parents and the Revolution at Home." In *Family in Transition: Rethinking Marriage, Sexuality, Child Rearing, and Family Organization*, edited by Arlene S. Skolnick and Jerome H. Skolnick. New York: HarperCollins.

Hojgaard, Lis. 1997. "Working Fathers—Caught in the Web of the Symbolic Order of Gender." *Acta Sociologica* 40:245.

Hollandsworth, Marla J. 1995. "Gay Men Creating Families through Surro-Gay Arrangements: A Paradigm for Reproductive Freedom." *American University Journal of Gender and Law* 3:183.

Holmes, Gilbert A. 1994. "The Tie That Binds: The Constitutional Right of Children to Maintain Relationships with Parent-Like Individuals." *Maryland Law Review* 53:358.

Hood, Jane C., ed. 1993. *Men, Work, and Family*. Newbury Park, Calif.: Sage.

hooks, bell. 1995. "Doing it for Daddy." In *Constructing Masculinity*, edited by Maurice Berger, Brian Wallis, and Simon Watson. New York: Routledge.

Horn, Wade F. 1997. "You've Come a Long Way, Daddy: After Being Pilloried and Left for Dead, the Fatherhood Ideal Is Making a Comeback." *Policy Review* 1997:24.

Howe, Ruth-Arlene. 1993. "Legal Rights and Obligations: An Uneven Evolution." In *Young Unwed Fathers: Changing Roles and Emerging Policies*, edited by Robert I. Lerman and Theodora J. Ooms. Philadelphia: Temple University Press.

Hutchison, Eliza B. 1998. "Improving Custody Law in Virginia Without Creating a Rebuttable Presumption of Joint Custody." *William and Mary Journal of Women and the Law* 4:523.

Hyde, Janet Shibley, Marilyn J. Essex, Roseanne Clark, and Marjorie H. Klein. 1996. "Parental Leave: Policy and Research." *Journal of Social Issues* 52:91.

Ihinger-Tallman, Marilyn, Kay Pasley, and Cheryl Buehler. 1995. "Developing a Middle-Range Theory of Father Involvement Postdivorce." In *Fatherhood: Contemporary Theory, Research, and Social Policy*, edited by William Marsiglio. Thousand Oaks, Calif.: Sage.

Ikemoto, Lisa C. 1996. "The Infertile, the Too Fertile, and the Dysfertile." *Hastings Law Journal* 47:1007.

Jackson, Robert Max. 1989. "The Reproduction of Parenting." *American Sociological Review* 54:215.

Jacobs, Michelle S. 1998. "Requiring Battered Women to Die: Murder Liability for Mothers under Failure to Protect Statutes." *Journal of Criminal Law and Criminology* 88:579.

Jacobs, Susan Beth. 1997. "The Hidden Gender Bias behind the Best Interest of the Child Standard in Custody Decisions." *Georgia State University Law Review* 13:845.

Jacobsen, Linda, and Brad Edmondson. 1993. "Father Figures." *American Demographics* 15:22.

Jaffe, Peter G., and Robert Geffner. 1998. "Child Custody Disputes and Domestic Violence: Critical Issues for Mental Health, Social Service, and Legal Professionals." In *Children Exposed to Marital Violence,* edited by George W. Holden, Robert Geffner, and Ernest N. Jouriles. Washington, D.C.: American Psychological Association.

Jennison, Judith Bond. 1991. "The Search for Equality in a Woman's World: Fathers' Rights to Child Custody." *Rutgers Law Review* 43:1141.

Johnston, Janet R. 1995. "Children's Adjustment in Sole Custody Compared to Joint Custody Families and Principles for Custody Decision Making." *Family and Conciliation Courts Review* 33:415.

Josephson, Jyl J., ed. 1997. *Gender, Families, and State: Child Support Policy in the United States.* Lanham, Md.: Rowman and Littlefield.

Joshi, Neela P., and Stanley F. Battle. 1990. "Adolescent Fathers: An Approach for Intervention." *Journal of Health and Social Policy* 1:17.

Kaufman, Michael. 1987. *Beyond Patriarchy: Essays by Men on Pleasure, Power, and Change.* New York: Oxford University Press.

"Keeping Pace with Change: Black Males and Social Policy." 1993. Washington, D.C.: Center for the Study of Social Policy.

Kelly, Joan B. 1993. "Current Research on Children's Postdivorce Adjustment: No Simple Answers." *Family and Conciliation Courts Review* 31:29.

Kidde, Andrew. 1997. "Non-Custodial Fathers: Why So Many Drop Out and What Can Be Done about It." *Oregon State Bar Bulletin* 57:15.

Kiecolt, Jill K., and Mark A. Fossett. 1997. "The Effects of Mate Availability on Marriage among Black Americans." In *Family Life in Black America,* edited by Robert Joseph Taylor, James S. Jackson, and Linda M. Chatters. Thousand Oaks, Calif.: Sage.

Kimbrell, Andrew. 1995. *The Masculine Mystique: The Politics of Masculinity.* New York: Balantine Books.

Kimmel, Michael S., ed. 1987. *Changing Men: New Directions in Research on Men and Masculinity.* Newbury Park, Calif.: Sage.

———. 1992. "Issues for Men in the 1990s." *University of Miami Law Review* 46:671.

———. 1995a. *The Politics of Manhood: Profeminist Men Respond to the*

Mythopoetic Men's Movement (And the Mythopoetic Leaders Answer). Philadelphia: Temple University Press.

———. 1995b. "Born to Run: Nineteenth-Century Fantasies of Masculine Retreat and Recreation (or The Historical Rust on Iron John)." In *The Politics of Manhood: Profeminist Men Respond to the Mythopoetic Men's Movement (And the Mythopoetic Leaders Answer)*, edited by Michael S. Kimmel. Philadelphia: Temple University Press.

———. 1996. *Manhood in America: A Cultural History*. New York: Free Press.

Kimmel, Michael S., and Michael Kaufman. 1995. "Weekend Warriors: The New Men's Movement." In *The Politics of Manhood: Profeminist Men Respond to the Mythopoetic Men's Movement (And the Mythopoetic Leaders Answer)*, edited by Michael S. Kimmel. Philadelphia: Temple University Press.

Kimmel, Michael S., and Michael A. Messner. 1992. *Men's Lives*. New York: Macmillan.

King, James R. 1998. *Uncommon Caring: Learning from Men Who Teach Young Children*. New York: Teacher's College Press at Columbia University.

King, Valerie. 1994a. "Variation in the Consequences of Nonresident Father Involvement for Children's Well-Being." *Journal of Marriage and the Family* 56:963.

———. 1994b. "Nonresident Father Involvement and Child Well-Being: Can Dads Make a Difference?" *Journal of Family Issues* 15:78.

Kirsch, John A. W., and James D. Weinrich. 1991. "Homosexuality, Nature, and Biology: Is Homosexuality Natural? Does It Matter?" In *Homosexuality: Research Implications for Public Policy*, edited by John A. W. Kirsch and James D. Weinrich. Newbury Park, Calif.: Sage.

Kisthardt, Mary Kay. 1991. "Of Fatherhood, Families, and Fantasy: The Legacy of Michael H. v. Gerald D." *Tulane Law Review* 65:585.

Knitzer, Jane, Eric Brenner, Stanley Bernard, and Vivian Gadsden. 1997. *Map and Track: State Initiatives to Encourage Responsible Fatherhood*. New York: Columbia University School of Public Health National Center for Children in Poverty.

Kolbo, Jerome R., Eleanor H. Blakely, and David Engleman. 1996. "Children Who Witness Domestic Violence: A Review of the Empirical Literature." *Journal of Interpersonal Violence* 11:2.

Kotre, John N. 1984. *Outliving the Self: Generativity and the Interpretation of Lives*. Baltimore: Johns Hopkins University Press.

Kovacic-Fleischer, Candace Saari. 1997. "*United States v. Virginia*'s New Gender Equal Protection Analysis with Ramifications for Pregnancy, Parenting, and Title VII." *Vanderbilt Law Review* 50:845.

Kraemer, Sebastian. 1991. "The Origins of Fatherhood: An Ancient Family Process." *Family Process* 30:377.

Krampe, Edythe M., and Paul D. Fairweather. 1993. "Father Presence and Family Formation: A Theoretical Reformulation." *Journal of Family Issues* 14:572.

Krause, Harry D. 1989. "Child Support Reassessed: Limits of Private Responsibility and the Public Interest." *University of Illinois Law Review* 1989:367.

Krugman, Steven. 1995. "Male Development and the Transformation of Shame." In *The New Psychology of Men,* edited by Ronald F. Levant and William S. Pollack. New York: Basic Books.

Kruk, Edward. 1994. "The Disengaged Noncustodial Father: Implications for Social Work Practice with the Divorced Family." *Social Work* 39:15.

Kurtz, Lynne R. 1997. "Protecting New York's Children: An Argument for the Creation of a Rebuttable Presumption against Awarding a Spouse Abuser Custody of a Child." *Albany Law Review* 60:1345.

Lacey, Linda J. 1996. "As American as Parenthood and Apple Pie: Neutered Mothers, Breadwinning Fathers, and Welfare Rhetoric." *Cornell Law Review* 82:79.

Lamb, Michael E. ed. 1987. *The Father's Role: Cross Cultural Perspectives.* Hillsdale, N.J.: Lawrence Erlbaum.

―――. 1994. "How Fathers Care for the Next Generation: A Four-Decade Study." *Human Development* 37:385.

―――. 1997. "The Development of Father-Infant Relationships." In *The Role of the Father in Child Development,* edited by Michael E. Lamb. New York: John Wiley.

Laqueur, Thomas W. 1990. "The Facts of Fatherhood." In *Conflicts in Feminism,* edited by Marianne Hirsch and Evelyn Fox Keller. New York: Routledge.

LaRossa, Ralph. 1997. *The Modernization of Fatherhood: A Social and Political History.* Chicago: University of Chicago Press.

Larson, Reed W. 1993. "Finding Time for Fatherhood: The Emotional Ecology of Adolescent-Father Interactions." *New Directions for Child Development* 62:7.

Larson, Reed, and Maryse H. Richards. 1994. *Divergent Realities: The Emotional Lives of Mothers, Fathers, and Adolescents.* New York: Basic Books.

Law, Sylvia. 1988. "Homosexuality and the Social Meaning of Gender." *Wisconsin Law Review* 1988:187.

Lawhon, Tommie. 1996. "Responsible Fathering: An Educational Approach." *Journal of Family and Consumer Sciences* 88:35.

Lazur, Richard F., and Richard Majors. 1995. "Men of Color: Ethnocultural Variations of Male Gender Role Strain." In *The New Psychology of Men,* edited by Ronald F. Levant and William S. Pollack. New York: Basic Books.

Lee, Patrick C., and Robert Sussman Stewart, eds. 1976. *Sex Differences: Cultural and Developmental Dimensions.* New York: Urize Books.

Legler, Paul K. 1996. "The Coming Revolution in Child Support Policy: Implications of the 1996 Welfare Reform Act." *Family Law Quarterly* 30:519.

———.1997. "Child Support Enforcement Reform." *Fair$Share* 17:8.

Lerman, Robert I. 1993. "A National Profile of Young Unwed Fathers." In *Young Unwed Fathers: Changing Roles and Emerging Policies,* edited by Robert I. Lerman and Theodora J. Ooms. Philadelphia: Temple University Press.

Lerman, Robert I., and Theodora J. Ooms, eds. 1993. *Young Unwed Fathers: Changing Roles and Emerging Policies.* Philadelphia: Temple University Press.

Levant, Ronald F. 1995a. *Masculinity Reconstructed: Changing the Rules of Manhood—at Work, in Relationships, and in Family Life.* New York: Penguin.

———. 1995b. "Introduction." In *A New Psychology of Men,* edited by Ronald F. Levant and William S. Pollack. New York: Basic Books.

———. 1995c. "Toward the Reconstruction of Masculinity." In *A New Psychology of Men,* edited by Ronald F. Levant and William S. Pollack. New York: Basic Books.

Levant, Ronald F., Linda S. Hirsch, Elizabeth Celentano, Tracy M. Cozza, Susan Hill, Mary MacEachern, Nadine Marty, and John Schnedeker. 1992. "The Male Role: An Investigation of Contemporary Norms." *Journal of Mental Health Counseling* 14:325.

Levant, Ronald F., and William S. Pollack, eds. 1995. *A New Psychology of Men.* New York: Basic Books.

Levesque, Roger J. R. 1993a. "The Role of Unwed Fathers in Welfare Law: Failing Legislative Initiatives and Surrendering Judicial Responsibility." *Law and Inequality Journal* 12:93.

———. 1993b. "Looking to Unwed Dads to Fill the Public Purse: A Disturbing Wave in Welfare Reform." *University of Louisville Journal of Family Law* 32:1.

———. 1994. "Targeting Deadbeat Dads: The Problem with the Direction of Welfare Reform." *Hamline Journal of Public Law and Policy* 15:74.

Levine, James A., and Edward W. Pitt. 1995. *New Expectations: Community Strategies for Responsible Fatherhood.* New York: Families and Work Institute.

Levine, James A., and Todd L. Pittinsky. 1998. *Working Fathers: New Strategies for Balancing Work and Family.* San Diego, Calif.: Harcourt Brace Longmans.

Levit, Nancy. 1996. "Feminism for Men: Legal Ideology and the Construction of Maleness." *University of California at Los Angeles Law Review* 43:1037.

———. 1998. *The Gender Line: Men, Women, and the Law.* New York: New York University Press.

Lewis, Charlie, and Margaret O'Brien, eds. 1987. *Reassessing Fatherhood: New Observations on Fathers and the Modern Family.* London: Sage.

Lewis, Robert A., and Robert E. Salt, eds. 1986. *Men in Families.* Beverly Hills, Calif.: Sage.

Li, Jiali, and Neil Bennett. 1996. *One in Four: America's Youngest Poor.* New York: Columbia University School of Public Health National Center for Children in Poverty.

Liebow, Elliot. 1967. *Tally's Corner: A Study of Negro Streetcorner Men.* Boston: Little, Brown.

Loewen, James W. 1988. "Visitation Fatherhood." In *Fatherhood Today: Men's Changing Role in the Family,* edited by Phyllis Bronstein and Carolyn Pape Cowan. New York: John Wiley.

Louv, Richard. 1993. "The Crisis of the Absent Father." *Parents Magazine* 68:54.

Loveridge, Judith. 1990. "Rethinking the Parenting Paradigm: Embodied Mothers and Fathers in Discourse/Practice." *Early Child Development and Care* 55:17.

Luker, Kristin. 1992. "Dubious Conceptions: The Controversy over Teen Pregnancy." In *Family in Transition: Rethinking Marriage, Sexuality, Child Rearing, and Family Organization,* edited by Arlene S. Skolnick and Jerome H. Skolnick. New York: HarperCollins.

Lupton, Deborah, and Lesly Barclay. 1997. *Constructing Fatherhood: Discourses and Experiences.* London: Sage.

Maccoby, Eleanor, and Robert Mnookin. 1992. *Dividing the Child: Social and Legal Dilemmas of Custody.* Cambridge: Harvard University Press.

Mackey, Wade C. 1985. *Fathering Behaviors: The Dynamics of the Man-Child Bond.* New York: Plenum Press.

———. 1995a. "The Fathering Incentive: A Hard Look." *Journal of Children and Poverty* 1:85.

———. 1995b. "U.S. Fathering Behaviors within a Cross-Cultural Context: An Evaluation by an Alternative Benchmark." *Journal of Comparative Family Studies* 26:443.

———. 1996. *The American Father: Bicultural and Developmental Aspects.* New York: Plenum Press.

Madhubuti, Haki R. (Don L. Lee). 1990. *Black Men: Obsolete, Single Dangerous? The Afrikan American Family in Transition. Essays in Discovery, Solution, and Hope.* Chicago: Third World Press.

Maravel, Alexandra. 1997. "Intercountry Adoption and the Flight from Unwed Fathers' Rights: Whose Right Is It Anyway?" *South Carolina Law Review* 48:497.

Mariani, Philomena. 1995. "Law-and-Order Science." In *Constructing Masculinity,* edited by Maurice Berger, Brian Wallis, and Simon Watson. New York: Routledge.

Marsiglio, William. 1988. "Commitment to Social Fatherhood: Predicting Adolescent Males' Intentions to Live with Their Child and Partner." *Journal of Marriage and the Family* 50:427.

———. 1993. "Contemporary Scholarship on Fatherhood: Culture, Identity, and Conduct." *Journal of Family Issues* 14:484.

———. 1995a. "Fathers' Diverse Life Course Patterns and Roles: Theory and Social Interventions." In *Fatherhood: Contemporary Theory, Research, and Social Policy*, edited by William Marsiglio. Thousand Oaks, Calif.: Sage.

———. 1995b. "Fatherhood Scholarship: An Overview and Agenda for the Future." In *Fatherhood: Contemporary Theory, Research, and Social Policy*, edited by William Marsiglio. Thousand Oaks, Calif.: Sage.

———. 1995c. "Stepfathers with Minor Children Living at Home: Parenting Perceptions and Relationship Quality." In *Fatherhood: Contemporary Theory, Research, and Social Policy*, edited by William Marsiglio. Thousand Oaks, Calif.: Sage.

———. ed. 1995d. *Fatherhood: Contemporary Theory, Research, and Social Policy*. Thousand Oaks, Calif.: Sage.

———. 1997. *Procreative Man*. New York: New York University Press.

Marsiglio, William, Randal Day, and Michael Lamb. 2000. "Exporing Fatherhood Diversity: Implications for Conceptualing Father Involvement." *Marriage and Family Review* 29:(forthcoming).

Mason, Mary Ann. 1994. *From Father's Property to Children's Rights: The History of Child Custody in the United States*. New York: Columbia University Press.

May, Larry. 1998. *Masculinity and Morality*. Ithaca, N.Y.: Cornell University Press.

May, Larry, and Robert Strikwerda. 1996. "Fatherhood and Nurturance." In *Rethinking Masculinity: Philosophical Explorations in Light of Feminism*, edited by Larry May, Robert Strikwerda, and Patrick D. Hopkins. Lanham, Md.: Rowman and Littlefield.

May, Larry, Robert Strikwerda, and Patrick D. Hopkins, eds. 1996. *Rethinking Masculinity: Philosophical Explorations in Light of Feminism*. Lanham, Md.: Rowman and Littlefield.

Maynes, Mary Jo, Ann Waltner, Birgitto Soland, and Ulrike Strasser, eds. 1996. *Gender, Kinship, Power: A Comparative and Interdisciplinary History*. New York: Routledge.

Mayo, Yolanda. 1997. "Machismo, Fatherhood, and the Latino Family: Understanding the Concept." *Journal of Multicultural Social Work* 5:49.

McAdoo, Harriet Pipes, ed. 1997. *Black Families*. 3d ed. Thousand Oaks, Calif.: Sage.

McAdoo, John L. 1988. "Changing Perspectives on the Role of the Black Father." In *Fatherhood Today: Men's Changing Role in the Family*, edited by Phyllis Bronstein and Carolyn Pape Cowan. New York: John Wiley.

———. 1993. "The Roles of African American Fathers: An Ecological Perspective." *Families in Society* 74:28.

McBride, Brent A. 1991. "Parental Support Programs and Paternal Stress: An Exploratory Study." *Early Childhood Research Quarterly* 6:137.

McBride, Brent A., and Johanna Darragh. 1995. "Interpreting the Data on Father Involvement: Implications for Parenting Programs for Men." *Families in Society: The Journal of Contemporary Human Services* 76:490.

McBride, Brent A., and Rebecca McBride. 1993. "Parent Education and Support Programs for Fathers." *Childhood Education* 70:4.

McCaffery, Edward J. 1997. *Taxing Women*. Chicago: University of Chicago Press.

McClain, Linda C. 1996. "Irresponsible Reproduction." *Hastings Law Journal* 47:339.

McConnell, Joyce E. 1998. "Securing the Care of Children in Diverse Families: Building on Trends in Guardianship Reform." *Yale Journal of Law and Feminism* 10:29.

McKenry, Patrick C., Sharon J. Price, Mark A. Fine, and Julianne Serovich. 1992. "Predictors of Single, Noncustodial Fathers' Physical Involvement with Their Children." *Journal of Genetic Psychology* 153:305.

McKenry, Patrick C., Theresa W. Julian, and Stephen M. Gavazzi. 1995. "Toward a Biopsychosocial Model of Domestic Violence." *Journal of Marriage and the Family* 57:307.

McLanahan, Sara. 1998. "Growing Up without a Father." In *Lost Fathers: The Politics of Fatherlessness in America,* edited by Cynthia Daniels. New York: St. Martin's Press.

McLearn, Christopher, Maggie Carey, and Cheryl White, eds. 1996. *Men's Ways of Being*. Boulder: Westview Press.

McNeely, Cynthia A. 1998. "Lagging behind the Times: Parenthood, Custody, and Gender Bias in the Family Court." *Florida State University Law Review* 25:891.

Meier, Catherine G. 1997. "Protecting Parental Leave: A Fundamental Rights Model." *Willamette Law Review* 33:177.

Meier, Joan. 1997. "Domestic Violence, Character, and Social Change in the Welfare Reform Debate." *Law and Policy* 19:205.

Melli, Marigold S., Patricia Brown, and Maria Cancian. 1997. "Child Custody in a Changing World: A Study of Postdivorce Arrangements in Wisconsin." *University of Illinois Law Review* 1997:773.

Messner, Michael A. 1992. "New Fathers, Wild Men, and Weeping Generals: Changing Men and Feminist Politics in the U.S." University of Southern California, Department of Sociology and Program for the Study of Women and Men in Society. Unpublished paper.

———. 1995. "Changing Men and Feminist Politics in the United States." In *The Politics of Manhood: Profeminist Men Respond to the Mythopoetic Men's Movement (And the Mythopoetic Leaders Answer),* edited by Michael S. Kimmel. Philadelphia: Temple University Press.

———. 1997. *Politics of Masculinities: Men in Movements*. Thousand Oaks, CA: Sage.

Meulders-Klein, Marie-Therese. 1996. "The Status of the Father in European Legislation." *American Journal of Comparative Law* 44:487.

Meyer, Daniel R. 1996. "Child Support Reform: Lessons from Wisconsin." *Family Relations* 45:11.

Meyer, Daniel R., and Steven Garasky. 1993. "Custodial Fathers: Myths, Realities, and Child Support Policy." *Journal of Marriage and the Family* 55:73.

Meyers, Steven A. 1993. "Adapting Parent Education Programs to Meet the Needs of Fathers: An Ecological Perspective." *Family Relations* 42:447.

Miccio, Kristian. 1995. "In the Name of Mothers and Children: Deconstructing the Myth of the Passive Battered Mother and the Protected Child in Child Neglect Proceedings." *Albany Law Review* 58:1087.

Miller, Robin Cheryl. 1998. "Right of Putative Father to Visitation with Child Born out of Wedlock." *American Law Reports* 58:669.

Mincy, Ronald B. 1989. "Paradoxes in Black Economic Progress: Incomes, Families, and the Underclass." *Journal of Negro Education* 58:255.

Mirande, Alfredo. 1988. "Chicano Fathers: Traditional Perception and Current Realities." In *Fatherhood Today: Men's Changing Role in the Family*, edited by Phyllis Bronstein and Carolyn Pape Cowan. New York: John Wiley.

———. 1991. "Ethnicity and Fatherhood." In *Fatherhood and Families in Cultural Context*, edited by Frederick W. Bozett and Shirley M. H. Hanson. New York: Springer.

Molvig, Dianne. 1998. "Debating the Standard in Child Custody Placement Decisions." *Wisconsin Lawyer* 71:10.

Monopoli, Paula A. 1994. "Deadbeat Dads: Should Support and Inheritance Be Linked?" *University of Miami Law Review* 49:257.

Moorehouse, Martha J. 1993. "Work and Family Dynamics." In *Family, Self, and Society: Toward a New Agenda for Family Research*, edited by Phillip A. Cowan, Dorothy Field, Donald A. Hansen, Arlene Skolnick, and Guy E. Swanson. Mahwah, N.J.: Lawrence Erlbaum.

Mosley, Jane, and Elizabeth Thomson. 1995. "Fathering Behavior and Child Outcomes: The Role of Race and Poverty." In *Fatherhood: Contemporary Theory, Research, and Social Policy*, edited by William Marsiglio. Thousand Oaks, Calif.: Sage.

Munson, Susan A. 1995. "Names—A Presumption Exists in Favor of the Surname Chosen for a Child by the Child's Custodial Parent." *Seton Hall Law Review* 26:490.

Nantell, Sharon C. 1997. "The Tax Paradigm of Child Care: Shifting Attitudes toward a Private/Parental/Public Alliance." *Marquette Law Review* 80:4.

"Natality Statistics." 1998. Atlanta: Center for Disease Control and Prevention/National Center for Health Statistics.

National Committee to Prevent Child Abuse. 1998. "Child Abuse and Neglect Statistics." Http://www.childabuse.org/facts97.html.

"National Crime Victimization Survey, Violence Against Women." 1994. *Bureau of Justice Special Report.* Washington, D.C.: Bureau of Justice.

"National Men's Health Week Survey." 1995. *Men's Health Magazine/CNN.*

National Study of the Changing Workforce. 1997. New York: Families and Work Institute.

Neela, Joshi P., and Stanley F. Battle. 1991. "Adolescent Fathers: An Approach for Intervention." *Journal of Health and Social Policy* 1:17.

Neville, Brian, and Ross D. Parke. 1997. "Waiting for Paternity: Interpersonal and Contextual Implications of the Timing of Fatherhood." *Sex Roles: A Journal of Research* 37:45.

Newman, Katherine S. 1992. "The Downwardly Mobile Family." In *Family in Transition: Rethinking Marriage, Sexuality, Child Rearing, and Family Organization,* edited by Arlene S. Skolnick and Jerome H. Skolnick. New York: HarperCollins.

Nugent, Kevin J. 1991. "Cultural and Psychological Influences on the Father's Role in Infant Development." *Journal of Marriage and the Family* 53:475.

Ofari, Earl. 1994. *Black Fatherhood II: Black Women Talk about Their Men.* Los Angeles: Middle Passage Press.

Oldham, Thomas J. 1997. "ALI Principles of Family Dissolution: Some Comments." *University of Illinois Law Review* 1997:801.

Olds, Sharon. 1992. *The Father.* New York: Knopf.

O'Neil, James M., Glenn E. Good, and Sarah Holmes. 1995. "Fifteen Years of Theory and Research on Men's Gender Role Conflict: New Paradigms for Empirical Research." In *The New Psychology of Men,* edited by Ronald F. Levant and William S. Pollack. New York: Basic Books.

Ostling, Richard N. 1997. "God, Football, and the Game of His Life." *Time* (Octobter 6).

O'Toole, Laura L., and Jessica R. Schiffman, eds. 1997. *Gender Violence: Interdisciplinary Perspectives.* New York: New York University Press.

Padawer, Ruth. 1999. "Gay Pair Win OK to Adopt 2d Child." *Bergen Record* (May 18).

Palkovitz, Rob. 1984. "Parental Attitudes and Fathers' Interactions with Their Five-Month-Old Infants." *Developmental Psychology* 20:1054.

Paradise, Jo-Ellen. 1998. "The Disparity between Men and Women in Custody Disputes: Is Joint Custody the Answer to Everyone's Problems?" *St. John's Law Review* 72:517.

Parke, Ross D. 1995. "Fathers and Families." In *Handbook of Parenting,* edited by Marc H. Bronstein. Mahwah, N.J.: Lawrence Erlbaum.

———. 1996. *Fatherhood.* Cambridge: Harvard University Press.

Parness, Jeffrey A. 1993. "Designating Male Parents at Birth." *University of Michigan Journal of Law* 26:573.

Pasley, Kay, and Marilyn Ihinger-Tallman, eds. 1994. *Stepparenting: Issues in Theory, Research, and Practice.* Westport, Conn.: Greenwood Press.

Pasley, Kay, Marilyn Ihinger-Tallman, and Cheryl Buehler. 1993. "Developing a Middle-Range Theory of Father Involvement Postdivorce." *Journal of Family Issues* 14:550.

Pasley, Kay, and Carmele Minton. 1997. "Generative Fathering after Divorce and Remarriage: Beyond the Disappearing Dad." In *Generative Fathering: Beyond Deficit Perspectives,* edited by Alan J. Hawkins and David C. Dollahite. Thousand Oaks, Calif.: Sage.

Pate, Alexs D. 1994. "The Invisible Black Family Man." *Journal of Blacks in Higher Education* 4:76.

Patterson, Charlotte J. 1995. "Lesbian and Gay Parenthood." In *Handbook of Parenting,* edited by Marc H. Bronstein. Mahwah, N.J.: Lawrence Erlbaum.

———. 1996a. "Gay Fathers and Their Children." In *Textbook of Homosexuality and Mental Health,* edited by Robert P. Cabaj and Terry S. Stein. Washington, D.C.: American Psychiatric Press.

———. 1996b. "Lesbian and Gay Parents and Their Children." In *The Lives of Lesbians, Gays, and Bisexuals: Children to Adults,* edited by Ritch C. Savin-Williams, William R. Savin, and Kenneth M. Cohen. Forth Worth, Tex.: Harcourt Brace.

Patterson, Charlotte J., and Raymond W. Chan. 1997. "Gay Fathers." In *The Role of the Father in Child Development,* edited by Michael E. Lamb. New York: John Wiley.

Pearson, Jessica, and Nancy Thoennes. 1988. "Supporting Children after Divorce: The Influence of Custody on Support Levels and Payments." *Family Law Quarterly* 22:319.

Pence, Alan R. 1998. "Fathers and Child Care: An Exploratory Study of Fathers with Children in Day Care." *Early Child Development and Care* 36:71.

Perrin, Ellen C., and Heidi Kulkin. 1997. "Pediatric Care for Children Whose Parents Are Gay or Lesbian." *Pediatrics* 97:629.

Phares, Vicky. 1995. "Fathers' and Mothers' Participation in Research." *Adolescence* 30:593.

———. 1996a. "Conducting Nonsexist Research, Prevention, and Treatment with Fathers and Mothers: A Call for More Change." *Psychology of Women Quarterly* 20:55.

———. 1996b. "Fathers and Developmental Psychopathology." *Current Directions in Psychological Science* 2:5 (October).

Phares, Vicky, and Bruce E. Compas. 1992. "The Role of Fathers in Child and Adolescent Psychopathology: Make Room for Daddy." *Psychological Bulletin* 111 (May): 387.

Phares, Vicky, and Bruce E. Compas. 1996. "The Education and Labor Market Outcomes of Adolescent Fathers." *Youth and Society* 28:236.

Pittman, Frank S. 1993. *Man Enough: Fathers, Sons, and the Search for Masculinity.* New York: G. P. Putnam.

Pittman, Joe F., and Jennifer L. Kerpelman. 1993. "Family Work of Husbands and Fathers in Dual-Earner Marriages." In *The Employed Mother and the Family Context,* edited by Judith Frankel. New York: Springer.

Piven, Frances Fox, and Richard A. Cloward. *Regulating the Poor: The Functions of Public Welfare.* New York: Vintage.

Pleck, Elizabeth H., and Joseph H. Pleck. 1997. "Fatherhood Ideals in the United States: Historical Dimensions." In *The Role of the Father in Child Development,* edited by Michael E. Lamb. New York: John Wiley.

Pleck, Joseph H. 1992. "The Theory of Male Sex-Role Identity: Its Rise and Fall, 1936 to the Present." In *The Making of Masculinities: The New Men's Studies,* edited by Harry Brod. New York: Routledge.

——— 1993. "Are Family-Supportive Employer Policies Relevant to Men?" In *Men, Work, and Family,* edited by Jane C. Hood. Newbury Park, Calif.: Sage.

———. 1995. "The Gender Role Strain Paradigm: An Update." In *A New Psychology of Men,* edited by Ronald F. Levant and William S. Pollack. New York: Basic Books.

Polikoff, Nancy D. 1996. "The Deliberate Construction of Families without Fathers: Is It an Option for Lesbian and Heterosexual Mothers?" *Santa Clara Law Review* 36:375.

Popenoe, David, 1996. *Life without Father: Compelling New Evidence That Fatherhood and Marriage Are Indispensable for the Good of Children and Society.* New York: Free Press.

Pronger, Brian. 1990. *The Arena of Masculinity: Sports, Homosexuality, and the Meaning of Sex.* New York: St. Martin's Press.

Quirion, Paul, Judith Lennett, Kristin Lund, and Chanda Tuck. 1997. "Protecting Children Exposed to Domestic Violence in Contested Custody and Visitation Litigation." *Boston University Public Interest Law Journal* 6:501.

Rabin, Bonnie E. 1995. "Violence against Mothers Equals Violence against Children: Understanding the Connections." *Albany Law Review* 58:1109.

Radin, Norma. 1988. "Primary Caregiving Fathers of Long Duration." In *Fatherhood Today: Men's Changing Role in the Family,* edited by Phyllis Bronstein and Carolyn Pape Cowan. New York: John Wiley.

———. 1994. "Primary Caregiving fathers in Intact Families." In *Redefining Families: Implications for Children's Development,* edited by Adele Eskeles Gottfried and Allen W. Gottfried. New York: Plenum Press.

Ramsey, Sarah H. 1994. "Stepparents and the Law: A Nebulous Status and a Need for Reform." In *Stepparenting: Issues in Theory, Research, and Practice,* edited by K. Pasley and M. Ihinger-Tallman. Westport, CT: Greenwood Press.

Rao, Radhika. 1996. "Assisted Reproductive Technology and the Threat to the Traditional Family." *Hastings Law Journal* 47:951.

Rawlings, Steve W. 1994. *Studies in Marriage and the Family, Singleness in America.* Washington, D.C.: Bureau of Census, U.S. Department of Commerce.

Real, Terrence. 1995. "Fathering Our Sons, Refathering Ourselves: Some Thoughts on Transforming Masculine Legacies." *Journal of Feminist Family Therapy* 7:27.

Rhode, Deborah, ed. 1990. *Theoretical Perspectives on Sexual Difference.* New Haven: Yale University Press.

Rhoden, J. Lyn, and Bryan E. Robinson. 1997. "Teen Dads: A Generative Fathering Perspective versus the Deficit Myth." In *Generative Fathering: Beyond Deficit Perspectives,* edited by Alan J. Hawkins and David C. Dollahite. Thousand Oaks, Calif.: Sage.

Riley, David. 1990. "Network Influences on Father Involvement in Childrearing." In *Extending Families: The Social Networks of Parents and Their Children,* edited by Moncrieff Cochran, David Riley, and Charles Henderson. Cambridge: Cambridge University Press.

Ritner, Gary. 1992. *Father's Liberation Ethics: A Holistic Ethical Advocacy for Active Nurturant Fathering.* Lanham, Md.: University Press of America.

Rivera, Rhonda R. 1991. "Sexual Orientation and the Law." In *Homosexuality: Research Implications for Public Policy,* edited by John C. Gonsiorek and James D. Weinrich. Newbury Park, Calif.: Sage.

Roberts, Dorothy E. 1995. "The Genetic Tie." *University of Chicago Law Review* 62:209.

———. 1998. "The Absent Black Father." In *Lost Fathers: The Politics of Fatherlessness in America,* edited by Cynthia Daniels. New York: St. Martin's Press.

Roberts, Paul, and Bill Moseley. 1996. "Fathers' Time." *Psychology Today* 29:48.

Roberts, Paula. 1993. "Establishing a Family: Blood Tests and the Paternity Determination Process." *Clearinghouse Review* 26:1019.

———. 1997. "The Family Law Implications of the 1996 Welfare Legislation." *Clearinghouse Review* 30:988.

Robinson, Bryan E., and Robert L. Barret, eds. 1994. *The Developing Father: Emerging Roles in Contemporary Society.* New York: Guilford Press.

Robinson, Margaret. 1997. "Fatherhood Reclaimed: The Making of the Modern Father." *Family Law* 27:466.

Robson, Ruthann. 1993. "Posner's Lesbians: Neither Sexy nor Reasonable." *Connecticut Law Review* 25:491.

Roman, Mel, William Haddad, and Susan Manso. 1978. *The Disposable Parent: The Case for Joint Custody.* New York: Holt Rinehart and Winston.

Roper, Pamela Forrestall. 1997. "Hitting Deadbeat Parents Where It Hurts: Punitive Mechanisms in Child Support Enforcement." *Alaska Law Review* 14:41.

Ross, John Munder. 1983. "Father to the Child: Psychoanalytic Reflections." *Psychoanalytic Review* 70:301.

———. 1994. *What Men Want: Mothers, Fathers, and Manhood*. Cambridge: Harvard University Press.

Rossi, Alice S., Frank F. Furstenberg Jr., and Martha T. Mednick. 1992. "Parents." In *Family in Transition: Rethinking Marriage, Sexuality, Child Rearing, and Family Organization*, edited by Arlene S. Skolnick and Jerome H. Skolnick. New York: HarperCollins.

Rotundo, E. Anthony. 1993. *American Manhood: Transformations in Masculinity from the Revolution to the Modern Era*. New York: Basic Books.

Rozie-Battle, Judith L. 1989. "Adolescent Fathers: The Question of Paternity." *Urban League Review* 12:129.

Rubin, Lillian B. 1992. "Sex and the Coupled Life." In *Family in Transition: Rethinking Marriage, Sexuality, Child Rearing, and Family Organization*, edited by Arlene S. Skolnick and Jerome H. Skolnick. New York: HarperCollins.

Ruddick, Sara. 1990. "Thinking about Fathers." In *Conflicts in Feminism*, edited by Marianne Hirsch and Evelyn Fox Keller. New York: Routledge.

Russell, Alan. 1997. "Mother-Son, Mother-Daughter, Father-Son, and Father-Daughter: Are They Distinct Relationships?" *Developmental Review* 17:111.

Russell, Diane E. H. 1984. *Sexual Exploitation: Rape, Child Sexual Abuse, and Workplace Harassment*. Thousand Oaks, Calif.: Sage.

Rutherford, Jane. 1998. "One Child, One Vote: Proxies for Parents." *Minnesota Law Review* 82:1463.

Sabo, Don. 1995. "Gazing into Men's Middles: Fire in the Belly and the Men's Movement." In *The Politics of Manhood: Profeminist Men Respond to the Mythopoetic Men's Movement (And Mythopoetic Leaders Answer)*, edited by Michael S. Kimmel. Philadelphia: Temple University Press.

Sanders, Herman A. 1996. *Daddy, We Need You Now: A Primer on African-American Male Socialization*. Lanham, Md.: University Press of America.

Santrock, John W., Karen A. Sitterle, and Richard A. Warshak. 1988. "Parent-Child Relationships in Stepfather Families." In *Fatherhood Today: Men's Changing Role in the Family*, edited by Phyllis Bronstein and Carolyn Pape Cowan. New York: John Wiley.

Schiff, Anne Reichman. 1994. "Frustrated Intentions and Binding Biology: Seeking Aid in the Law." *Duke Law Journal* 44:524.

———. 1997. "Arising from the Dead: Challenges of Posthumous Procreation." *North Carolina Law Review* 75:901.

Schmidt, Leigh Eric. 1995. *Consumer Rites: The Buying and Selling of American Holidays*. Princeton: Princeton University Press.

Schoenfeld, Elizabeth. 1996. "Our Foundering Fathers." *Policy Review* 75:18.

Schoonmaker, Samuel V., IV. 1997. "Consequences and Validity of Family Law

Provisions in the Welfare Reform Act." *Journal of the American Academy of Matrimonial Lawyers* 14:1.

Schrof, Joannie. 1995. "Unhappy Girls and Boys." *U.S. News and World Report* (October 23).

Schultz, Vicki. 1990. "Telling Stories about Women and Work: Judicial Interpretations of Sex Segregation in the Workplace in Title VII Cases Raising the Lack of Interest Argument." *Harvard Law Review* 103:1749.

Schwebel, Andrew I. 1988. "Clinical Work with Divorced and Widowed Fathers: The Adjusting Family Model." In *Fatherhood Today: Men's Changing Role in the Family*, edited by Phyllis Bronstein and Carolyn Pape Cowan. New York: John Wiley.

"Science and Society." 1995. *U.S. News and World Report* (October 23).

Scott, Elizabeth S. 1992. "Pluralism, Parental Preference, and Child Custody." *California Law Review* 80:615.

———. 1994. "Rehabilitating Liberalism in Modern Divorce Law." *Utah Law Review* 1994:687.

Scott, Elizabeth S., and Robert E. Scott. 1995. "Parents as Fiduciaries." *Virginia Law Review* 81:2401.

Sedgwick, Eve Kosofsky. 1995. "Gosh, Boy George, You Must Be Awfully Secure in Your Masculinity." In *Constructing Masculinity*, edited by Maurice Berger, Brian Wallis, and Simon Watson. New York: Routledge.

Sedlak, Andrea J., and Diane D. Broadhurst. 1996. "Executive Summary of the Third National Incidence Study of Child Abuse and Neglect." Washington, D.C.: U.S. Department of Health and Human Services.

Segal, Lynne. 1990. *Slow Motion: Changing Masculinities, Changing Men*. New Brunswick: Rutgers University Press.

Segell, Michael. 1995. "The Pater Principle: Fathers and Sons Face a Lifetime of Unfinished Business." *Esquire* (March 1).

Seibold, Douglas. 1995. "Reinventing Fatherhood." *Our Children* 1:6.

Sells, Marcia. 1994. "Child That's Got Her Own." In *The Public Nature of Private Violence: The Discovery of Domestic Abuse*, edited by Martha Albertson Fineman and Roxanne Mykitiuk. New York: Routledge.

Selmi, Michael. 1999. "The Limited Vision of the Family and Medical Leave Act." *Villanova Law Review* 44:395.

Seltzer, Judith A., and Yvonne Brandreth. 1994. "What Fathers Say about Involvement with Children after Separation." *Journal of Family Issues* 15:49.

Senate Committee on the Judiciary. 1993. "Violence against Women Act of 1993," Senate Report no. 138, 103d Congress, 1st Session.

"Sex Differences in Violent Victimization." 1997. *Bureau of Justice Special Report*. Washington, D.C.: Bureau of Justice.

Shanley, Mary L. 1994. "Fathers' Rights, Mothers' Wrongs? Reflections on

Unwed Fathers' Rights, Patriarchy, and Sex Equality." Paper presented at the Feminism and Legal Theory Workshop, Columbia University Law School, March 24–26.

———. 1995. "Unwed Fathers' Rights, Adoption, and Sex Equality: Gender-Neutrality and the Perpetuation of Patriarchy." *Columbia Law Review* 95:60.

Shapiro, Jerrold Lee, Michael J. Diamond, and Martin Greenberg, eds. 1995. *Becoming a Father: Contemporary, Social, Developmental, and Clinical Perspectives*. New York: Springer.

Shelton, Beth Anne, and Daphne John. 1993. "Ethnicity, Race, and Difference: A Comparison of White, Black, and Hispanic Men's Household Labor Time." In *Men, Work, and Family*, edited by Jane C. Hood. Newbury Park, Calif.: Sage.

———. 1995. "Does Marital Status Make a Difference? Housework among Married and Cohabiting Men and Women." *Journal of Family Issues* 14:401.

Shon, Steven P., and Davis Y. Ja. 1992. "Asian Families." In *Family in Transition: Rethinking Marriage, Sexuality, Child Rearing, and Family Organization*, edited by Arlene S. Skolnick and Jerome H. Skolnick. New York: HarperCollins.

Shulman, Samuel, and W. Andrew Collins, eds. 1993. *Father-Adolescent Relationships*. San Francisco: Jossey-Bass.

Shulman, Samuel, and Inge Seiffge-Krenke. 1997. *Fathers and Adolescents: Developmental and Clinical Perspectives*. London: Routledge.

Shuster, Claudia. 1994. "First-Time Fathers' Expectations and Experiences Using Child Care and Integrating Parenting and Employment." *Early Education and Development* 5:261.

Silverstein, Louise B. 1996. "Fathering Is a Feminist Issue." *Psychology of Women Quarterly* 20:3.

Silverstein, Louise B., and Vicky Phares. 1996. "Expanding the Mother-Child Paradigm: An Examination of Dissertation Research 1986–1994." *Psychology of Women Quarterly* 20:39.

Simpson, Mona. 1992. *The Lost Father*. New York: Knopf.

Singer, Jana B., and William L. Reynolds. 1988. "A Dissent on Joint Custody." *Maryland Law Review* 47:497.

Skolnick, Arlene S., and Jerome H. Skolnick. 1992. "Introduction: Family in Transition." In *Family in Transition: Rethinking Marriage, Sexuality, Child Rearing, and Family Organization*, edited by Arlene S. Skolnick and Jerome H. Skolnick. New York: HarperCollins.

Smart, Carol, ed. 1992. *Regulating Womanhood: Historical Essays on Marriage, Motherhood, and Sexuality*. London: Routledge.

Snarey, John. 1993. *How Fathers Care for the Next Generation: A Four-Decade Study*. Cambridge: Harvard University Press.

Snyder, Thomas. 1996. *Youth Indicators, 1996: Trends in the Well-Being of American Youth*. Washington, D.C.: Office of Education Research and Improvement.

South, Scott J., and Stewart E. Tolnay, eds. 1992. *The Changing American Family: Sociological and Demographic Perspectives*. Boulder: Westview Press.

Spalter-Roth, Roberta M., and Heidi I. Hartmann. 1990. *Unnecessary Losses: Costs to Americans of the Lack of Family and Medical Leave*. Washington, D.C.: Institute for Women's Policy Research.

Stampfer, Judah. 1983. *Fathers and Children*. New York: Schocken Books.

Stamps, Leighton E., Seth Kunen, and Robert Lawyer. 1996. "Judicial Attitudes regarding Custody and Visitation Issues." *Journal of Divorce and Remarriage* 25:23.

Staples, Robert, ed. 1994. *The Black Family: Essays and Studies*. Belmont, Calif.: Wadsworth.

Stark, Barbara. 1997. "Guys and Dolls: Remedial Nurturing Skills in Post-Divorce Practice, Feminist Theory, and Family Law Doctrine." *Hofstra Law Review* 26:293.

Stark, Evan. 1995. "Re-Presenting Woman Battering: From Battered Woman Syndrome to Coercive Control." *Albany Law Review* 58:973.

Starrels, Marjorie E. 1994. "Gender Differences in Parent-Child Relations." *Journal of Family Issues* 15:148.

Stearns, Peter N. 1991. "Fatherhood in Historical Perspective: The Role of Social Change." In *Fatherhood and Families in Cultural Context*, edited by Frederick W. Bozett and Shirley M. H. Hanson. New York: Springer.

Stein, Terry S. 1996. "Homosexuality and Homophobia in Men." *Psychiatric Annals* 26:37.

Steinman, Susan. 1983. "Joint Custody: What We Know, What We have Yet to Learn, and the Judicial and Legislative Implications." *University of California at Davis Law Review* 16:739.

Stephens, Linda S. 1996. "Will Johnny See Daddy This Week?" *Journal of Family Issues* 17:466.

Sternberg, Kathleen J. 1997. "Fathers, the Missing Parents." In *The Role of the Father in Child Development*, edited by Michael E. Lamb. New York: John Wiley.

Stier, Haya, and Marta Tienda. 1993. "Are Men Marginal to the Family? Insights from Chicago's Inner City." In *Men, Work, and Family*, edited by Jane C. Hood. Newbury Park, Calif.: Sage.

Stoltenberg, John. 1989. *Refusing to Be a Man: Essays on Sex and Justice*. Portland: Breitenbush Books.

Strader, Scott C. 1993. "Non-Custodial Gay Fathers: Considering the Issues." Paper presented at 101st Annual Convention of the American Psychological Association.

Sullivan, Mercer L. 1989. "Absent Fathers in the Inner City." In *The Ghetto Underclass: Social Science Perspectives*, edited by William Julius Wilson. Newbury Park, Calif.: Sage.

Sverne, Tor. 1993. "Children's Rights in Scandinavia in a Legal and Historical Perspective." *Family and Conciliation Courts Review* 31:299.

Swomley, John. 1996. "Watch on the Right: Promises We Don't Want Kept." *Humanist* 56:35.

Taylor, Robert Joseph, Linda M. Chatters, M. Belinda Tucker, and Edith Lewis. 1992. "Developments in Research on Black Families: A Decade Review." In *Family in Transition: Rethinking Marriage, Sexuality, Child Rearing, and Family Organization*, edited by Arlene S. Skolnick and Jerome H. Skolnick. New York: HarperCollins.

Taylor, Robert Joseph, M. Belinda Tucker, Linda M. Chatters, and Rukmalie Jayakody. 1997. "Recent Demographic Trends in African American Family Structure." In *Family Life in Black America*, edited by Robert Joseph Taylor, James S. Jackson, and Linda M. Chatters. Thousand Oaks, Calif.: Sage.

Taylor, Robert Joseph, James Sydney Jackson, and Linda M. Chatters, eds. 1997. *Family Life in Black America*. Thousand Oaks, Calif.: Sage.

Testa, Mark, Nan Marie Astone, Marilyn Krogh, and Kathryn M. Neckerman. 1989. "Employment and Marriage among Inner-City Fathers." In *The Ghetto Underclass: Social Science Perspectives*, edited by William Julius Wilson. Newbury Park, Calif.: Sage.

Thevenin, Tine. 1993. *Mothering and Fathering: The Gender Differences in Child Rearing*. Garden City Park, N.Y.: Avery Publishing Group.

Tiedje, Linda Beth, and Cynthia Darling-Fisher. 1996. "Fatherhood Reconsidered: A Critical Review." *Research in Nursing and Health* 19:471.

Tolman, Richard M. 1996. "Expanding Sanctions for Batterers: What Can We Do Besides Jailing and Counseling Them." In *Future Interventions with Battered Women and Their Families*, edited by Jeffrey L. Edleson and Zvi C. Eisikovits. Thousand Oaks, Calif.: Sage.

Tripp-Reimer, Toni, and Susan E. Wilson. 1991. "Cross Cultural Perspectives on Fatherhood." In *Fatherhood and Families in Cultural Context*, edited by Frederick W. Bozett and Shirley M. H. Hanson. New York: Springer.

Trost, Jan. 1996. "Family Studies in Sweden." *Marriage and Family Review* 23:723.

Tuttle, Robert C. 1994. "Determinants of Father's Participation in Child Care." *International Journal of Sociology of the Family* 24:113.

Umberson, Debra. 1993. "Divorced Fathers: Parental Role Strain and Psychological Distress." *Journal of Family Issues* 14:378.

United States Congress, Senate Committee on Labor and Human Resources, Subcommittee on Labor. 1988. *Day Care—A National Priority*. Washington, D.C.: United States Government Printing Office.

United States Congress, Senate Committee on Labor and Human Resources, Subcommittee on Children and Families. 1996. *Encouraging Responsible Fatherhood: Hearing before the Subcommittee on Children and Families of the Committee on Labor and Human Resources, United States Senate, 104th Congress, Second Session, on Examining Initiatives to Encourage Responsible Fatherhood.* Washington, D.C.: United States Government Printing Office.

U.S. Department of Health and Human Services. 1996a. "Trends in the Well-Being of America's Children and Youth: 1996."

———. 1996b. "Child Maltreatment 1996: Reports from the States to the National Child Abuse and Neglect Data System."

U.S. Office of Juvenile Justice and Delinquency Prevention. 1997. *Responsible Fatherhood*, edited by Eileen M. Garry. Washington, D.C.: United States Department of Justice.

Valdes, Francisco. 1995a. "Queers, Sissies, Dykes, and Tomboys: Deconstructing the Conflation of Sex, Gender, and Sexual Orientation in Euro-American Law and Society." *California Law Review* 83:3.

———. 1995b. "Sex and Race in Queer Legal Culture: Ruminations on Identities and Inter-Connectiveness." *Southern California Review of Law and Women's Studies* 5:25.

Vance, Carole S. 1995. "Social Construction Theory and Sexuality." In *Constructing Masculinity*, edited by Maurice Berger, Brian Wallis, and Simon Watson. New York: Routledge.

Vega, William A. 1992. "Hispanic Families in the 1980s: A Decade of Research." In *Family in Transition: Rethinking Marriage, Sexuality, Child Rearing, and Family Organization*, edited by Arlene S. Skolnick and Jerome H. Skolnick. New York: HarperCollins.

Ventura, Stephanie J. 1995. *Births to Unmarried Mothers: United States 1980–92.* Washington, D.C.: National Center for Health Statistics.

Veum, Jonathan R. 1993. "Interrelation of Child Support, Visitation, and Hours of Work." *Social Science* (September): 229.

"Violence against Women: Estimates from the Redesigned Survey." 1995. *Bureau of Justice Special Report.* Washington, D.C.: Bureau of Justice.

Volling, Brenda L., and Jay Belsky. 1991. "Multiple Determinants of Father Involvement during Infancy in Dual-Earner and Single-Earner Families." *Journal of Marriage and the Family* 53:461.

Wade, Jade C. 1994. "African American Fathers and Sons: Social, Historical, and Psychological Considerations." *Families in Society: The Journal of Contemporary Human Services* 94:561.

Wall, Jack C., and Carol Amadio. 1994. "An Integrated Approach to Child Custody Evaluation: Utilizing the Best Interest of the Child and Family Systems Frameworks." *Journal of Divorce and Remarriage* 21:39.

Wallerstein, Judith S., and Sandra Blakeslee. 1989. *Second Chances: Men, Women, and Children a Decade after Divorce, Who Wins, Who Loses—and Why.* New York: Ticknor and Fields.

Walters, Lynda Henley, and Steven F. Chapman. 1991. "Changes in Legal Views of Parenthood: Implications for Fathers in Minority Cultures." In *Fatherhood and Families in Cultural Context,* edited by Frederick W. Bozett and Shirley M. H. Hanson. New York: Springer.

Warshak, Richard A. 1996. "Gender Bias in Child Custody Decisions." *Family and Conciliation Courts Review* 34:396.

Wattenberg, Esther. 1990. "Unmarried Fathers: Perplexing Questions." *Children Today* 19:25.

———. 1993. "Paternity Actions and Young Fathers." In *Young Unwed Fathers: Changing Roles and Emerging Policies,* edited by Robert Lerman and Theodora Ooms. Philadelphia: Temple University Press.

Wax, Amy. 1996. "The Two-Parent Family in the Liberal State: The Case for Selective Subsidies." *Michigan Journal of Race and Law* 1:491.

Wedgeworth, Cicely. 1997. "Divorce and Identity." *Patriot Ledger* (August 11).

Wehner, Karen C. 1994. "Daddy Wants His Rights Too: A Perspective on Adoption Statutes." *Houston Law Review* 31:691.

Weiner, Merle H. 1997. "We Are Family: Valuing Associationalism in Disputes over Children's Surnames." *North Carolina Law Review* 75:1625.

Weiss, Robert S. 1990. *Staying the Course: The Emotional and Social Lives of Men Who Do Well at Work.* New York: Free Press.

Werner, Craig. 1997. "Daughters: On Family and Fatherhood." *African American Review* 31:168.

Whithead, Barbara Dafoe. 1996. "Women and the Future of Fatherhood." *Wilson Quarterly* 20:30.

"Why Fathers Count." 1995. *Men's Health* (September).

Wideman, John Edgar. 1994. *Fatheralong: A Meditation on Fathers and Sons, Race and Society.* New York: Pantheon.

Williams, Joan. 1999. *Unbending Gender: Market Work and Family in the Twenty-first Century.* New York: Oxford University Press.

Williams, Lucy A. 1997. "Rethinking Low-Wage Markets and Dependency." *Politics and Society* 25:541.

———. 1998. "Welfare and Legal Entitlements: The Social Roots of Poverty." In *Politics of Law: A Progressive Critique,* edited by David Kairys. New York: Basic Books.

Williams, Victoria Schwartz, and Robert G. Williams. 1989. "Identifying Daddy: The Role of the Courts in Establishing Paternity." *Judges' Journal* 28:2.

Willinger, Beth. 1993. "Resistance and Change: College Men's Attitudes toward

Family and Work in the 1980s." In *Men, Work, and Family,* edited by Jane C. Hood. Newbury Park, Calif.: Sage.

Wilson, Melvin N. 1992. "Perceived Parental Activity of Mothers, Fathers, and Grandmothers in Three-Generational Black Families." In *African American Psychology,* edited by A. Kathleen Hoard Burlew, W. Curtis Banks, Harriette Pipes McAdoo, and Daudi Ajani ya Azibo. Newbury Park, Calif.: Sage.

Wolchik, Sharlene A. 1996. "Residential and Nonresidential Parents: Perspectives on Visitation Problems." *Family Relations* 45:230.

Woodhouse, Barbara Bennett. 1993. "Hatching the Egg: A Child-Centered Perspective on Parents' Rights." *Cardozo Law Review* 14:1747.

———. 1994. "Out of Children's Needs, Children's Rights: The Child's Voice in Defining the Family." *Brigham Young University Journal of Public Law* 8:321.

———. 1995. "Are You My Mother? Conceptualizing Children's Identity Rights in Transracial Adoptions." *Duke Journal of Gender Law and Policy* 2:107.

———. 1996. "Toward a Communitarian Theory of the Nontraditional Family." *Utah Law Review* 570:569.

"Workers on Flexible and Shift Schedules in 1997." 1998. Washington, D.C.: Bureau of Labor Statistics (news release).

Yaeger, Patricia, and Beth Kowaleski-Wallace, eds. 1989. *Refiguring the Father: New Feminist Readings of Patriarchy.* Carbondale, Ill.: Southern Illinois University Press.

Yaffe, Nancy Ellen. 1994. "A Fathers' Rights Perspective on Custody Law in California: Would You Believe It If I Told You That the Law Is Fair to Fathers?" *Southern California Interdisciplinary Law Journal* 4:135.

Yanez, Luisa. 1999. "Suit to Challenge Ban on Gay Adoptions." *Sun-Sentinel* (May 26).

Yeager, Catherine A. 1996. "The Intergenerational Transmission of Violence and Dissociation." *Child and Adolescent Psychiatric Clinics of North America* 5:393.

Yogman, Michael W., James Cooley, and Daniel Kindlon. 1988. "Fathers, Infants, and Toddlers: A Developing Relationship." In *Fatherhood Today: Men's Changing Role in the Family,* edited by Phyllis Bronstein and Carolyn Pape Cowan. New York: John Wiley.

Zietlow, Rebecca E. 1996. "Two Wrongs Don't Add Up to Rights: The Importance of Preserving Due Process in Light of Recent Welfare Reform Measures." *American University Law Review* 45:1111.

Zimmerman, Marc A., Deborah A. Salem, and Kenneth Maton. 1995. "Family Structure and Psychosocial Correlates among Urban African-American Adolescent Males." *Child Development* 66:1598.

Zinman, Daniel C. 1992. "Father Knows Best: The Unwed Father's Right to Raise His Infant Surrendered for Adoption." *Fordham Law Review* 60:971.

Zinn, Maxine Baca. 1992. "Family, Race, and Poverty in the Eighties." In *Family in Transition: Rethinking Marriage, Sexuality, Child Rearing, and Family Organization*, edited by Arlene S. Skolnick and Jerome H. Skolnick. New York: HarperCollins.

CASES

Armstrong v. Manzo. 1965. 380 U.S. 545.

Bowen v. Gilliard. 1987. 483 U.S. 587.

Bowers v. Hardwick. 1986. 478 U.S. 186.

Bradwell v. Illinois. 1873. 83 U.S. 130.

Caban v. Mohammed. 1979. 441 U.S. 380.

Califano v. Jobst. 1977. 434 U.S. 47.

Califano v. Westcott. 1979. 443 U.S. 76.

Clark v. Jeter. 1988. 486 U.S. 456.

Davis v. Davis. 1992. 842 S.W.2d 588.

Department of Health and Rehabilitative Services v. Privette. 1993. 617 So.2d 305.

EEOC v. Sears, Roebuck and Company. 1988. 839 F.2d 302.

Fiallo v. Bell. 1976. 430 U.S. 787.

Frontiero v. Richardson. 1973. 411 U.S. 677.

Gantt v. Gantt. 1998. 716 So.2d 846.

Gomez v. Perez. 1973. 409 U.S. 535.

Griswold v. Connecticut. 1965. 381 U.S. 479.

In re Adoption of Baby E.A.W. 1995. 658 So.2d 961.

International Union, UAW v. Johnson Controls, Inc. 1991. 499 U.S. 187.

J.E.B. v. Alabama. 1994. 511 U.S. 127.

Jimenez v. Weinberger. 1974. 417 U.S. 628.

King v. Smith. 1968. 392 U.S. 309.

Lalli v. Lalli. 1978. 439 U.S. 259.

Lehr v. Robertson. 1983. 463 U.S. 248.

Levy v. Louisiana. 1968. 391 U.S. 68.

Lewis v. Martin. 1970. 397 U.S. 552.

Linda R.S. v. Richard D. 1973. 410 U.S. 614.

Little v. Streater. 1981. 452 U.S. 1.

Loving v. Virginia. 1967. 388 U.S. 1.

Mathews v. Lucas. 1976. 427 U.S. 495.

Meyer v. Nebraska. 1923. 262 U.S. 390.

Michael H. v. Gerald D. 1989. 491 U.S. 110.

Miller v. Albright. 1998. 523 U.S. 420.

Mills v. Habluetzel. 1982. 456 U.S. 91.

Moore v. City of East Cleveland, Ohio. 1977. 431 U.S. 494.

Morey v. Peppin. 1985. 375 N.W.2d 19.

Norton v. Mathews. 1976. 427 U.S. 524.

Palmore v. Sidoti. 1984. 466 U.S. 429.

Parham v. Hughes. 1979. 441 U.S. 347.

Pickett v. Brown. 1983. 462 U.S. 1.

Pierce v. Society of Sisters. 1925. 268 U.S. 510.

Planned Parenthood of Central Missouri v. Danforth. 1976. 428 U.S. 52.

Planned Parenthood of Southeastern Pennsylvania v. Casey. 1992. 505 U.S. 833.

Quilloin v. Walcott. 1978. 434 U.S. 246.

Rivera v. Minnich. 1987. 483 U.S. 574.

Skinner v. Oklahoma. 1942. 316 U.S. 535.

Smith v. Organization of Foster Families for Equality and Reform. 1977. 431 U.S. 816.

Stanley v. Illinois. 1972. 405 U.S. 645.

Trimble v. Gordon. 1977. 430 U.S. 762.

United States v. Clark. 1983. 712 F.2d 299.

United States v. Virginia. 1996. 518 U.S. 515.

Van Lare v. Hurley. 1975. 421 U.S. 338.

Weinberger v. Wiesenfeld. 1975. 420 U.S. 636.

Zablocki v. Redhail. 1978. 434 U.S. 374.

Index

About the Author

Nancy Dowd is a member of the faculty of the University of Florida Levin College of Law, where she has taught since 1989. She holds the position of University Research Foundation Professor and Trustee Research Scholar. Her first book, *In Defense of Single-Parent Families,* was published by New York University Press in 1997, and is now in paperback. She has published extensively in the area of work and family policy, and family law. She teaches Constitutional Law, Gender and Law, Employment Discrimination Law, and Family Law. She is the mother of two children, and an avid sailor.